Praise for *Finally Out*

"A must-read. Provides insight into a hidden population of men who have sex with other men but may not wish to identify themselves as gay." — Abraham Morgentaler, M.D., FACS, Author of *Testosterone f~ ¯   'harge Your Vitality, Sex Drive, Muscle Mass, and O~·*   n's Health Boston; Associate Professor, Harvan

"*Finally Out* is a much-needed book ɩ   gay men come to terms with the apparen   .–ıı their rational assumptions about the two sexes and   ...ıı set of sexual attractions that do not fit that norm. Loren Olson blends the story of his own experience of coming out and an array of scientific information to develop his thesis. An insightful read." — Amity P. Buxton, PhD, author of *The Other Side of the Closet: The Coming-Out Crisis for Straight Spouses and Families*; Founder of the Straight Spouse Network

"For those who have struggled with coming out, Olson's expert combination of private struggle and professional reflection will prove invaluable. His down-to-earth, conversational tone makes the work even more accessible, and his story will likely be embraced by anyone facing the same issues or even just intrigued by the topic." — *ForeWord Reviews*

"*Finally Out* resonated for me on many levels as a gay man who married, raised children and came out at fifty-one. Loren Olson's own story of coming out in middle-age touches on universal truths that speak to a generation of gay men who have left the closet later in life or are contemplating that journey." — John Riley Myers, author of *Prince of the Pharisees*

"*Finally Out* goes far beyond a coming out story of a married, middle-aged gay man. It represents a carefully reasoned book about all human sexuality. Dr. Olson is so honest and direct that any reader will soon get the impression that he knows what he writes about. Lay readers, both gay and straight, will relate his ideas to their own lives, and professionals in social work, religion, psychology, and sociology will find this book invaluable." — Dr. Bernard J. Brommel, Professor Emeritus, Northeastern Illinois University, and co-author of *Family Communication: Cohesion and Change*

Finally Out

Published by inGroup Press, a division of inGroup Marketing, LLC.

inGroup Press and the inGroup Press logo are trademarks of inGroup Marketing, LLC. The inGroup Press logo was designed by Shelly Rabuse (www.rabusedesign.com).

Book cover design by Cypress House (www.cypresshouse.com).

ISBN-13: 978-1935725039

Visit our website: www.inGroupPress.com

Finally Out

Letting Go of Living Straight,
A Psychiatrist's Own Story

Loren A. Olson, M.D.

inGroup Press

Chicago, IL

This book is dedicated to the men and women who remain tormented by their same-sex

attractions, and to those who have lost their lives—or stand at risk of doing so—just because

they loved someone of the same sex.

CONTENTS

Acknowledgments

One man from East Africa wrote to me and asked, "Do people who condemn us for our same-sex attractions know how we feel?" An attempt to answer this question has been the driving force behind this book. Although *Finally Out* is about my story, a chronicle of my life would be insignificant except for the fact that it resonates with the histories of so many other men whose stories have never been told.

At the beginning of this three-year project I believed that there were many men like me, who for a variety of reasons had either delayed their coming out or had chosen not to come out at all. The project began with an online survey. I wish to thank those who completed it—their responses encouraged me to move forward. Only after seeing these responses did I begin to realize how many men there are who find themselves trapped in a life between gay and straight.

I am exceedingly grateful that so many men from around the world trusted me with the intimate details of their lives, despite taking tremendous risks in doing so. Their stories have enriched my life as well as this book. Many expressed gratitude for having an opportunity for the first time to unburden themselves by speaking with someone who would accept them without judgment. All of them expressed hope that their investment in this book would help others who ask, "Why do I feel something with a man that I don't feel with a woman? What can I do about it?"

I want to express my gratitude to several people who with a very few words changed the course of my life. First there was Edell Petersen, who said to me when I was seventeen, "Loren, I've always hoped you'd be a doctor." Dr. Julie Silver, in her course at Harvard Medical School on writing for physicians, inspired me by saying, "There's a book inside you." My agent, Linda Konner, encouraged me by saying, "This just might work if you put your story into it." I am grateful to Anthony DiFiore at inGroup Press for taking a chance on an unknown author writing about a controversial topic.

I deeply appreciate the helpful comments and support of several people who read the manuscript, or portions of it: Dr. Jack Drescher, Dr. Abraham Morgentaler, Dr. Amity Pierce Buxton, Dr. Bernard J. Brommel, Dr. Carl J. Ratner, Tim Turner, Leslie Wolfe Arista, Judith Gustafson, and

John Riley Myers. I am grateful to my attentive editors, Anna Sternoff and Karen Levy, who respected what I wrote while making it better.

I am indebted to the men in the gay fathers' support group, especially Bruce, who helped me believe that it was possible to be both gay and good. I am grateful for supportive friends and colleagues who have endured three years of my talking about nothing much beyond writing this book. I also want to acknowledge the welcoming community I have found at Plymouth Church.

Writing about my life inevitably exposed others whose lives have intersected with mine; none of them discouraged me from doing so. I have been blessed with a family that has supported me through some difficult life transitions: my daughters, Whitney and Krista, their husbands and my grandchildren, and my siblings and their families. I also wish to thank my former wife, Lynn, whom I still think of as family. I am also grateful to the Mortimer family for welcoming me.

Finally, I want to thank my husband, Doug Mortimer. Never once did he express doubt that I could write this book, nor did he ever complain about the enormous amount of time it took to write it. This book is also his.

Foreword

Jack Drescher, M.D.

What does it mean to come out as gay? In the mid-1990s, I wrote a professional book to answer that question. My goal was to explain the psychology of homosexuality and provide an alternative to the rigid dogma that used to inform psychiatric and psychoanalytic discussions of lesbian, gay, bisexual, and transgender (LGBT) lives. In that book, *Psychoanalytic Therapy and the Gay Man*, I offered a range of stories that define some gay men's identities without offering any singular definition of what it means to be gay. I knew from both personal and professional experiences that gay men of my generation were not like those of previous ones, and that the sensibilities of gay men younger than me differed in other ways. To paraphrase the anthropologist Gilbert Herdt, gay identities are not static and vary according to time, place, and culture.

Loren A. Olson's *Finally Out*, the story of a psychiatrist and self-described "late-blooming" gay man, is a welcome addition to our understanding of gay identities. Coming out late in life has its own special set of challenges, and Dr. Olson's book, part memoir and part self-help, poignantly addresses many of them. He speaks to older men who are struggling to come out, to those who already have done so, and to those who know and love such individuals. He recounts his own coming-out process, draws from his own psychiatric experiences with gay men he's treated, and offers helpful professional advice to individuals and families engaged in similar midlife struggles. All of this practical help is sprinkled with his far-ranging and insightful thoughts about neuroscience, sex research, psychopharmacology, psychiatry, issues of aging, literature, philosophy, politics, religion, gay culture, and human relationships.

As Dr. Olson's story illustrates, the decision to call oneself gay is not just about one's sexual orientation. It is also about social identity. It is not just about sex but also about learning to develop intimate relationships with other men. While developing intimate relationships may seem perfectly natural to some heterosexuals, for many gay men it is a process that requires practice. And there are numerous socially sanctioned outlets for heterosexual youngsters that serve the purpose of modeling or role-playing the part of future heterosexual adults. Teenage dating, high school dances, and adult supervision of coed activities help preteens and teens develop interpersonal skills required for later life and relationships. If and when they manage these interactions successfully, an adolescent's confidence may grow.

Yet those same rituals intended for heterosexual adolescents can generate confusion, shame, and anxiety in kids who grow up to be gay. The closet, which requires that gay people pretend to be straight, imposes a heavy burden. Not only does being in the closet interfere with learning needed social skills, but for many it also may lead to the development of hiding and other coping mechanisms that make it difficult to develop relationships after coming out.

Ironically, younger gay men who come out during their late teens and twenties can appear "adolescent." They form social cliques characterized by in-groups and out-groups. They place a strong emphasis on style, conformity to standards of dress, a hierarchy of popularity based on looks, and athleticism and affability, and they take advantage of opportunities for experimentation with sex, alcohol, and drugs. For many younger men, this "delayed gay adolescence" is a chance to catch up, in a manner of speaking, with the social skills of heterosexual peers who engaged in similar behaviors years earlier.

The person who comes out later in life faces different challenges. Common points of entry into the open gay community, like gay bars and dance clubs, are usually designed for the pleasure of younger people. Gay men who come out in midlife, having lived in an inauthentic way for a long time and often in need of interpersonal skill-building, may not be welcome in venues mainly catering to younger men. As a result, a pre-existing sensation of alienation from the straight community sometimes can turn into feelings of alienation from the more visible younger gay community, which some mistakenly believe to be the entire gay community.

For these and other reasons, coming out is not always easy for older gay men. Yet the courage to come out is best defined as choosing to do the right thing, not because one has no fear and anxiety but despite having fear and anxiety. In fact, those who come out late do so regardless of the difficulties of making a new gay life for themselves because the painful inauthenticity of the closet is more unbearable. Fortunately, as social acceptance of homosexuality has increased and as more people come out, there is a growing gay infrastructure for older people. These include LGBT community centers and national organizations like SAGE.

Of course, not everyone is fortunate to live close enough to a supportive gay infrastructure, but the Internet has eased the isolation of many gay people who rightly or wrongly believe they are the only gay person in a five-hundred-mile radius.

Finally Out is full of helpful advice for gay men coming out late in life and should be counted among the resources for those men who feel they are alone, their families, and their counselors. Dr. Olson has written an invaluable survival guide for older gay men with a clarity that is both highly accessible and greatly appreciated.

Jack Drescher, M.D., is a Distinguished Fellow of the American Psychiatric Association and a member of the APA's DSM-5 Workgroup on Sexual and Gender Identity Disorders. He is a past chair of the APA's Committee on GLB Issues and a past president of the APA's New York County Branch. He is president-elect of the Group for Advancement of Psychiatry, training and supervising analyst at the William Alanson White Institute in New York, clinical associate professor of Psychiatry and Behavioral Sciences at New York Medical College, and adjunct clinical assistant professor at the New York University Postdoctoral Program in Psychotherapy and Psychoanalysis. He is author of *Psychoanalytic Therapy and the Gay Man* and has edited more than twenty volumes dealing with gender, sexuality, and the health and mental health of LGBT communities.

Introduction

I didn't intend to write a book. After all, I'm just your average gay, close-to-retirement psychiatrist, living with my husband on a farm in rural Iowa. All I wanted were some answers. A 2007 article by Jane Gross in the *New York Times*, "Aging, Gay, and Facing Prejudice," had attached itself to my brain like a barnacle. She wrote that older gay men and women were being forced to go back in the closet because geriatric social service agencies were discriminating against them. Having not come out until I was forty, I was flooded with anxiety. Now in my sixth decade, I imagined that I would need those services before long. I did not want to let go of the feeling of freedom that first surged through me when, in the middle of my life, I recognized and accepted that I am gay.

So I did what any physician would do. I researched the medical literature to see what I could find about mature gay men and women. But my search of both the medical and the lay presses frustrated me; research almost entirely ignored the subject of coming out in midlife, and what little information I found didn't resonate with my own experience or the experiences of most of the mature gay men I know. The absence of answers led to more questions, which eventually led to this book.

I have chosen to tell my story, not because it is unique, but because it is one that I have heard over and over again from tormented men. They feel alone, and they are frightened about sharing their conflict with anyone. As I searched psychiatric literature to find answers for myself, I found that almost everything written addressed issues faced by young men; however, almost nothing was written for and about men who delayed their coming out until midlife. Except for a few high-profile men whose secret life has led to public exposure, these men are mostly hidden from view.

My goal in writing this book is to use my psychiatric training and experience to shed psychological insights into how the brain develops and operates, how self-identity is formed in both functional and dysfunctional ways, and how gay men have the power to change how they feel about their lives. It is my desire to help the younger LGBT community understand mature gay men and help mature gay men see younger gay men as something more than the stereotype. My intent is to offer hope to these men and their families, to tell them they can heal, and to let them know through my own experience that life doesn't always have to be as painful as it has been.

i

Finally Out: Letting Go of Living Straight

I am frequently asked—sometimes quite angrily—two questions: "How could you not know you were gay until you were forty years old?" and "Wasn't your first marriage just a sham designed to protect yourself, and at your wife and children's expense?" The second question is easier to answer. Although I know that my sexual orientation and my decision to come out deeply hurt my wife and children, I never intended to use them as a shield to protect me. As a psychiatrist, the focus of my life has been to relieve pain, not to cause it. Before I was forty, there was never a time in my life when I was committed to anything more than to being a good husband and a devoted father.

My decision to leave my family came about because I was losing the battle to control the feelings that raged inside me. I worried that my secret life would be exposed. Right or wrong, my judgment was that if I were outed while still married, the potential for humiliating my family and bringing shame on myself loomed larger than the pain I would inflict by leaving. Cheating on my wife, whether with a man or a woman, was wrong, and recognizing I was gay did not absolve me from the guilt I felt about it. Perhaps my reasoning was only twisted rationalization, but I absolutely believed that I faced a choice between only two unacceptable outcomes: either break a deeply held commitment to marriage and family, or inflict shame and embarrassment on the people I love.

The other question, "How could you not know?" is much more difficult to answer. Probing for an answer is ultimately what led to this book. All memories are but reconstructions, but what I can affirm without qualification or reservation is that until I was forty, I had no idea I was gay. Before that, I suffered from a sense that things weren't right inside me. It seemed that I had to work harder to feel like a man than other men appeared to, but I could never speak of my confused feelings to anyone. I believed that my father's death when I was three years old had crippled me. It was as if his death created negative space around me, like the optical illusion of Rubin's vase. Was I really a man or just the illusion of one, defined by that negative space surrounding me?

Jonah Lehrer, in his book *How We Decide*, captivated my attention as he described how our minds contain two distinct systems of thought: rational thought and feeling thought. Although we prefer to believe that as humans we operate exclusively through rational thought,

ii

according to Lehrer, our feeling thought makes up the majority of our thinking and operates continuously and usually unconsciously:

> That deep need to repress inner contradictions is a fundamental property of the human mind. Even though the human brain is defined by its functional partitions, by the friction of all these different perspectives, we always feel compelled to assert its unity. As a result, each of us pretends that the mind is in full agreement with itself, even when it isn't. We trick ourselves into being sure.

That need for harmony in our thinking is why men like me who experience a significant conflict between their rational thought (men should love women) and their feeling thought (I am attracted to men) search for a way to find accord in our thoughts—deceiving ourselves about our sexual attractions. To protect ourselves from unacceptable feelings, we instinctively erect barricades in our brains so that we may hoodwink ourselves into absolute assurance that we are heterosexual. In the process, we unknowingly perpetrate a hoax on our spouses, our children, and everyone we know. If that partition develops even a small crack, it is not a fissure that enlightens our conscious minds; it is a fault line in the darkening lens we've constructed that blocks the blinding light of unwanted feelings.

In high school, I was captivated with the idea of becoming a flight attendant, with "flight" being the important word. On domestic airlines in the 1960s, flight attendants were young, beautiful women called stewardesses. Men were only hired as stewards on international flights, and the airlines required fluency in a foreign language. My one year of poorly taught high school Spanish did not qualify me for the job. Looking back, I can see that this, too, was the unconscious operations of my mind, pushing me to break free of the fences created by my traditional upbringing to explore the world that lay beyond Nebraska's prairies.

Inquisitiveness about how the mind works and why people become who they are, including a curiosity about understanding myself, drew me into psychiatry. As I finished medical school, the unconscious forces in my brain were pushing me to consider continuing my training in New York, Chicago, or New Orleans, but my rational brain told me to get married and remain in Nebraska. A young doctor and a beautiful and educated wife with similar backgrounds and values should have been a perfect match.

During medical school and my psychiatric residency I read—with what I thought was only intellectual curiosity—everything I could find about the "psychopathic deviancy" of homosexuality. Very early in my practice I displayed too much interest in the life of one of my homosexual patients. He came into my office one day and, before I could sit down, stripped off all his clothes. Stunned, I said, "Put your clothes on again, then sit down and we'll talk about what just happened." The implications were obvious; unchecked empathy creates what psychiatrists call "counter-transference," something I should have worked out with a supervisor in training. But, unfortunately, I had been too afraid to discuss any of this with anyone. What led to my earlier study of homosexuality proved to be driven far more by the forces of my unconscious mind than I ever imagined. This incident with my patient served as a wake-up call to me; my interest in homosexuality was much more than just an intellectual curiosity.

Some may read into my story the psychological defense mechanism of "dissociation," a disruption of consciousness, memory, and identity. A simpler explanation is a child's belief in Santa Claus. Very young children have no difficulty accepting the fantasy of Santa Claus, no matter how improbable it is. As the child becomes a little older, he or she begins to be suspicious that it isn't true but wants so badly to believe that the child dismisses all evidence to the contrary. As the child grows even older, the evidence becomes overwhelming and the child must forfeit the belief.

Dr. Jack Drescher, in *Psychoanalytic Therapy and the Gay Man*, provides a thorough discussion of the phenomenon of dissociation, focusing on two principles originated by Dr. Harry Stack Sullivan, a gay psychiatrist: "the good me, the bad me, and the not me" and "selective inattention." Drescher describes one of his patients who referred to his religious beliefs as the "good me," his sexual feelings as the "bad me," and the dreaded homosexual feelings as "not me." Focusing almost exclusively on one experience prohibits awareness of other unacceptable experiences.

Loren A. Olson, M.D.

Used in this context, dissociation is a ubiquitous defense central to everyone's growth, and it was certainly a part of my own. The hysteria around sexual abuse during the 1980s and '90s, however, has tainted the concept of dissociation. The symptoms of dissociation are easily dramatized, and therapists became obsessed with it. Unskilled therapists pronounced to their patients that if they couldn't remember aspects of their childhood, they must have been sexually abused, and together they created false memories of horrific abuse that resulted in unwarranted accusations toward "perpetrators," often unsuspecting family members. Abuse is not a part of my life experience.

I never considered myself pathological, so I did not identify with gay men whom psychiatrists and society as a whole considered sick. I briefly questioned if my intensifying feelings for men meant I might be bisexual, but at a psychiatry conference when one of the speakers proclaimed, "Bisexuality is nothing more than a state of transition," I immediately dismissed that radical idea as having nothing to do with me. I was not willing to loosen my grasp on heterosexuality if it meant I was going to slip right past bisexuality into being gay. I was heterosexual—with a little quirk.

In 1985, when I learned of a gay fathers' support group, I went to that first meeting with Alfredo, the Argentinean man I had secretly been seeing while I was married. For the first time in my life, within that small group of men I felt a sense of sanctuary, a feeling of being at peace with myself among men who accepted me without the pretenses that by then had become so automatic. It was like being welcomed home for a holiday. Our common experiences created an immediate sense of intimacy, an insurgent connection with other men that I had never before experienced. After forty years, I had finally found a group of men with whom I felt I belonged. It transformed me from wondering if I might be gay to knowing without ambivalence or reservation that I was gay. Next I had to figure out what I was going to do about it. I knew that coming out was going to be a long and complicated process.

There were moments during the years I was transitioning from living a heterosexual life to being an openly gay man that I began to wonder, "What have I done to my life?" Harvey Milk, the first openly gay man elected to any significant political office, was murdered on November 27, 1978. In June of 1981, the Centers for Disease Control and Prevention in its *Weekly Morbidity and Mortality Report* reported an outbreak of a fatal disease subsequently named Acquired Immunodeficiency Syndrome (AIDS). In 1988, Ken Eaton was murdered, the victim of a hate crime. Ken was one of my friends in the gay fathers' support group.

But in spite of these events, I never seriously questioned the legitimacy of my decision to leave my family and begin my new life as a gay man. I saw a video clip on television of Harvey Milk saying, "If every man who is gay would just come out, we would win this battle." My mind was beginning to find a peace and unity that I had never before known, and to come out in more and more areas of my life began to feel like a moral obligation.

As my circle of gay friends expanded, I learned that many of them had been married, and all of them took their roles as fathers very seriously. None had abandoned their families in pursuit of a stereotypical hedonistic gay lifestyle. For some time I thought that my experience as a gay father was uniquely Midwestern, and that men who knew they were gay early in their lives would have moved to the urban coastal areas, leaving behind those of us who were more tightly bound to traditional values, married and with families.

Any envy I felt toward those who had come out as young men and had become a part of the gay community was offset by the incredible joy I felt at being a father. I also discovered many men enjoyed sex exclusively with other men, but found it impossible to identify with the "out and proud" values of the activist gay community. Many of them who, like me, lived in a heterosexual world and passed as "straight" were sheltered from the diversity of the gay community, and our prejudices toward gay people persisted, unchallenged.

I discovered that there is no universal pathway to accepting that you are gay and coming out, and traditional values are not the exclusive property of heterosexuals. Many men who truly honored their strong religious and cultural experiences believed that the losses they would experience if they came out were far greater than continuing to lead a duplicitous life. They chose to maintain their struggle against the undertow of their attraction to men.

Despite the comfort I felt in finding a community, I still believed that, at forty years of age, I was over the hill as a gay man, clueless about what being gay meant, and suddenly alone. It seemed I had all the prerequisites for clinical depression. A lecture in a class for physician executives at the University of Arizona given by Dr. Harry Levinson, an emeritus professor of psychology in the Department of Psychiatry at Harvard, dispelled that idea. As I studied his remarks, I realized that I would never achieve lasting self-esteem if the person I wanted to be was so far removed from the person I considered myself to be. I had to let go of pretending to be straight and work toward becoming the best gay man I could be. Dr. Levinson pointed out that lasting self-esteem never comes through seeking approval from others. In other words, the only way to improve the way you feel about yourself is to take charge of the person you want to be—make it your own, actively attempt to reach that ideal, and be realistic about the progress you are making toward it. You also need to stop beating up on yourself for not being the person someone else wants you to be.

As Anna Freud, daughter of Sigmund Freud and a psychoanalyst herself, said, "I was always looking outside myself for strength and confidence, but it comes from within. It is there all the time." It was a moment of tremendous insight for me. Letting go of the need for approval allows the coming-out process to begin.

Over the years, as I spoke to more and more men who were attracted to other men, I found some who had resolved their inner contradictions in their own way. Those who resolved this conflict had successfully done so by developing a moral integrity—an authentic relationship between who they wanted to be and who they thought they were. They had let go of being preoccupied with trying to please others. Many men had only begun to deal with their homosexual attractions later in life, and many others had no idea how or where to begin to find that congruence.

As I spoke about my ideas of writing a book, I heard over and over again, "I wish your book had been written when I was trying to find myself." So it is with that purpose that this book is being written. It is not only for those men who are still engaged in the struggle but also for those who love them or want to understand them. Too often what has been written about sexual orientation suggests that every person must be either gay or straight; no allowance is made for those who are struggling in a state of confusion, a kind of sexual purgatory. In fact, some gay

vii

activists appear to have forgotten their own experience of locking horns with this issue, and have suggested that gay people don't want to include "those hypocrites" as a part of the gay community. Have they grown insensitive to the fact that attempting to resolve conflicts about sexual orientation is a process that can go on for many years, and for some never ends?

When I first met with my agent, Linda Konner, one of the first things she said to me was, "Loren, people don't want to read charts and graphs; they want to read stories." I knew immediately that she was right. I was drawn to psychiatry because I wanted to know people's stories. But doctors are first and foremost scientists, and our training teaches us to be objective, to question, to look for data. Medicine teaches doctors how to cure illness. It doesn't teach them how to heal people. Healing involves much more than data.

I began the research that led to this work to see if there was evidence to support what I believe to be true of mature men who have sex with men. The research was composed of two parts: 1) an online convenience survey of mature men who have sex with men, and 2) biographical interviews to add depth to the survey findings. Convenience sampling is done by recruiting respondents from people known to the researcher and then asking them to recruit others. A convenience sampling is not scientific. Conclusions cannot be generalized to a larger population, but they still can be useful. I initially got in touch with personal friends and contacts through Internet social networks; they recruited others.

To test my hypotheses, I conducted an online survey of 132 of these men; the participants were not recruited from my psychiatric practice. I promoted the survey by requesting respondents from men who have sex with men. I avoided using the word "gay" because I believed then, as I do even more now, that there are many men who have sex with men who, for a variety of reasons, wish to avoid being labeled gay. I was interested in reaching men who might still be living a heterosexual life but who felt an irresistible pull toward sexual relationships with men. I chose to have people self-define "mature men." Although some of the men in the survey and interviews had been involved in counseling or psychiatric treatment, none of them had been former patients of mine.

Some of the interviews were conducted face to face; others were via the Internet. Contacts through social media allowed me to interview men from a wide variety of cultures, both within and outside the United States. Through this series of formal biographical interviews and informal conversations in person and online, I found that the men I interviewed had a "rational" explanation for why they felt different from other men, and often they attributed it to some historical event in their life, usually one over which they had no control. Just as I had used my father's death to explain my feelings of difference, each man had also found some experience in his own life that fulfilled his need to bring his thinking into accord.

The questions in the survey were drawn primarily from two sources. I wanted to compare men in today's society to men surveyed at the time I was first dealing with my own homosexuality. I drew heavily upon survey questions from John Dececco's *Gay and Gray: The Older Homosexual Man*. The second source was "A Brief Male Sexual Function Inventory" developed by O'Leary and colleagues in 1995 to study adult male sexual functioning.

Respondents ranged from twenty-four to ninety-one years of age, with a median age of sixty. Purely by chance, the respondents broke nearly evenly between men who were twenty years old or younger at the time of Stonewall (1969) and those who were older than twenty. The respondents were also almost equally divided between those who are or have been married and those who have not.

Respondents came from twenty-two states and three countries outside of the United States. They were both urban and rural. The vast majority of respondents to the survey were Caucasian. By design, those who were interviewed were a more diverse group of men.

A description of survey respondents follows. Any attempt at interpreting the data or comparing the findings to previous studies goes beyond the scope of this book.

Relationship Status
Have you been married to a woman?

Yes	53.4%
No	46.6%

Of those previously married:
Average times married: 1.02
     Range of times married: 1—4
     Median times married: 1

Do you have children?

Yes	43.5%
No	56.5%

Do you have a partner or lover?

Yes	70.2%
No	29.8%

How many previous relationships have you had?
Average number of previous relationships: 2.24
Range of previous relationships: 0—12
Median number of previous relationships: 2

With whom do you currently live?

I live alone.	42.7%
I live with a partner or lover .	32.1%
I live with a roommate.	6.1%
I live with family (spouse, children, relatives).	14.5%
Other	4.6%

Comfort with Sexual Orientation

At the present time, how would you rate your sexual orientation?

Exclusively heterosexual	0.0%
Primarily heterosexual, only slightly homosexual	0.0%
Primarily heterosexual, but more than slightly homosexual	0.8%
Just about equally homosexual and heterosexual	5.3%
Primarily homosexual, but more than slightly heterosexual	4.6%
Primarily homosexual, only slightly heterosexual	16.0%
Exclusively homosexual	71.8%
Other	1.5%

I wish that I were not homosexual.

Strongly agree	4.6%
Agree	6.1%
Not sure	10.7%
Disagree	33.6%
Strongly disagree	45.0%

I would not want to give up my attraction for men, even if I could.

Strongly agree	52.7%
Agree	26.7%
Not sure	12.2%
Disagree	6.9%
Strongly disagree	1.5%

Who knows about your homosexuality?

Family	91.8%
Work	52.7%
Straight friends	62.6%
Gay Friends	84.0%

I don't care who knows about my homosexuality.

Strongly agree	26.7%
Agree	26.0%
Not sure	13.0%
Disagree	19.1%
Strongly disagree	15.3%

Physical Health, Mental Health, and Sexual Health

In general, how would you describe your health?

Excellent	25.2%
Very good	38.9%
Good	22.1%
Fair	12.2%
Poor	1.5%

In the past, have you ever consulted a counselor or mental health professional?

Yes	56.5%
No	43.5%

Are you now or have you in the past taken medication for anxiety or depression on a regular basis?

Yes	32.1%
No	67.9%

Over the past six months, how satisfied have you been with your sex life?

Very dissatisfied	9.9%
Mostly dissatisfied	23.7%
Neither satisfied nor dissatisfied	16.8%
Mostly satisfied	35.9%
Very satisfied	13.7%

Socioeconomic Status

How would you describe your political views?

Very liberal	32.8%
Somewhat liberal	30.5%
Progressive	13.0%
Moderate	15.3%
Somewhat conservative	6.1%
Very conservative	2.3%

What has been your work status during the past 12 months?

Retired	32.1%
Work full time	50.4%
Working part time	14.5%
Disabled	3.1%

What is your current household income from all sources?

Less than $25,000 per year	11.5%
$25,000—50,0000	35.9%
$50,000—$100,000	35.1%
More than $100,000	17.6%

Appropriately, attention is being focused on the mental-health crisis of gay American teens. They often experience bullying, rejection, and depression. They have a nearly twofold increase in the likelihood of using alcohol and drugs and a fourfold increase in the likelihood of successful suicide over their non-gay cohorts. I am not aware of any research on suicide rates in more mature men who are experiencing similar issues, but there are logistical, financial, and ethical issues in attempting to study a hidden group of men who have sex with men. The secretive nature of these men's lives would make such research very difficult, and perhaps society isn't motivated to find the answers. Many of the men I have studied turned to alcohol and other drugs as a solution, but the number of men receiving counseling appears to be increasing.

This book is not intended as a polemic of what must be done. My thoughts and experiences are presented only as an example of what has worked for me. It is my hope that sharing my story will help men like me, the families who love us, and the people who counsel us, to have a better understanding about the lives of men who delay their coming out or perhaps choose not to come out at all.

It was a lonely birthday in March 1987, shortly after my divorce, when I went to a gay bar in Des Moines, still uneasy about my newly discovered sexual orientation. Sitting at the other end of the bar was a handsome young man to whom I was immediately attracted. But I was paralyzed by my lack of experience in negotiating this new gay world. Just as I was about ready to give up, he came over, taking the bar stool next to me. His name was Doug, he told me, and he easily started chatting with me, telling me he was from Arizona and visiting Des Moines only for a short time. "Damn," I thought. "Not much long-term potential here, but I'll make the most of it, even if it's just for tonight."

We spent that night together, and as Doug was leaving in the morning, I asked him if I could call him. He gave me his number, and even before he got home, I was already on the phone calling to see if he would see me again. On our second date, Doug told me, "I'm monogamous. *Very* monogamous." Those words were magical because what I, too, wanted was a committed, enduring, and exclusive relationship.

Doug felt drawn to return to Arizona, and I had planted deep roots in my new psychiatric practice in Des Moines; it seemed like an impasse for us. For several months, I kept pressing him for a long-term commitment. Once he said to me, "If I'm still here in the morning, you'll know I'm still committed." I needed him to say the words he couldn't say.

One night I was on my way to meet him for dinner, feeling rather hopeless and discouraged about our relationship. I counseled myself in the same words I say to my patients: "What are the facts? Your feelings tell you that you're going to lose him because they *always* tell you that you will lose what you love. Today, he is here with you. Those are the facts." An arresting sense of peace descended over me, and I stopped asking him if he was committed. A full year after we began dating, we moved in together.

Twenty-three years after our relationship began, the Iowa Supreme Court found, in a unanimous decision, that the Iowa statute limiting civil marriage to a union between a man and a woman violates the equal protection clause of the Iowa Constitution. Over and over we have heard, "Iowa? Of all places?" But Iowans are aware that we have a long tradition of equality and justice, and we expect that eventually places like California and New York will catch up.

Thirty years ago I could never have imagined that two people of the same sex who love each other and share the same values of love, commitment, and family would be able to marry, here or anywhere else.

On September 26, 2009, Doug and I were married in Des Moines at Plymouth Church, United Church of Christ, in the presence of our families, including my daughters and their husbands and several of our grandchildren, my sisters and their families, and several very close friends. My best man was my best friend, Bruce, a man I'd met many years before in the gay fathers' support group. As Doug placed the wedding band on my finger, I began to realize that my coming-out process was starting all over again. I knew that a shiny, new wedding band, on a finger that had been naked for more than twenty-five years, would be obvious to patients who were always asking, "How's your wife?" After the ceremony, Doug's brother and his best man gave me a hug and said, "Brother-in-law, welcome to the family." Marriage changes the line in the family tree from a dotted line to a solid one.

My former wife and I have reached a rapprochement, and she, Doug, my daughters, their husbands, and our grandchildren frequently spend holidays and celebratory events together. This did not happen immediately or easily, and it required that all of us examine our inner contradictions, remove partitions within our brains, and smooth out the frictions both within and between us. Coming out as a mature gay man is complicated and never ending.

In *Prescriptions for the Mind: A Critical View of Contemporary Psychiatry*, Dr. Joel Paris wrote, "Memories of the past are rarely factually accurate. We tell old stories in new ways, re-creating and reinterpreting the past in light of the present." In this book, I have reconstructed my memories to create with as much accuracy as possible a narrative of my past. I could not have written this book earlier in my career; it is far too personal.

Because many of the men whose stories I have related are not yet open about their sexual orientation in every area of their lives, most of the names have been changed. I have not made any attempt to write about this experience as it relates to women. Some of the same principles may apply to them, but I found it necessary to limit the scope of this project. Since it began with a search for my own answers, I have focused on mature gay men. Mature gay women will surely wish to define themselves.

No universal blueprint exists, and each individual must work out his own solution. My hope is that some of the answers I have found will offer others insights into why some men who love other men might marry and have families, choose to come out or not, or delay it until midlife or beyond. My primary message is one of hope, encouraging others to discover who it is they want to be. I'd like to help them take responsibility for working out their own solutions so that they, and the families and friends who love them, will believe that happiness is attainable, although perhaps in a different way than they had once expected.

Loren A. Olson, M.D.

Chapter 1
I Am Not Gay, but I Might Be a Little Bit Queer

*That fear had been inside him for many years, if it lived with him,
it had been another shadow cast over his own shadow ever since the night
he awoke, shaken by a bad dream, and realized that that was not only a
permanent probability, as he had always believed, but an immediate
reality.*

—*Love in the Time of Cholera*,
Gabriel García Márquez

I know precisely the moment I became gay. As Cary Grant said as Dr. David Huxley in the 1938 movie *Bringing Up Baby*, "I just went gay all of a sudden!"

Of course, my transformation did not occur suddenly. Nothing much about my life had changed, at least not yet. But at the very precise moment when I was forty years old, things shifted inside my head. I went from thinking of myself as straight to knowing that I am gay. Only then did I begin to realize how my gayness had cast a shadow over me my entire life.

On August 28, 2007, United States senator Larry Craig, after having been arrested for making sexual advances in a men's bathroom at a Minneapolis airport, stood before the microphones of the national media, his wife, Suzanne, at his side, and declared, "I am not gay! I never have been gay!" What he did *not* say overshadowed what he did say. He did not say, "I have never had sex with a man." Senator Craig's voting record had earned him top ratings from social conservative groups. He had voted in favor of the Defense of Marriage Act, which denies federal recognition to same-sex marriages and prevents states from being forced to recognize the marriages of gay and lesbian couples legally performed in other states. He had supported a federal constitutional amendment banning same-sex marriage.

> **When Cary Grant said, "I just went gay all of a sudden!" it was one of the first on-screen uses of the word "gay" to mean something other than happy.**

1

Reactions to Senator Craig's announcement varied. Some gay activists smiled smugly, believing that one more hypocritical, closeted gay man had just been exposed. Religious conservatives, often intolerant of any homosexual behavior, countered that gay activists proved their own hypocrisy; they said gay people only support the separation of a person's public from their private lives when it serves their purposes. Now the activists were viciously smearing someone's private behavior. They claimed that the senator had supported legislation as a matter of public policy and he had not targeted anyone's personal behavior. Others thought police had wasted their time entrapping otherwise honorable male citizens. Some felt that Senator Craig should resign; as a married man, he had cheated on his wife, lied to his family and constituents, and broken the law.

And a considerable number of men thought, "Man, that could have been me!" Countless numbers of ordinary men live with the fear of being exposed and discredited, humiliating themselves and their families, their friends, and their coworkers. The exposure of the underground sexual activity of celebrities and politicians like Senator Craig briefly generates a media commotion. Men arrested for having sex with other men in public places are usually referred to as "gay." However, a significant portion of these men, like Senator Craig, would not define themselves as homosexual. Many of them are married to women. Why would anyone choose to risk so much and behave in ways that potentially can be so destructive?

First of all, does anyone really behave rationally when they are having sex? Sexual desire operates within the very primitive levels of our brains, and truthfully the scientific community knows very little about how sexual desire affects our judgment. Perhaps more powerfully, the use of psychological defense mechanisms like denial, repression, and rationalization protect the conscious mind from awareness of unacceptable desires. Sex is not rational, but it is rationalizing.

Senator Craig's situation became fodder for late-night TV comedians until the next scandal bumped it aside. A much larger issue emerged: according to a 2006 study of men in New York City published in *The Annals of Internal Medicine*, 10 percent of working-class and immigrant men who labeled themselves as heterosexual have sex *only* with other men. They also found that 10 percent of all married men in this study have had sex with another man in the past year. It appears possible that there are more men who refer to themselves as straight who are having sex with other men than men who call themselves gay.

Although the study describes a limited population in New York City and cannot be generalized to an entire country's population, it does suggest that the number of men having sex with men is much greater than most imagine. These men who have sex with men come from all communities, all ethnicities, and all socioeconomic levels of society. Both single and married, they lead hidden lives. Society colludes to lock these men inside its collective closet. It ignores, denies, or represses the fact that men have sex with other men.

Several forces operate in our culture to sustain the misperception that men are not having sex with men. Many people believe that homosexual behavior is sinful and undermines "traditional family values." They believe it would just go away if we would return to the "natural and timeless values" of small-town America of the 1950s. Oddly, many of these older men who have sex with men were raised in and still live in these mythic small towns. Spouses and families fear that homosexuality threatens to destroy the institution of the family.

In 2010, the U.S. Centers for Diseases Control and Prevention (CDC) estimated that men who have sex with other men account for 4 percent of the population over the age of thirteen. Since many of these men do not use condoms, women justifiably fear that they serve as a bridge for the transmission of HIV and other sexually transmitted diseases; this fear is supported by CDC statistics. In the 1980s, the CDC sought to expand their education to all men at risk for transmitting HIV and other sexually transmitted diseases, and they initiated use of the term "men who have sex with men," or "MSM," to incorporate men who are straight-identified but still have sex with men, not just those who are gay-identified. Initially the gay community reacted negatively to the category "men having sex with men." They felt it rejected their hard-fought, self-affirming label of "gay." Many in both the gay and the straight worlds believe that only gay men have sex with men. MSM, however, is a very diverse group of men, potentially much more diverse than the gay community. Many have discovered their homosexuality buried deep within themselves and want to expel themselves from the life that has held them thus far. In the survey that I conducted as well as in conversations and correspondence with other mature men, I have found that some experience no sense of shame about their hidden homosexual activities, while others live with significant conflict about their sexuality. Many MSM never consider the possibility of public disclosure of their homosexual behavior and refuse to identify themselves as gay. In fact, many of these men are repelled by the idea of being called gay and have barricaded themselves in a heterosexual world because they have incorporated an inaccurate and stereotypic view of gay men. Many of them see the gay community as a radical counterculture defined primarily by sexual behavior, the same way much of the heterosexual community sees it. They don't want to be a part of it.

Some men do seek only casual man-on-man sex—an impersonal orgasm—with no interest in any emotional connection with their sexual partner. They consider it an easy, "no strings," way of obtaining sexual gratification, as if their sexual partner is nothing more than a genderless sex organ. They believe that soliciting sex from another man does not make them gay; only feminine, deviant, and abnormal men who respond to the solicitation are gay. Even though they may be having sex exclusively with men, they do not consider themselves to be gay or bisexual because they claim, and often firmly believe, that their interest in men is secondary to their primary affection-based interests in women. One man said to me, "My wife is a wonderful woman. I love her, but I only want to have sex with men." The behavior of these men may even be overlooked by society if they are meeting the heteronormative masculine responsibilities of being overworked and stressed out. That was my own personal rationalization when I first discovered the reality of my sexual attraction to other men.

> **Homosexuality may be overlooked and excused by society when men are overworked and stressed out—in other words, living out their "masculine responsibilities."**

Although society evolves, sexism persists, and it plays a significant role in men's conflicts about sexual orientation. Successfully competing with other men often defines masculinity more than a relationship with a woman does. Rigid cultural conventions concerning men prescribe that men have a wife and family, aggressively pursue their careers, participate in contests of strength, and demonstrate prowess with women, even to the point of objectifying them. Several conservative religious groups demand a dominant role for men over women.

When I was ten years old, one of our neighbors bought me a gas-powered lawnmower that, in the 1950s, only a few people had. The agreement was that I would mow their lawn and ours, and I could use the lawnmower to mow other people's yards to earn some money for our family. The lawnmower frustrated me considerably. I had a great deal of difficulty with any machine, and I always had difficulty getting that John Deere lawnmower started. One day it just would not start. In frustration, I called my widowed mother at work, crying, "Mom, I can't get the lawnmower started!"

Helpless to know what to do, she said to me, "Of course you can! You're a man, aren't you?" I felt as if one of my testicles had just been torn away. Men start machines. I couldn't start mine. I was not a man. Inside I was feeling, "If only my dad hadn't died, I could have fixed it." I desperately wanted someone to teach me to be a man. I needed a counterweight to my mother. Masculinity, I thought, is never nuanced. This feeling of being incompetent at accomplishing manly tasks embedded itself in my brain and penetrated every aspect of my life.

I hadn't considered that I might be gay; my masculinity was like a child's stick figure drawing of a man. Call me anything, but do not call me a sissy. I do not remember any reference to homosexuality as a child other than "Don't wear yellow on Tuesday because it means you're queer." We called each other "fairy," but we were thinking Tinker Bell, not faggot. Although we derided others with these terms, they had little to do with sexuality—we only knew it was not good to be called one.

The Complexity of Sex

Mature men know what arouses them sexually, but why those things arouse us remains foggy. A growing consensus of scientists believes that genetics determines sexual attraction. Research may help inform the debate about whether or not sexual orientation is innate, environmental, or both, but those who oppose homosexuality use the same research to make same-sex attraction appear pathological. One psychoanalyst, Jeffrey Satinover, a leading spokesperson for the "reparative therapy" movement, purporting to offer an objective criticism to the question of the genetic basis of homosexuality, wrote that if we were determined to find an

5

answer to the question of the genetic basis of homosexuality, "We would soon develop better ideas on what homosexuality is *and how to change, or better, prevent* it [his emphasis]." The exact causes of homosexuality may be unknowable, but our society's tendency to describe things in terms of black and white, all or nothing, disallows thoughtful consideration and dialogue.

One young Chinese student wrote me and asked, "What am I? For whom and what do I live in this world?" His questions are similar to many I have received. Many men want to know if they are gay or not, how it will impact their lives, and why they prefer one type of man over another. Most men who are attracted to sex with other men are not concerned about an explanation for the attraction they have. If pressed, they almost inevitably say, "I was born this way." They have a sense of being different from other men, but many of them do not consider themselves to be gay. They profile themselves as "masculine" and "straight-acting," code words for "passing" in a heterosexual world. They emphasize "no kissing and no anal" when they seek male partners. They believe these self-imposed limits set them apart from being "gay." Even though they may desire kissing and anal sex, these are boundaries beyond which they cannot go, or they risk slipping inescapably into the pit of homosexuality. These barriers allow them to avoid emotional connection to their sexual partner, maintaining their imperfect grasp on being straight. If they have begun to explore anal sex, by limiting their sexual behavior to being the inserting partner in the sexual relationship, they can then look at their receptive partner as the "feminine" one, the *real* queer. They feel they have left their masculinity intact. In *Secret Historian: The Life and Times of Samuel Steward, Professor, Tattoo Artist, and Sexual Renegade*, Justin Spring quotes Steward's description of one of his regular sex partners: "[I imagine him] standing there, cock uplifted, his hands clasped behind his head (fearful that if he should touch me while I kneel before him, that some of my queerness will rub off on him)."

These men are from diverse backgrounds—some are raised in the traditions of conservative religions, some are from minority or immigrant cultures and lower socioeconomic groups. They fear the potential consequences of exposure of their behavior. They have made strong commitments to "traditional values" that they believe belong exclusively to the heterosexual community. They often say they do not

6

want to be a part of "the scene." By the scene they are referring to the homosexual subculture. Their perceptions are dominated by the gay stereotype of young men who dance and drink excessively, go to the gym relentlessly, are narcissistically preoccupied with their bodies and physical appearance, and hedonistically spend all their money on clothes, travel, and restaurants.

These men may marry, not because of some reductionist idea that they are using women to cover up their sexuality, but because they honestly believe this will resolve all their ambiguities of love and sexual expression. They believe in love, romance, and long-term commitment. As one of the men I interviewed said, "Masculine men are attracted to other masculine men for a reason that is stronger than just sex, a big cock, or a beautiful body."

For those who have internalized the cultural constructs of masculinity (strong, heterosexual) and femininity (weak, sissy), life is complex and difficult. They experience a silent and secret sense of difference from the masculine ideal. Shame and secrecy, lying, self-blame, and self-hatred inform their sexual activities with other men. They experience a sense of dissonance between who they know they are and who they think they should be, and the greater the difference, the greater the self-hatred.

Sexuality is a far more complex issue than body parts. It includes sexual fantasy, sexual behavior, sexual preference, sexual orientation, and sexual identity; it also includes emotionality and romance. At times, these forces contradict each other even within the same individual. One eighty-five-year-old man who responded to my survey said now he is exclusively homosexual and quite sexually active: "My married life for fifty-four years was the most wonderful imaginable. I never had any gay leanings that I was aware of. I can discern incidents in my earlier life that I now see as [red] flags. However, I was so happy in my married life that I never gave them a thought. I never even thought about the gay life until age eighty-two." Initially, his story grabbed my attention, but now I have heard it repeatedly.

I was born in 1943 on a small farm in a rural community in Nebraska. Everyone seemed to have the same values, those same values that some conservatives idealize and think we should return to. Conversations about human sexuality rarely occurred, and when they did, they were met with discomfort, embarrassment, and disapproval. Discussions of homosexuality, if they occurred at all, focused on its being unnatural and an invitation to deviancy. Not only were we innocent about sex, but we also were innocent about almost everything. We did as we were told and independent thought was discouraged. The roles for men and women were rigidly defined. Bombing drills, where we hid under our desks to prepare for attacks by the Russians, became a kind of metaphor for our lives. It felt as if the entire world beyond the 1,035 people in my hometown was a very threatening place.

One of the guys in my high school had more difficulty hiding his effeminacy than I did. We all made fun of him. I hoped that by joining in, people would overlook any similarities I had with him. I was thankful he was there to divert any suspicions about me. I made a very conscious effort to be as unlike him as I could be. He refused to come to a class reunion, saying, "You didn't like me then. I doubt that I would like any of you now." I always felt like a man-imposter. I wondered why I had to work so hard at masculinity when it seemed to come so naturally to everyone else.

Of the men that I interviewed, those from my generation described being the best in their class at playing jacks, jumping rope, and twirling a baton, but their pride in their achievements at the time was diminished by a sense of shame at being the best at something a boy should not even want to do at all. I felt similarly.

At age fourteen, had I known there was such a thing as homosexuality, I might have understood my life better. All of the sexual experiences with other boys that I had had up to that time—mostly mutual masturbation—seemed perfectly normal to me, and I presumed were seen as normal by my partners. As I grew older, their interests were changing, and I questioned the tardiness of my own attraction to girls. And as for the other adolescent boys' fascination with "tits," I just didn't get it.

The Good Me and the Bad Me

Psychologists and psychiatrists call it "cognitive dissonance" when anxiety is created because there is an inconsistency between what people believe and their actions. One man wrote to me, "I had always been taught that homosexuality was bad, but as I began to accept that I am gay, I could not make myself believe that I had become a bad person." Life no longer fit with what he thought he knew and his actions were no longer consistent with his previously held opinions. Dissonance creates anxiety that varies in intensity depending upon the importance of the issue and the degree of the disparity. Becoming aware of the potential consequences of behavior that departs from traditional expectations only adds to the discomfort. This intense anxiety often drives people to seek a sense of wholeness either by changing their behavior or by changing their beliefs.

Factors that contribute to cognitive dissonance:
- The longer beliefs are held
- The more important the issue
- The greater the inconsistency between beliefs and actions
- The greater the degree of difficulty in reversing a decision
- The greater the anticipation of future problems as a result of the belief

Dissonance, when it occurs in those who experience same-sex attraction, is usually attributed in gay literature to "internalized homophobia," that is, an adoption of the majority culture's fear of or prejudice against gay, lesbian, bisexual, and transgendered (LGBT) people. Self-hatred derives from believing and internalizing those factually unsupported preconceptions about homosexuality. I am not a fan of the term "homophobia." For one thing, it appears double-dealing to be angry about the struggle to replace the term "psychopathic deviants" with "gay," while at the same time labeling the straight community perversely pathologically homophobic. For another, the term

> **"Homophobia" is really nothing more than the prejudice experienced by anyone who is an "outsider," and all outsiders bleed the same when wounded.**

homophobic collapses all opposition to homosexuality into one overly simplistic explanation. Finally, prejudice is not a uniquely gay experience. People are discriminated against because of their language, their religion or skin color, or anything else that confers on them the status of an "outsider." All outsiders bleed the same blood when they are wounded by prejudice.

The gay community appropriately promotes coming out as essential for personal authenticity and social justice. It is hard to argue against that point. In my experience, relationships with openly gay people do help remove prejudices. My mother had never met anyone she knew was gay until I came out to her. My stepfather was a stern but loving Swede, who lived into his deep, unexamined religious faith and who would never knowingly hurt anyone, but he would say some of the most outrageously insensitive things about others. When his granddaughter began seriously dating an African American, the family became nervous about how my stepfather would react. After they gathered their courage and told him the news, his response was, "Thank God he's not Norwegian." I can only imagine what he might have said about gay people. My parents were not homophobic, but they were homo-naïve.

As a young teenager I read muscle magazines that I stole from the Rexall drugstore. I wanted to be like the men pictured in those magazines. (Now I wonder who the other men in my small town reading those magazines were.) Once I ordered a small, white spandex bathing suit from an ad in the back of one of those magazines. I wore it to the swimming pool to teach swimming lessons, thinking the suit itself would create muscle definition, thereby making me appear more masculine. The senior lifeguard, a very handsome young man who had a body like the one I wanted, called me aside and told me the suit was not appropriate to wear to the pool. He sent me home, humiliated. I couldn't seem to get anything right about being a man.

Until I was able to afford corrective plastic surgery, I was always ashamed of having gynecomastia, or "man boobs." It was as if they betrayed a secret about me. Once my high school football coach shouted at me in front of all my teammates, "Olson, with tits like that, you should wear a bra!" The only word any of us had learned up to that point that suggested an alternative existed to being either a boy or a girl was "hermaphrodite," and suddenly my coach had just called me one.

Binary reasoning dominates contemporary American society—the idea that there are only two alternatives—particularly in religion, politics, and advertising. The polar definitions of masculinity and femininity have been deeply ingrained in our psyches. The Marlboro man has become

10

iconic of the tough, muscular man, always ready to get the girl. For the older man, the Viagra man, a little blue pill promises to rescue him from impotence and failure. The pill promises him an adolescent-like erection that with any luck will last just under four hours, right before you need to call the doctor.

Any movement away from the entrenched image of masculinity could begin a chain reaction of events that culminates inevitably in membership in the despised sissy out-group. These values are among the longest and most deeply held. Consequently, they yield to change slowly, and only with great difficulty. Men may not know why they feel a sense of difference, but they do know they cannot talk about it. Saying "I think I might be gay" is like unbridling a mustang. Anyone who says "I think I might be gay" is assumed to be gay, otherwise those thoughts would never enter his mind. It is a remark that does not allow a retraction the following morning.

> In the early twentieth century, the world was not divided into gay and straight; men had to be a lot of things, but being heterosexual was not one of them.

Men having sex with other men in the early twentieth century was not considered abnormal as long as those men abided by gender-conforming characteristics, according to George Chauncey, author of *Gay New York: Gender, Urban Culture, and the Making of the Gay Male World 1890–1940*. Interest in homosexual encounters did not preclude interest in heterosexual ones, as is insisted today. Achieving orgasm was a more powerful motivator than the gender of one's partner.

The schoolboys I grew up with were not the first to call men fairies. In the early 1900s the term "fairy" was applied to effeminate men and the men who had impersonal sex with these "fairies" were referred to as "trade," the same word prostitutes used to describe their customers. "Rough trade" were men of working or criminal class and were often chosen as sexual partners of middle- and upper-class men. Men having sex with men did not indicate abnormality or deviance. The word "gay" referred to pleasure, not an identity, and later came to mean primarily immoral pleasure. Prior to the middle of the twentieth century, coming out of the closet did not exist, because the closet did not exist. Men had to be a lot of things, but being exclusively heterosexual in terms of sexual practices was not one of them.

The world at that time was not divided, as it is today, into gay and straight, and having sex with other men didn't come with a value judgment. Chauncey writes:

> Whether homosexuality is good or bad, chosen or determined, natural or unnatural, healthy or sick is debated, for such opinions are in the realm of ideology and thus subject to contestation, and we are living in a time when a previously dominant ideological position, that homosexuality is immoral or pathological, faces a powerful and increasingly successful challenge from an alternative ideology, that regards homosexuality as neutral, healthy, or even good.

The Stonewall Revolution

Although some resistance to the oppression of homosexuality existed earlier, many believe that the Stonewall riots defined the beginning of the gay liberation movement. Police raided the Stonewall Inn, a popular gay bar in New York City, on June 27, 1969. The street filled with violent protesters and people at the bar fought back.

Following Stonewall, homosexual men and women adopted the word "gay" as a form of self-affirmation. They replaced their shame with pride and staked out a place for themselves in the midst of a hostile society. Gay men rejected the effeminate caricature of their sexuality associated with "fairies"—at least in public. Many adopted a uniform of flannel shirts, Levi's, and work boots as a means of expressing a new sense of "masculine" self. They advanced values and identities different from those prescribed by the dominant culture. The Village People became the archetypes of the new gay masculinity. "It's Raining Men" became their new national anthem. The gay community developed sovereignty within the larger community, and gay men found a visibility, solidarity, and mutual emotional support that they had not previously experienced.

But for some, the radicalized counterculture was too much. As one man I spoke to—one who chose not to label his sexual orientation although he only has sex with men—said, "I think the gay community is like a club with exclusive membership. If you don't wear the uniform, you cannot belong. I really don't understand the advantage of belonging, except [gay people] do help each other out."

Following the Stonewall riots, more men and women publicly disclosed their sexual orientation, but not all men welcomed the higher visibility of the gay community. Baby boomers, those men and women born in the explosion of births following World War II, spent their childhoods in a pre-Stonewall society. Having been so deeply closeted prior to Stonewall, many were hesitant to begin to explore their adult lives in a more tolerant post-Stonewall culture.

The "Not Me"

We have a fundamental need to repress inner contradictions to bring our thinking into alignment. We use powerful defense mechanisms that operate outside of the conscious mind to prevent unacceptable and intolerable feelings or behaviors from coming into awareness. Not uncommonly, men explain their same-sex indiscretions by saying, for example, "Oh God, was I drunk! You'll never believe what I did!" or "All I really wanted was a blow job and my wife wouldn't do it." These rationalizations are used to justify behavior that might otherwise be unacceptable.

The psychological defense mechanism called "denial" prevents information, ideas, fantasies, or impulses from reaching the conscious mind; "repression" banishes them in the event they momentarily reach consciousness. "Rationalization" seeks to justify them in an acceptable way while hoping to make them appear reasonable. Defense mechanisms can be adaptive and allow us to function normally, and can help control anxiety when a person's desires are doing battle with his or her own values. They also can be unhealthy when they are overused in order to avoid dealing with problems.

Psychological defense mechanisms prevent unacceptable thoughts from entering our conscious mind:
- Denial—believing that unacceptable attractions do not really exist
- Repression—pushing back unacceptable thoughts after stealing a look at them

- Rationalization—justifying unacceptable thoughts
  in an acceptable way

During my final year of medical school, I took a trip to St. Louis with my brother. We were exploring a gentrifying neighborhood of the city, and I went into an antiques store. My brother remained outside because he was in a wheelchair and the store was not accessible to him. I stood in the musty-smelling store examining a piece of Red Wing stoneware that I would have collected if I'd had any money. The young, attractive man who owned the store approached me. He was obviously intelligent and well educated, and I enjoyed visiting with him. He asked me a few questions, and I told him I was in medical school in Nebraska and just visiting. As we talked, he had his thumbs hooked inside the pockets of his Levi's with his fingers extending below. Suddenly, he flared out his fingers and touched my crotch. I thought, "How clumsy of him!"

When I moved away from him, he followed, engaging me in more friendly conversation. He invited me to a party that evening. As he spoke this time, he touched me once again, this time a little more assertively. I ignored him, and did not allow myself to accept the reality of his actions. In my mind, I was not ready to accept that these were sexual advances.

I walked away, looking at some other stoneware. He started to touch me for a third time. It was as if I suddenly discovered that I had forgotten to put my clothes on when I left the hotel that morning. I was aghast as I finally awakened to what was happening. I fled the store and ruminated all day about it. My first thought was, "I should call the cops!" I never confided to my brother what had happened, unconsciously believing that he would hold me responsible for inviting temptation. Although I abhorred what had happened, I was terrified that I could not hide my sense of excitement. Was it possible to feel violated while at the same time welcoming it? I focused on the abhorrence while discounting the excitement.

Inside my head was an attempt to avoid what was clear and available evidence that I had played a role in what had happened. Believing I had invited this, even in some small way, was completely unacceptable on a conscious level. In order to continue to affirm my heterosexuality, I had to alter any evidence to the contrary and ignore

14

everything that suggested I might have been accountable for what had happened. Examining the undercurrents of my unconscious might have swept me in a direction I was unwilling to go. The experience amplified my cognitive dissonance; I needed to relieve the overpowering anxiety.

It was not until much later that I could begin to accept that I had unconsciously contributed to what had happened. As long as I could be angry with the proprietor of the antiques shop, I did not have to accept my responsibility. We legitimize anger directed at injustices, but now I do not find injustice in what happened in St. Louis. Each individual must ultimately take responsibility for the way his or her sexual impulses reach expression. Blaming others for our problems does not transform us. As long as I portrayed myself as the victim and felt anger toward the perpetrator, I was able to continue to use denial, repression, and rationalization to maintain a façade of heterosexuality. As one interviewee said, "We as individuals are responsible for the course of our lives, in bed and out."

Redefining the "Bad Me"

In 1973, the American Psychiatric Association (APA) reversed itself and took the scientific position that homosexuality is not a mental disorder. Ultimately, most other professional organizations came to the same decision. In 2000, the APA joined other professional mental health associations in opposition to "reparative therapies," issuing a position statement published on their Web site that says, in part:

> In the past, defining homosexuality as an illness buttressed society's moral opprobrium of same-sex relationships. In the current social climate, claiming homosexuality is a mental disorder stems from efforts to discredit the growing social acceptance of homosexuality as a normal variant of human sexuality. Consequently, the issue of changing sexual orientation has become highly politicized. The integration of gays and lesbians into the mainstream of American society is opposed by those who fear that such an integration is morally wrong and harmful to the social fabric. The political and moral debates surrounding this issue have obscured the scientific data by calling into

15

question the motives and even the character of individuals on both sides of the issue. This document attempts to shed some light on this heated issue.

The validity, efficacy, and ethics of clinical attempts to change an individual's sexual orientation have been challenged. To date, there are no scientifically rigorous studies to determine either the actual efficacy or the harm of "reparative" treatments. There is sparse scientific data about selection criteria, risks versus benefits of the treatment, and long-term outcomes of "reparative" therapies. The literature consists of anecdotal reports of individuals who have claimed to change, people who claim that attempts to change were harmful to them, and others who claimed to have changed and then later recanted those claims.

"Reparative therapists" seek to change men from a homosexual orientation to a heterosexual one. They have based their work on the psychological theories of a distant era, when homosexuality was seen as a developmental arrest, severe psychopathology, or some combination of both. They base their theories of treatment upon an assumption that a person can and should change her or his sexual orientation.

Those who practice reparative or conversion therapy cling to the pre-Stonewall word "homosexual" and avoid using "gay." By doing so, they attempt to create an image that homosexuality is not an identity that is immutable but rather a behavior that can be changed. Most gay people believe that their sexual orientation is an innate part of their sexuality. They consider the term "sexual preference" offensive because "preference" implies a choice.

In 1948, Alfred C. Kinsey published *Sexual Behavior in the Human Male*, which described sexual orientation on a seven-point continuum, from exclusively heterosexual to exclusively homosexual. He suggested that male sexual behavior was far more diverse than held by tradition. As Justin Spring said in *Secret Historian*, "Through statistics, Kinsey had presented these individuals with a whole new way of understanding the sexual self. Among those with a homosexual orientation, feelings of guilt, shame, anxiety, and depression could be particularly intense, and so Kinsey's findings were profoundly enlightening—and, by extension, healing—to these people."

16

Viewpoints about Kinsey's research are as diverse as his description of sexuality. Opinions range from elevating him as a pioneering researcher in an age of moral hypocrisy to chastising his work as a pseudo-intellectual exercise intended on shredding the moral fabric of the nation by wrecking the family. Kinsey's work had an unintended consequence, according to Spring: "Only as society became more conscious of the nature and statistical prevalence of homosexuality within the general population did it become more violently repressive of it."

Reverend Peter Sprigg, director of marriage and family studies for the Family Research Council (FRC), a conservative lobbying group, wrote on the FRC's Web site, "We know the formula for sexual health—that is, sex within a monogamous, lifelong relationship. Studying permutations of it is an effort like Kinsey's to change the sexual mores of society, so that what most people consider deviant behaviors look more normal." Sprigg's intent was to show that gay men and women are incapable of sexual health and monogamous, lifelong relationships, something that has been disproved repeatedly.

Some men who have sex with men feel quite comfortable with Kinsey's nonbinary description of sexuality because they do not see themselves as exclusively homosexual or heterosexual. They often express that they feel more normal and comfortable in their sexual relationships with men than they do in sexual relationships with women. One man commented, "It isn't a matter of who penetrates who. Making love is way different than hook-up sex or a blow job, although some people think it's the same. It is about passion, something that just happens. No rules or agendas. There must be some kind of mutual feeling." Many straight-identified men have difficulty with labeling themselves as gay, although they are not homophobic. Some have experienced crushes on other men in their youth and accept that their emotional desire is for a romantic relationship with another man. Other men may have romantic attachments only to women but primarily have sexual attraction to men. They may have examined coming out, but they do not feel that "the gay life" is a true fit with who they are. Some simply reject society's restriction on whom they can choose to have as a sexual partner.

John Howard, discussing men who have sex with men in *Men Like That: A Southern Queer History*, wrote:

[Straight-identified men who have sex with men] should not be read as essentialized gay men unable to accept it . . . male-male sexualities happened within complicated worlds of myriad desires. To experience or act on homoerotic appetites did not necessarily define the person as gay. Male-male desire functioned beside and along with many other forms of desire—all at some times, in some places, privileged, oppressed, ignored, overlooked, spoken silenced, written, thought, frustrated, and acted upon.

I have often been asked, "How could you not know you were gay until you were forty?" I have been called a liar and a cheat by heterosexuals, and a gay man once said to me, "You have no balls. You're a liar and a hypocrite. There is no way you could not have known you were gay." However, in a society where binary logic dominates, one can be only good (straight) or evil (gay). Ambiguity, nuance, and moderation on ethical issues do not exist; at least they did not exist for me. It was not until midlife that I could finally accept that it is possible to be both gay and good.

I met my first gay lover at the gym at Iowa State University when I was forty. One day, when dressing after my shower, I noticed Alfredo, an attractive younger man, staring at me and smiling. I looked away nervously, but when I looked back at him he was still looking at me and smiling. Finally, he nodded toward the hallway door as he left the locker room and walked down the hall. As if his smile were pulling me by a magnetic force, I was unable to resist following him. In his very broken English, he invited me to come to his apartment on the next Thursday at 3 p.m. He was quite specific about the time. In my excitement to see him, I arrived about a half hour early. I was stunned when his wife greeted me at the door. Even though I, too, had a wife at home, I was astonished to learn that it was a married man that had seduced me.

Despite our marriage vows, we met each other regularly over the course of about two years. In some ways it was more acceptable to me that he was married because we shared this duplicitous life and it placed boundaries on the extent of our relationship. Knowing that he would eventually return to his home in Argentina assured me this affair would eventually come to an end. I would not be forced to make unacceptable

18

choices. Then one day he kissed me. It felt as if I'd never been kissed before.

The kiss betrayed my unconscious desires. I knew I had too much interest, not only in the sex but also in the romance. Although Alfredo and I had had sex, we followed the rules: no kissing, no anal. When he finally kissed me, I loved the kiss for what it represented about our relationship, but I hated it for the ways it might change my life. At that moment, "I just went gay all of a sudden." The kiss forced me to discover the hidden panel separating my conscious and unconscious mind, and it jarred it open so that it could never be closed again. With a rush of insight, a great deal of my life that I had not understood until then suddenly made a great deal of sense. How would I get the tiger back in the cage?

My relationship with the thirty-two-year-old Alfredo was romantic, passionate, and volatile, as many forbidden relationships are. I experienced a range and intensity of loving and erotic feelings I had never before experienced. Although my adolescent friends' captivation with women's breasts had escaped me, the excitement of an erect penis did not.

Late one evening when my mother and stepfather were visiting from Nebraska, I received a phone call from the emergency room at the hospital where I worked. "Dr. Olson, there's a young international graduate student here who says that you know him. He has asked us to contact you."

"Yes, I know him."

"He's been in a bicycle accident and has fractured his hip. He doesn't have insurance and we need to transfer him to the University Hospital in Iowa City."

Alfredo's wife had returned to Argentina. He was alone, in a great deal of pain, and he had no one. "I'll be right there," I replied.

With far too little explanation to anyone, I abandoned our guests and left for the hospital. The ambulance waited and with no further thought about consequences, I climbed in after they put him on board. His pain intensified with each little bump in the freeway on the ninety-mile trip to Iowa City. I lovingly tried to do what I could to ease it. I spent the entire night helping to get Alfredo registered and consent papers for his surgery signed. I arrived home just in time to go to work the next morning.

I visited Alfredo several times during his stay in Iowa City. After his discharge, his wife remained in Argentina. I attended to his needs

19

daily, as much as I possibly could. This emotionally intimate time intensified our investment in each other, but soon the relationship began to deteriorate. With his wife still in Argentina, Alfredo became more and more possessive of my time and grew increasingly jealous of the hours I spent away from him. We also became more realistic about the fact that he would need to return to Argentina very soon. Combined, the strain was too much.

At the same time, my wife, Lynn, finally broke through her own unconscious denial about the nature of my relationship with Alfredo. She and I began to talk about divorce, and eventually I moved out of our home into my own place.

Alfredo and I continued to see each other, and I had given him a key to my condo. One night I came home late from the hospital to find him in my apartment. He had been waiting and watching for me from the roof, and refused to accept my explanation for where I had been. He became increasingly enraged and demanded I confess to an infidelity I had not committed. Suddenly, he attacked me with his fists. I demanded that he give me back my key and leave. He angrily threw the key across the room and slammed the door so hard as he left that it rattled the dishes in the kitchen cabinets. As I looked at my bruised and swollen face in the mirror, I searched for the lies I would tell the hospital staff the next day.

> **As long as you perceive your sexual partner as nothing more than a body part, it is difficult to see yourself as anything more than an instrument for sex.**

A few weeks later, I took my daughters for a vacation at Lake Okoboji in northwest Iowa, where we planned to meet my Nebraska family. While there I received a phone call from the psychiatric unit where I worked, telling me that a young international graduate student had attempted suicide. He had asked them to call me. I replied, "Yes, I know him. Tell him I'm not available." With that, our relationship was over.

Once my relationship with Alfredo ended, so did the dissonance I felt about my sexual orientation. I began to accept that, for me, loving another man was as normal as loving a woman is for other men. This was no longer about sex but about loving, and the sex was just an expression of that love. As long as I perceived a sexual partner as nothing more than a body part with which I might achieve an impersonal orgasm, it was hard to see myself as anything more than an instrument for sex. But when I discovered that the body part was attached to a person I loved and whom I wanted to love me, everything changed.

When the moment came that I knew I was gay, insights exploded inside my mind. It immediately became obvious to me that I had found the answers to questions I'd been asking for forty years. I began to reinterpret my past in the context of my new reality. I no longer felt that being a man was contingent upon accepting the cultural definition of masculinity. It was within my power to define it for myself. I could now go to a party with gay men and talk about football, china patterns, or someone's cute butt. I still found my "man boobs" unattractive, but I no longer felt that they revealed some sexual ambiguity. There were other men who couldn't fix machines. My testicles had been restored.

Chapter 2
It's Just Common Sense

Out beyond ideas of right-doing and wrong-doing there is a field.
I'll meet you there.

—Jelaluddin Rumi

"Am I gay? Bisexual? A latent homosexual? Or a heterosexual with issues?" While hiding as they search for answers to these questions, mature men who are sexually attracted to other men find themselves caught in the crossfire between those who consider them an abomination and those who think of them as hypocritical, self-hating, closeted gay men. Those searching for answers, however, might not be asking the right questions. Rather than searching for a label that fits them, these men could be asking: "How can I understand, accept, and experience the complexities of my sexuality and align it with my values?" But it is easier just to choose a label and let the label define you.

One steamy hot day in August when I was three years old, my dad was making hay. My father had a well-trained team of horses but wanted to break in a new, partially trained horse he'd just purchased. He hitched the inexperienced horse with the steadiest and best one in his mature team, trying to train the new addition. My father was alone with the team in the hayfield when suddenly something spooked the horses. They bolted, running at full speed down the lane and back to their barn, dragging the hay—and my father who was trapped in the harnesses beneath them. As they reached the barn, they found themselves stopped abruptly because the hay wagon was too wide to fit through the doorway. My father died several days later, never having regained consciousness.

To reconstruct some image of my father I created a montage from other people's memories of him. When I was young, I would ask my mother about him, but she had canonized him and her description was more divine than mortal. I knew that I could never be just like him. Once when I was in a high school play, I needed to wear an outdated suit. My mother said that she still had my father's suit in a trunk. We went to the attic together. As she dug through the chest, she found his suit under her mother's wedding veil and old pictures of relatives I didn't remember. She removed it from the trunk and pulled it to her chest. She began to cry softly, and said, "I can still smell your dad on his suit." I tried the suit on for size, but it was too small for me. I was too big for the suit, but I could never fill my father's shoes.

I didn't know what my father looked like. I didn't know the sound of his voice. I envied my mother's ability to remember the smell of my father, for I didn't even have that memory. I needed a father as a hero and a mentor. The biased and fractured template of a man provided by my mother was all I had to use for a role model. Long before I questioned being gay, I believed that it was my father's death—and the lack of a role model—that informed my feelings of being an unfinished man.

After I had been married several years I asked a cousin, Gaylund, to tell me about my father. Our conversation lasted well into the night. "Tell me some dirt," I said. "I need some balance, something to bring him down to earth." I thought my cousin might have heard something in his family that would pluck a few feathers from the wings my mother had given him. I needed to make him more accessible to me as a human being. I needed to remove his shroud.

In the Chariot Allegory, Plato described our minds as a chariot pulled by two horses. The charioteer represents rationality, and he holds the reins and uses the whip to assert his authority. One horse in the team is well bred and well behaved. The other is obstinate and difficult to control, barely yielding to the whip. As a man experiencing sexual attraction to other men, that desire was like the obstinate and difficult-to-control horse. Once a man discovers that meeting another man eye to eye—and holding that contact for just a moment too long—betrays his interest, he can neither unlearn it nor stop doing it. He forever becomes a participant in this silent communication between men, and therefore is always at risk of losing control over the obstinate and high-spirited horse.

Some have suggested that my father, then only thirty-two, was no match for the spirited team of horses that killed him. But my Uncle Glen, who knew my father best and loved him as much as I do, insists that my father was an excellent horseman. He and my dad would get wild mustangs through the Bureau of Land Management and bring them to our farm in Nebraska. They would break the untamed animals so they could be ridden and later be sold as well-trained horses.

Pope Benedict XVI, while still Cardinal Ratzinger, apparently didn't put much stock in Plato's allegory. He wrote that the essence of being human resides in one's reason, and our conscience must guide our physical passions. Homosexual "inclination," according to Ratzinger, is not a sin, but homosexuality is "intrinsically disordered." Cardinal Ratzinger said that homosexual behavior is not a right. He also said that no one should be surprised if violence is directed at those who engage in homosexual behavior—an all too feint condemnation of violence based on hate.

Many gay men believe that once a man has been tempted to homosexual behavior, he has little choice but to give in to it. Charles Darwin thought sexuality was biologically determined. In *The Descent of Man*, Darwin wrote: "At the moment of action, man will no doubt be apt to follow the stronger impulse; and though this may occasionally prompt him to the noblest deeds, it will far more commonly lead him to gratify his own desires at the expense of other men." The subtext of Darwin's message is evident: we frequently do not operate using only rational thought even when our decisions have painful consequences to others.

When we speak of the "self," we are talking about the core of our being, the uniting principle that underlies all of our subjective experiences. The self incorporates our genetic programming with the lessons our parents and culture have taught us. We cannot change our genetic makeup, at least not as of yet, but as humans we can use our gifts for self-examination and analytical thinking to examine our values and what we have been taught. Buddha got it right when he wrote in the *Dhammapada*, "Your worst enemy cannot harm you as much as your own mind, unguarded. But once mastered, no one can help you as much, not even your father or mother."

Many resist Darwin's idea that humans aren't always capable of operating with rational thought. They believe that God gave man a special gift—the gift of reason—that elevates us above other animals. With it, they believe, we always have the capacity to deliberate and decide, to analyze the alternatives, and to weigh the pros and cons. But decisions aren't made using a series of computer chips. While we may wish to ignore our feelings, we respond as flesh and blood engaged in a palpable world. We have the capacity to deconstruct our inherited value system, analyze it, and reconstruct a value system of our own making; in fact, it is essential that we do so. But too much thinking can also lead us astray or paralyze us into stagnation.

Those who believe that there are absolutes of right and wrong and good and evil have had their thinking done for them. A book like this won't be of help to those people, because they will sort their experiences in the world, including what they read, to conform to rigid, preordained beliefs. For me, successfully understanding, accepting, and deciding how to live into my sexuality required questioning, analyzing, and reassessing some fossilized values that I had never questioned before.

> **If you believe there are absolutes of right and wrong, someone else has done your thinking for you.**

Gay Men Are Born, Not Made

In the mid-1800s, Gregor Mendel chose a small set of traits in pea plants to develop what would become the foundation of modern genetics. Mendel studied discrete characteristics that fit into only one of two different classes with no overlap or blending—green peas versus yellow ones, tall stalks versus dwarf varieties, etc. I have what my family calls the "Koester nose." At family reunions, cousins, aunts, and uncles in the clan all stand in line for pictures, profiles exposed. Cameras click and cousins joke about the dubious heritage of those who don't have "the nose." In looking at those photos, it certainly does not require an understanding of Mendel's peas to have a basic grasp of the power of genetics.

Our fate is not determined exclusively by genes. Although noses may be similar, they cannot be separated into only two characteristic types. Sir Francis Galton, a contemporary of Mendel and a close relative of Darwin, studied the inheritance of characteristics that could be quantified along a continuum—for example, height and intelligence. Galton's work was the beginning of understanding "multifactorial inheritance." He discovered that development of any trait requires a combination of genetic predisposition and environmental features, such as nutrition. When I was a teenager, all of the boys hoped to reach the magical height of six feet tall; now that height is common for boys. Girls were never six feet tall as they occasionally are now. Genetics didn't change, but our environment has. But no matter how favorable the environment, if the genetics aren't present for height, some men will never be tall enough to play basketball for the NBA. Many diseases and most physical and personality traits likely have several genes that trigger their development, but the context in which they develop also significantly influences the way those traits unfold. It is possible that being gay is a consequence of the presence or absence of multiple genes, each with a limited effect but collectively influenced by the environment.

Homosexuality is a complex behavioral trait that Stella Hu and her colleagues in a 1995 article for *Nature Genetics* reported to involve multiple genetic factors of DNA on the X chromosome. Even before the ink had dried, the theological press began to consider testing fetuses for the "gay gene" and speculated that abortion could "cleanse" society of the homosexual curse.

Most gay men accept a genetic explanation for homosexuality because they believe they were born, not made. And a growing consensus of human sexuality researchers and mental health professionals concede that we do not choose our sexual orientation. Homosexual orientation is increasingly acknowledged to be a human trait, like being left-handed. And, as studies of twins separated at birth show, there is strong evidence that genetics determines a significant part of our personality—including such things as sexuality.

However, biology is necessary but not sufficient to explain the occurrence of being gay. In fact, correlations exist between being gay and being left-handed. Correlations also exist between being gay and being the younger sibling of older brothers, or having hair that forms a whorl in a counterclockwise direction. But correlations only establish linkages, and several steps must be taken before causation can be established. After researchers combine correlations with biologic plausibility, they look for models in the animal kingdom. These studies support a growing belief that a person's sexual attractions are a combination of genetic factors decided at the moment of conception and triggered by the environment. Interestingly, child psychiatrists who interview kids in many cases can determine by the age of five which children will grow up to be gay. And mothers always seem to know.

A few studies of questionable validity have shown that some gay people can change their sexual behavior, but a real change in self-identity in most cases does not occur. While sexual *behavior* may be chosen, the preponderance of evidence suggests that sexual *attraction* is dictated by biology, with little or no demonstrated contribution from social factors. Religious conservatives and "reparative" or "transformational" therapists who are committed to changing sexual orientation vehemently protest such proclamations. They do not want homosexuality to be intrinsically human, just intrinsically evil. Either homosexuality is abnormal, chosen, changeable, and hated by God more than all other sins, or it is innate and created by a God who doesn't make mistakes. If being gay is innate, it cannot be changed; if it is a behavior, it is one from which a person can choose to abstain, however difficult reining in the untamed animal might be.

Genes contain DNA that forms a blueprint for making proteins that influence behavior. In 1990, a cooperative effort among international partners launched the Human Genome Project, whose goal was to sequence all three billion base pairs of DNA in the human body. Completed in 2003, this project sequenced and mapped all the genes in the human genome, forming a genetic master plan that makes up each and every human being. Genes occur in pairs, and from one person to the next, 99 percent of these pairs are identical. The remaining 1 percent of gene pairs accounts for the possibility of millions of potential variations between the genomes of two people. All of us are much more alike than different, but those differences are many and important. The challenge is to determine how to read the blueprint and understand how all these many and complex parts work together to make us the people we are.

Figure 1: The nucleus of our self-identity

When a single gene determines the presence or absence of a trait, that gene is rather easily discovered. However, no single gene, or even a combination of genes, dictates whether or not someone will have a specific behavioral trait. In other words, even if a gene is present, it won't necessarily express itself. Additionally, genes can be switched off and on. A good example is schizophrenia, which was once thought to be caused by mothers. We now know there are genetic correlates. Although schizophrenia occurs more frequently in identical twins than in fraternal twins, schizophrenia does not occur in all identical twins because of what is called "gene penetration." In other words, although identical twins have the same genetic code, if one develops schizophrenia, the other twin is at higher risk but may or may not have symptoms of this disorder.

According to Justin Spring, Alfred Kinsey's work in the 1950s supported the idea that sexual variations were entirely consistent with genetic theories. In *Secret Historian: The Life and Times of Samuel Steward, Professor, Tattoo Artist, and Sexual Renegade*, Spring wrote:

> [Kinsey's] findings suggested that variations in sexual behavior were not based on acts of will and individual choice, as religious teachings had always insisted. Rather they were based on widespread biological variations existing within the human population: in other words, on genetic variation.

Genes vary in their expression. In a 1991 study of identical and fraternal twins, Bailey and Pillard found that if one identical twin is gay, the chance of the other being gay is 52 percent. In fraternal twins, however, the chance is only 22 percent. In identical twins, if one is gay, the other is much more likely also to be gay, but one may be gay and the other straight. Many people believe that this is because homosexuality is related to several genes, all of which vary in their degree of expression.

Evolutionary theory would seem to predict that homosexuality should be rare or nonexistent because only those humans with the strongest genes for survival and reproduction would spread their advantageous genes throughout whole populations. Those who oppose the idea that homosexuality is genetic use the logic that gay men presumably don't spread their DNA very far, because they aren't traditionally reproducing. "How could their combination of 'gay genes' be passed on?" these critics ask. Arguments that homosexuality cannot be genetic because it is "non-procreative," and therefore would eventually be extinguished, have been countered by the study of other species in the animal kingdom in which non-procreative individuals exist. Felix Warneken and Michael Tomasello say they have found an "altruism gene," which suggests that a group in which reproductive and non-reproductive members cooperate may be much stronger than groups composed only of selfish members who look exclusively after their own interests.

In evolutionary biology, an organism is said to behave altruistically when its behavior benefits other organisms, but it does so at its own expense. By behaving altruistically the unselfish worker bee produces no offspring, but at the same time, the bee enhances the health of the entire bee community. Its behavior boosts the reproductive capabilities of the queen bee and increases the chances of survival of the entire bee colony.

The survival of an entire population has advantages over the survival of an individual. Individuals are expendable. Homosexuality in most cases leads into an evolutionary blind alley, but some scientists believe that homosexuals serve an altruistic purpose in the larger population. Homosexuals may contribute to the survival of their genetic base by assisting in the care and survival of their families who share their DNA. In this way, families that contain a homosexual gene—if there is one—might have better survival rates than families that don't, even though each individual homosexual might be an evolutionary dead end.

Ignorance and Common Sense

People who intentionally avoid or disagree with facts—no matter how well founded—simply because those facts oppose or contradict their personal beliefs, exhibit "willful ignorance." Some conservative religious and political groups are suspicious of all science, including the big bang theory, evolution, and global warming. They consider science to be driven by a conspiracy of liberal academics, the media, and Hollywood. Several years ago, they had a fit when headlines exclaimed, "Gay Gene Found."

It is unlikely that such skeptics will accept any genetic explanation for homosexuality based on a study such as counterclockwise hair whorls. They often attempt to dismiss these studies with sarcasm rather than facts. They are correct, however, when they argue that even when a correlation exists, those correlations do not establish causality. The gay community, eager to establish an innate basis for sexual orientation, too frequently lifts up these studies as proof, drawing conclusions beyond those that can be supported by the data in the study. Both sides of the argument remain in an ideological gridlock.

Until 2007, polls generally found that a majority of Americans believed gay people could change their sexual orientation if they so desired. Now, a majority believes homosexuality is inborn. As a psychiatrist, I understand the exploitation of facts on both sides of the genetic debate. Both proponents and skeptics manipulate well-founded arguments in order to maintain the stability of their beliefs. Discrediting one deeply held belief threatens the security of all other beliefs. Accepting a fact or an argument that contradicts one's personal beliefs cracks the barrier that separates good from evil. So, for example, if one accepts that our world was created through evolution rather than by God as described in Genesis, everything that follows Genesis in the Bible comes into question. Thinking only in black and white simplifies an understanding of the world.

Moral issues are ostensibly decided on the basis of solid logic, but that is rarely the case. Morality is strongly related to our feelings and outlook on the world. And feelings most often come before reason. Arguments are invented. Like a snowball fight, as one argument is hurled at the opposition, it is deflected, only to be followed repeatedly by another. Haidt, Koller, and Dias, in a 1993 paper referred to as "Is it wrong to eat your dog?" use the term "moral dumbfounding" to describe how, when people run out of reasons and have exhausted their list of moral justifications, they start arguing without substance. They make comments like, "Because it's just wrong and disgusting. That's why." Their research dissects moral psychology into two parts: emotion and cognition. They discovered that we feel answers first and then search for moral arguments to justify the wrongness to back up our instinctual beliefs. Their findings have major implications for the theological arguments on the morality of homosexuality. When we feel it is wrong, we seek arguments to defend our belief. Almost nothing will convince us to change those emotionally charged beliefs.

Psychiatrists have learned through their study of the psychological development of children that values originate in the intimate lives of families, in whose presence they initially feel defenseless. Families socialize us into our communities; friends and loved ones teach us how to participate in our small corner of the world. A system of rewards and punishments directs how we should live. A young child absorbs these "truths," knowing almost as if by instinct what is expected of him. He does not wish to disappoint his parents whom he depends upon for love, approval, and security. He feels tremendous pressure to conform to their values, ideals, and goals, even when they have not been explicitly stated.

For all of us, this pressure forms the basis for our self-esteem, and we internalize it as our conscience, the standard against which we measure all of our behavior. Freud named it the super-ego. Parents call it "common sense," the knowledge that they believe most people consider practical and sensible. Albert Einstein is reported to have said, "Common sense is the collection of prejudices acquired by age eighteen."

Theories evolve over time. The classic psychodynamic explanation for the development of male homosexuality—always presented in terms of pathology—that I read over and over in medical school and in my psychiatric training was a distant father and a close binding mother. Reparative therapists continue to blame fathers primarily for creating their gay sons. They believe that homosexuality is caused by the absence of a happy, warm, and intimate relationship with a father who has been "repeatedly disappointing." According to these theories, the son detaches from the father in order to protect himself from the pain of those disappointed expectations, and he seeks to replace the "encircling arms" of the father with a sexual relationship with another man.

My father wasn't distant. He was dead. Even though reparative therapists do make exceptions for boys whose fathers have died, I cannot fathom having my wish for an intimate personal and rewarding sexual relationship with a man to be trivialized by considering it nothing more than a need for the "encircling arms" of my father. How can the complexities of sexuality be reduced to such a simplistic interpretation? If it were that simple, wouldn't a warm and loving relationship with his mother draw a young man toward a similar relationship with a woman? Although many of the men whom I have interviewed have had some difficult relationships with their fathers, the pseudo-science of the reparative therapy movement has confused correlation—difficult father-son relationships—with causation—men developing same-sex attraction. And their theory ignores entirely those gay men who have perfectly warm relationships with their fathers. Could it be that some fathers pull away from their sons simply because they don't know how to be a father to a gay son? During the years before I came out while thinking of myself as an "incomplete" man, I believed I might be more successful as a father of daughters rather than sons; after coming out and feeling complete, I recognized that those worries were invalid.

Although far from universal, some themes about the relationship of gay sons with their mothers and fathers come up repeatedly in the stories of the lives of men I have talked with:

1. Sometimes mothers do sense that their son is different from other boys-will-be-boys male children, and may have early valid concerns that their child needs protection from bullies.
2. Some sons may share interest in more traditionally female activities.
3. Sometimes fathers do have difficulty finding common ground with their gay sons, and pull away, preferring other sons whose interests are more compatible with their own.

33

However, even if some correlation between homosexuality and mother-son/father-son relationships exists, these themes don't prove that homosexuality is a disorder that must be treated, as opposed to a variance that must be understood. The task is not to redefine an individual man, molding him into the heterosexual masculine stereotype, but to redefine the boundaries of what it means to be a man.

Apparently others in my hometown felt that I needed masculine role models, just as I thought I did. I remembered how as a child, I was dragged to a father-son banquet at our church by some childless old man who smelled of stale cigarette smoke. I scarcely knew him and we barely spoke to each other. Neither of us wanted to be reminded that we didn't really belong there, and he was definitely not a man I would have chosen to use to model my life after.

My brother was a gifted athlete, just as my father had been, and I knew that I couldn't be like either of them. I was a chubby kid who preferred twirling a baton to throwing any kind of ball. When I was nine years old, my brother was seriously injured in a car accident, which led to his becoming a quadriplegic. For a time after he was injured, I thought, "I've got to be a good baseball player because now he can't be one." No matter how hard I tried, the coaches always put me out in right field, the place where they thought I would do the least damage to the team. Although no one ever said it directly to me, I assumed others were thinking that the wrong brother had been injured, as if two lives were now wasted. Being a man in my family was difficult and dangerous, and I felt my training had been insufficient.

Throughout my entire adolescence, I consciously searched for men I could model myself after. I felt I had only a fragmented sense of the person I should be. I wasn't looking for sex, but a way to be initiated as a member into the fraternity of men, and my ideas of what it meant to be a man were very superficial and idealistic. I feared, "If I don't know how to be a man, how can I ever hope to hang on to someone I love?" Being called a "sissy" or a "faggot" only really hurt me because I already believed it to be true. As a young man, I didn't know that the struggle for my identity was the same struggle many

> **Being called a "sissy" or a "faggot" only hurts if one already believes it to be true.**

other young men were having, albeit with different explanations and outcomes.

One seventy-two-year-old man from Georgia, still married to a woman, but self-identified as gay, remembered how he began to hide his interest in art and classical music after being called a sissy. He played tennis in high school and college, hardly a match for playing football in the South. His youthful rationalization for feeling different from other young men was that he had had a more genteel, Southern upbringing, one that led him to be more "cultured" than his friends. After revealing to me that his first crush was on Roy Rogers, he said, "I know I was born this way and I expect someday a gene will be discovered to explain it."

When I was in my psychiatry residency, I turned thirty-two years old—my father's age at the time of his death. I also had a daughter who was three, my age when he died. My mother and I became very close after my father's death, but the void he left was always present. One day the director of my residency asked me about my father. I began to cry. He referred me to a psychiatrist to help me deal with the grief issues that had haunted me for thirty years.

The psychiatrist and I did some work with dreams. I had dreamt that my mother was lying in her bed as I entered her room. The bed was dressed in satin sheets. She was propped up on pillows, her hair dyed the color of carrots and tied with a pink ribbon. She wore too much makeup, theatrically applied. As I approached the bed she said, "Before we kill the fatted calf, let's have a couple of bonbons." Distant father? Check. Close binding mother? Check. I saw my psychiatrist for several months, but my grief was only part of the problem. Even after repairing those damaged fragments of my psychological self in psychotherapy, I still had no understanding of my sexual self.

Around this time I traveled to New York City for a meeting. While I was there, I visited a friend of mine who I knew was gay. After having several drinks, we went out for dinner and continued to drink. It was clear to me that I shared his enthusiasm for getting me drunk. I offered no resistance, and when we got back to his apartment, I had sex with a man for the first time as an adult. And for the second and third time, too.

I knew I had to disclose what had happened to my therapist. My revelation very clearly made him uncomfortable. He recommended that I read Allen Drury's *Advise and Consent*. One of the main characters in the story is plagued by his homosexual past and jumps off a bridge to his death. Why did my therapist recommend this book? Was he predicting an untimely death if I continued my "destructive" behavior? To be fair to him, at the time, the American Psychiatric Association was still debating whether or not homosexuality was a pathologic deviancy.

Although my therapist's handling of the situation still baffles me, I am grateful that he did not treat it as harshly as he could have; he had the power to end my career in psychiatry. We never spoke of the incident in New York again, and soon after we both agreed that I should terminate psychotherapy.

After more than thirty years of thinking about it, I can now confidently reject the empty claims made by the psychiatrists who trained me. Perhaps gay sons have rejected their fathers so that the father doesn't discover their secret wish to play with their sister's Barbie dolls. Even those boys who can throw a football like a bullet may find it hard to be around their father if they find themselves attracted to his best friend. Neither my father's death nor having a strong but loving mother made me gay. I am gay, and I always have been gay. My life was transformed as I discovered this truth about myself, and in the process, the lives of others who love me were also changed by their discovery of it.

Chapter 3
God Hates Fags: In Bondage to Dogma

Everyone has a holy place, a refuge,
where their heart is purer, their mind clearer,
Where they feel closer to God or love of truth or whatever it is they
happen to worship.

—*The Tender Bar*,
J. R. Moehringer

"If you don't believe that Jonah could reach out and touch the walls of that fish's stomach, you are not a Christian." Those were the words I heard from the preacher when I attended services in one of those new big box churches in Ohio a few years ago. Earlier in his sermon about Jonah and the whale, he had established—at least to his own satisfaction—that Jonah had been swallowed by a fish, not a whale. His message was quite clear: believe as I believe or you will go to hell. No ambiguity, no nuance, no discussion. No thought or introspection was required, only obedience. During the sermon he made several jokes about "hom-o-SEX-u-als." Obviously, he hated my sin, but I couldn't feel any love for the sinner either. By the time I heard him speak these words, I had grown confident enough in my own sexuality and my faith that I couldn't be shaken by his remarks. But I felt tremendous anger toward him and empathy for his congregants who were being told that to think for themselves would send them straight to hell.

Although the message about homosexuals from the preacher in Ohio was subtle, the message of the Westboro Baptist Church of Topeka, Kansas, is anything but subtle. In fact, they are known widely for their "God hates fags" message. In October 2010, the U.S. Supreme Court heard arguments in a classic case to determine whether or not the First Amendment guarantees the rights of members of this congregation to exploit a bereaved family. Albert Snyder of York, Pennsylvania, claimed he was harmed by a protest by this church held at the funeral of his son, Lance Cpl. Matthew Snyder, who died in a Humvee accident in 2006. Margie Phelps, an attorney who happens to be the daughter of Fred

Phelps, the pastor of the church, argued in front of the Court that the Constitution protects unpopular speech as well as conventional views. Reverend Fred Phelps and other church members of the Westboro Baptist Church picketed Snyder's funeral, carrying signs that read, "Thank God for Dead Soldiers" and "God Hates Fags." The protestors were not claiming that Snyder was gay, but that all war deaths are God's punishment of a country that tolerates homosexuality. The congregation has held their protests at a number of funerals for fallen soldiers— ironically, the very ones who have died to protect their freedom of speech.

The congregation of the Westboro Baptist Church published this on their Web site: "Since 1955, the Westboro Baptist Church has taken the precious from the vile . . . [The] WBC took her ministry to the street, conducting over 43,851 peaceful demonstrations (to date) opposing the fag lifestyle of soul-damning, nation-destroying filth."

I grew up in Nebraska in a town of just over one thousand people, a number that has remained nearly the same for more than one hundred years. Doors were never locked in anyone's home. I once asked my mother why she left the keys in her car, and she responded, "You never know who might need to borrow your car." In my hometown, there were several churches, all Protestant, with more churches in the rural countryside. The church was the center of most social activities; a deceased person's worth was measured by the number of people who attended his or her funeral service. We had only a handful of Roman Catholic families. One Jewish person lived there, but he later became a Lutheran. Church attendance was expected. During Lent, the entire school let out for lunch served at my Lutheran church. Each morning in school the Pledge of Allegiance was followed by the Lord's Prayer. No one ever questioned singing Christmas carols at school Christmas programs.

Every Saturday during my seventh- and eighth-grade years, I attended confirmation classes at my Lutheran church. Our class was taught by a stern and childless Scandinavian minister. His wife was the organist and my mother directed the choir. In our confirmation class, anyone who could play the piano was required to learn a hymn and play it while the class sang. One of the boys in my class told the pastor that I could play even though I'd never taken any lessons. Perhaps because my mother was so musical, the pastor believed my friend rather than me and insisted I learn a hymn. I could not escape the humiliation of stumbling through a hymn, amid the laughter of my classmates. At the conclusion of our confirmation classes, we had a public examination in front of the congregation. All of the confirmands sat in the choir loft at the front of the church as the pastor drilled us on *Luther's Catechism*. We were expected to testify to our beliefs and our commitment to the faith.

This was the world in which mature men like me, men who have sex with men, were born. Because I was raised a Lutheran, I assumed I would always be a Lutheran. I believed that if my life didn't conform to the dogma, it was my life that needed to be changed, not the dogma. For many years, these beliefs remained unexamined and unchallenged. My failure to challenge these inherited beliefs contributed significantly to my coming out late in life.

The Bondage of Dogma

Marcus J. Borg, in *Meeting Jesus Again for the First Time: The Historical Jesus and the Heart of Contemporary Faith,* wrote that "the internalized voice of culture" forms a core value system that impacts all of our later life experiences. It provides a set of rules that serve the interest of all society and forms guidelines by which the majority live. When any subsequent event in one's life occurs, it is filtered through this belief system. Ultimately it affects the way we feel and the way we respond to everything.

Figure 2: Each event in our lives is filtered through an internalized belief system that affects the way a person responds to that event.

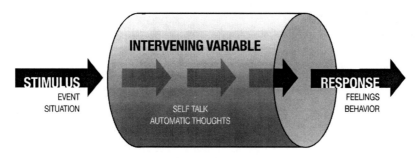

When it comes to religion, the media often presents to us only the two extremes: either homosexuality is an abomination or homophobia is the real evil. Conflict leads to tension, tension lends drama, and drama creates interest. Intermediate positions between the extremes are usually overlooked. Most Americans, even those who find homosexuality morally unacceptable, see the actions taken by the Westboro Baptist Church as extreme and unacceptable. Those who take a more neutral position on the morality of homosexuality may feel that it is acceptable, but only if a person remains celibate or if same-sex behavior occurs only in the context of a committed relationship.

The position of right wing Christianity and of most fundamentalist religions is that everyone is essentially heterosexual and that there is no such thing as homosexual orientation. Homosexuality is seen as a "lifestyle," as if it were a choice between living in the city or at the beach. Homosexual feelings and homosexual behavior are seen as equally sinful. Homosexuality is seen as a product of original sin, a perversion that traps people in a lifestyle of lust. They believe that because homosexuals are driven by lust that they are incapable of a loving, nonexploitive relationship. When debating the morality of homosexuality, religious conservatives isolate and lift up biblical verses as "proof texts" to prove that homosexuality is an abomination. Many in the gay community think of these as "the clobber passages."

The most conservative religions preach that all of God's truths have already been revealed, are recorded in the words of the prophets, and are governed by objective criteria for right and wrong. Fundamentalist Christians define homosexuality in terms of what gay people do, not who they are. They believe that men who have sex with men *should* experience dissonance because they are living lives contrary to God's laws. Religious conservatives consider the capacity to reason as the essence of being human and

> **"Clobber passages," – or biblical texts often cited as God's condemnation of homosexuality:**
> - **Genesis 19:1—5**
> - **Leviticus 18:22 and 20:13**
> - **Deuteronomy 23:17**
> - **Romans 1:21—31**
> - **1 Corinthians 6:9—10**
> - **1 Timothy 1:9—10**
> - **Jude 1:6—7**

that reason and conscience should be a guide to dealing with the power of physical passions. For the first forty years of my life, I believed that, too.

40

Many who have been unable to reconcile their sexuality and their religious beliefs have abandoned religion altogether. But one cannot presuppose that everyone who assumes a gay identity sheds his spiritual identity. I receive a lot of correspondence similar to this one from a young man in Indonesia, edited slightly for easier reading:

> Yes, I am a Muslim and I do not so well as Muslim, just enough for me, common of men in my age. So I'm not so bad. I am hav[ing] an [attraction to men] but I am not a gay. I keep it safe from my friend, family also. I'm not lie to myself, but I want to marry woman to doing what my religion teach . . .

The most progressive view of homosexuality is that sexual orientation is not a moral issue. Morality is seen as having nothing to do with what we do sexually but by how we care for and about others. Sexual behavior, whether homosexual or heterosexual, must be judged as moral or immoral only in the context in which sexuality is expressed. It is moral if it is consensual, noncoercive, and safe. Some even believe that if these criteria are met, a loving and committed relationship is not essential for sexual behavior to be considered moral.

Can More Than One Road Lead to Heaven?

For about twenty years I struggled with attempting to reconcile being gay with my religious faith. After I recognized my homosexuality and accepted that I would always be gay, I found it increasingly difficult to practice my faith in the manner it was handed down to me. Like so many other gay men, I began to feel that the only way for me to feel good about myself was to remove myself from the persistent condemnation I felt. Yet being without a spiritual base also left me feeling unsettled, and I made repeated but unsuccessful attempts to return to the church I had known. Like the horses involved in my father's death, I was frightened and sought to return to the security of the only barn I knew, but my sexuality wouldn't let me through the door.

I was raised a Lutheran, and it was a critical part of my identity for many years. In my last attempt to practice, I visited a large and growing Lutheran church in Des Moines. After the service, I sent the minister an e-mail, asking him about their gay and lesbian outreach efforts. His response was brief. "None. We are a family church." Even after many years as an openly gay man, I was taken aback. How could I possibly join a church that so clearly was unwelcoming to me, one that insisted I remain anxious and afraid to love someone of the same sex? I was saddened, and could not understand why I should be required to live only half a life while others could live theirs completely. Since I knew my attraction to men wouldn't go away, and my success in suppressing it had been only moderately successful for the first forty years of my life, I left the Lutheran Church.

Religious institutions, like religious people, are toiling with the morality of homosexuality, and the struggle has resulted in divisions within these institutions just as it has resulted in estrangement within families. Between the two extreme positions on the morality of homosexuality, churches have come to different conclusions. Some believe that homosexuality is a behavior that can be changed, and therefore *must* be changed, and the individual who feels he cannot change must remain celibate. Other churches have taken the position that, while homosexuality is not acceptable, when weighed against promiscuity, it is less sinful if it occurs in the context of a loving and committed relationship. Still other churches, like the United Church of Christ and the Unitarian Universalist churches, have taken the stance that homosexuality is morally neutral and that homosexual and heterosexual loving and committed relationships are equivalent.

Marcus J. Borg wrote, "[Life in this world] is a life of bondage to the dominant culture." Values and religious traditions are so totally incorporated as a part of us that they seem almost inherited from our families. Anything so deeply ingrained is extremely difficult to change. But when you are gay and your church and family say it is wrong, that is where the change must begin. With increasing maturity, we can begin to see the imperfections in our parents; our heroes fall from grace and the framework of our religious dogma weakens. We learn that prejudices and prohibitions often are based on incorrect assumptions. We begin to realize that social values and traditions are not fixed but rather evolve over time. Rigid and restrictive religion is responsible for much of the shame that gay men feel about their sexual orientation, and many of them have left all religious tradition behind because of it.

Religious institutions hold power over their congregants, and the effects of religious dogma can be devastating. This has created a significant backlash against religion in the gay community. For some, however, spiritual identity is more highly valued than sexual orientation. In my interviews some men expressed the view that it can be easier to come out as gay in their communities of faith than it is to come out in the gay community as religiously oriented. Douglas C. Haldeman suggests in "Gay Rights, Patient Rights: The Implications of Sexual Orientation Conversion Therapy" that it is as ethically irresponsible to ask people to abandon their religion in favor of their sexual orientation as it is for conversion therapists to suggest that people can give up their sexual orientation because of their religious convictions. Suggesting that people must choose between their sexual orientation or their religious beliefs can only prolong their internal dissonance.

After my mother died, while I was searching for clothes for her burial, I found a drawer in her dresser filled with books that she had hidden. The books were for parents who were trying to understand their child's homosexuality, religious books recommended by her pastor that condemned my behavior. My grief for her passing was

> **Jesus and Muhammad didn't have common sense; they both challenged the conventional wisdom of their time.**

compounded by an incredible sadness. She had never hinted to me that my behavior had put her Christian faith to such a test. Her anxiety was created by her love for me, and an unflinching dedication to a faith that told her I was going straight to hell. Rather than rejecting me, she had tried to understand me.

Uncommon Sense

What people think of as "common sense" is all of those beliefs that we feel should be shared by everyone. What Jesus and Muhammad taught is that what we should have is *un*common sense, not common sense. Both Marcus J. Borg and Reza Aslan, who wrote *No god but God: The Origins, Evolution, and Future of Islam*, make the case that what contributed to the greatness of both Jesus and Muhammad was the fact that both challenged the conventional wisdom of their time, and they did so not by producing a new set of laws but by offering insights that challenged people to develop greater understanding.

In recent years, religious conservatives promoted "abstinence pledges" for teens as a way of discouraging premarital sex, but teenagers who pledged to remain virgins until marriage were just as likely to have premarital sex as those who did not promise abstinence. I knew that no matter what kind of promises I made not to respond to my sexual attraction to other men, I would fail. Whether teenage heterosexuals or mature homosexual men, it seems that when reason and passion battle, the one driving the chariot often loses control.

I began to realize that I didn't have to act on all of my sexual inclinations, but I wanted to act on some of them. I came to believe that moral standards are imperfect and change as societies evolve. I found that there are progressive churches where homosexuality is seen as morally neutral and natural for a minority of people. I learned that the only resolution to my conflict in values was to unhitch the horses from the wagon.

The bigger the secret, the greater its impact once it is finally revealed. Reverend Ted Haggard was president of the National Evangelical Association, representing thirty million evangelical Christians, when he was disgraced for having a sexual relationship with a male prostitute. Although he preached sermons with anti-gay messages, he was preaching one thing and doing another. When he left his church and his church leadership positions, he said, "There is a part of my life that is so repulsive and dark that I've been warring against it all of my adult life." Evangelical leaders abandoned Haggard as he left the church he had founded. Haggard has been widely criticized by the gay community because, as Jon Stewart said on *The Daily Show*, "People like you [Haggard] make it really hard for, quite frankly, people like you."

Appearing to believe he is more unique than he really is, Haggard told Oprah Winfrey on her show, "I do believe I don't fit into the normal boxes. I do think there are complexities associated with some people's sexuality, but it just wasn't as simple as I wanted it to be." In the documentary movie *The Trials of Ted Haggard*, Haggard appears to be a man struggling to be honest with himself, the world, and his God. Asked whether he could define his sexual identity, Haggard said, "I just thought a spiritual solution would be the solution to everything that's internal. That turned out not to be the case." When he said the familiar gay mantra, "I am what I am," he followed it with, "I was born an evangelical." Shame is the public exposure of private guilt, and recently Haggard has claimed that his homosexual escapades were because as a child he was sexually abused by an adult male. According to his wife, Gayle, through his therapy, he no longer has "those compulsions."

The conflict for men and women who come out in midlife is no more or less difficult than it is for young people, but in some ways, because they have been passing as heterosexual in a heterosexual world, it is more complicated, and reconciliation of their contradictory values has been put on hold. The conflict for the mature man usually isn't about whether or not to change—most know they cannot. The conflict is about losing a wife and kids, a job, family and friends, and in some cases, religious faith. Although many of the risks of a vaguely perceived future are more imagined than real, coming out in midlife can lead to an almost total loss of the family and religious community support that was previously enjoyed.

I feel some empathy and compassion for Haggard, and the judgment and intolerance he has received from both his church and the LGBT community are disturbing. The power of his story should not come from watching a dogmatic hypocrite fall! It could easily be lost in the ideological gridlock between religious conservatives and liberal supporters of gay rights. Such contradictions are echoed over and over in the lives of millions of men who struggle to beat back their natural homosexual urges. When they fail to do so, they lose their families and friends, only to find themselves rejected by the gay community, the very ones who should welcome and embrace them.

Although Haggard preached his fire and brimstone deceptions from a national pulpit, all gay men have lied about their sexuality at some point. In the mid-1980s, I sat on a committee to define benefits that would be covered by an HMO. One of the managers said that they were developing a health questionnaire that was designed to identify gay men so they could deny them insurance because of the potential high costs of HIV treatment. Pretending to speak in a whisper, one physician asked, "What do you ask them? Do you like to take it up the ass?" I sat there in stunned disbelief. I had just left my wife and children, was not out professionally, nor was I sure I could be, and I needed a job to pay alimony and child support. I was paralyzed. The painful, personal awareness that I had not lived up to my own moral standards by speaking up has never left me, but my failure to respond was the result of a conflict between my fears of what I might lose and my underexamined sexuality. Coming out is not an event, nor is it a linear process. It is like Odysseus's ship, sailing from point to point, but driven time and again off course.

Gay men and women waste a lot of energy hating a homophobic culture and blaming it for the guilt and shame they feel. As Reverend Candace Chellew-Hodge writes in *Bulletproof Faith: A Spiritual Survival Guide for Gay and Lesbian Christians*, "Work out your own demons, and the perceived demons in others suddenly disappear." If one wishes freedom and peace about same-sex attractions, the homophobic bondage inside one's head is the first thing that must be addressed.

Are Morals Relative or Fixed?

Attitudes in the United States are changing. More and more people believe the criteria by which to judge the morality of homosexual relationships are the degree of commitment, a lack of coercion and manipulation, safety, permanence, and fidelity. The Values and Beliefs Survey completed by Gallup in May 2010 found that acceptance of gay relationships has continued to increase in the United States. Those considering gay and lesbian relations morally acceptable exceeded 50 percent in that survey for the first time. In the same survey, Americans who are opposed to homosexual relationships dropped to 43 percent, the lowest in Gallup's decade-long trend. Attitudes among men, particularly men younger than fifty, accounted for the greatest change. In fact, changes in attitudes of young men accounted for almost all of the increase in acceptance in that survey. The survey also found that fewer and fewer people are attributing homosexuality to their upbringing or environment. If one does not accept an inherent sinfulness of homosexuality, justice demands that both homosexual and heterosexual relationships be judged by the same standards of morality.

When I became a member of my church, I asked the senior minister, "How can you have a conversation with a fundamentalist Christian without getting cross-wise with them?" He thought for a while, and then he responded, "I have not found it difficult to have these conversations as long as we focus on the meaning of the Scripture instead of the details of it." This is the model that can be used in resolving the conflict in our consciences between the good and evil of homosexuality, the meaning rather than the explanation of it. For some, homosexual activity may simply be one more way to achieve sexual satisfaction. For many more, the meaning is about a deep and committed love for another person.

But introspection and analytical thinking can help individuals resolve inner conflicts. Some may choose to remain homosexually celibate, but that will often require guarding every aspect of one's life to avoid being dragged by a team of horses like my father was. When one horse in a team is high-spirited (and, in this case, driven by primitive sexual urges), the horse continuously challenges the skills of the charioteer, waiting for just the right moment to break away. Spiritual beliefs can be a source of comfort but can also prove an irresolvable conflict. Unless a person can begin to understand his homosexuality in the context of a reconstructed value system, the only option may be to pray for a miracle.

Sadly, religion has been used to justify hate, but it is not easy to hate people you know. The more gay men and women publicly acknowledge their sexual orientation, the more tolerant our society will become. However, on an individual basis the decision to come out is a painful struggle no matter how old you are. It can be made less painful by getting to know those who believe that being both gay and religious is acceptable. The LGBT community walks a delicate line between justifiable and appropriate anger, and intolerance and vengeful rage. Both sides of this divisive argument must begin to find common ground. Freedom from the bondage of this internalized ideological conflict comes when one begins to realize on a very personal level that good and gay are not mutually exclusive.

Chapter 4
Out from the Shadows: You're Not the Man You Thought You Were

We stand before a hundred doors, choose one, where we're faced with a hundred more and then we choose again.

—*Bridge of Sighs*,
Richard Russo

I didn't know my mother's father had shot himself until twenty years after it happened, despite the fact that we lived under the same roof with him when he took his life. I only found out as my brother and I passed the home of an old woman who had difficulty with depression and had resisted treatment. I asked him how she was doing.

"She hung herself," my brother said.

"Oh, no," I responded. "I just don't see how anyone could ever do that."

"Well," he said, "I guess it was sort of like Grandpa Koester."

"What do you mean?" I half questioned, half shouted.

"You know, like when Grandpa shot himself."

"What! Why didn't anyone ever tell me?" I demanded.

"I guess we thought you knew," he said.

Years later my sister told me that early one morning our mother had heard a gunshot. When Mother went to the basement, she found Grandpa. She rushed us off to school so we wouldn't be there when the police and ambulance arrived. News travels fast in a small town, and my older sister learned what had happened from her friends when she arrived at school that morning. My younger sister didn't hear about his suicide until several years later; one of her friends told her. I only now have a hazy memory of being told Grandpa had wanted to go to sleep and not wake up, probably enough of an explanation for a five-year-old. I remember wondering how someone could have known he was going to die, but I had no reference for understanding suicide. I remember riding in the family car following the hearse. As we drove past the school

49

playground I stared out the window at my friends' tiny figures, which seemed to be moving in slow motion.

My mother never talked about Grandpa's suicide, at least not to me. When a cousin—many years later—asked about Grandpa's death at a family reunion, my mother looked terror-stricken. "We don't talk about that," she responded. An uncomfortable silence fell upon the room, and the topic was dropped. By then I knew that Grandpa had taken his own life, and I understood that she couldn't talk about it because the blood-spattered memories choked her. Finding Grandpa so soon after her husband had been dragged to his death must have ripped her apart.

Shortly after my father's death, my mother's mother simply withered away and died without explanation, as people seemed to do in those days. Now that my mother and my grandfather were both alone, we moved in with him just after the end of World War II. My grandparents had both immigrated as teenagers, arriving in the United States from Germany in the late 1800s. None of their eight children was allowed to speak German at home because the older ones had been harassed about their nationality at school. Speaking a different language is enough to confer outsider status, particularly when it is the voice of the enemy. In the fall of 1948, about a year after we moved into Grandpa Koester's house, Grandpa Koester returned to Germany alone for a visit. He arrived back in Nebraska on a Friday and killed himself Sunday night. Depression was a terrorist in our family, unpredictably detonating explosive devices.

I would later learn from my sister that during World War II, according to our mother, Grandpa had not believed in the Holocaust. As a German, he could not accept that the people of his homeland could have perpetrated such a heinous crime. During his trip to Germany he learned the truth about the Nazis, and he came home unable to bear the shame. The power of denial can be very strong when we need it to be. Grandpa's wartime denial must have been profound, but it wasn't strong enough to conquer the truth when he saw it.

I sometimes wonder if he had known that thousands of homosexuals were imprisoned by the Germans, and that some were castrated because they could not or would not have sex with a female prostitute. Did he know about the medical experiments performed on them, that the majority died, and how the ones who did survive were too frightened to talk about their experiences?

People become depressed when they experience significant losses or if their expectations aren't realized. Although affected to some degree by family environment, each person has an individual, highly heritable degree of vulnerability or resistance to depression. Research has increasingly proved that some of us are simply genetically more prone to depression. Some people simply find it easier than others to be happy. In a 2008 article for the *BMJ*, James Fowler and Nicholas Christakis found that people's happiness depends on the happiness of others with whom they are connected. Happiness, like health, is a collective phenomenon. Happy people have more friends, happier marriages and fewer divorces, more successful careers, and longer lives. They learn more easily and recover more quickly from adversity.

For those who are particularly susceptible to depression, antidepressant medications sometimes can raise their depressive set point. Happiness is not a birthright, but neither are we doomed to the level of happiness we have inherited. It is easier to change our thinking than to change the world. In my work, I often hear patients say, "I just want to be happy," and my response is, "What are you willing to do to make that happen, and how will you measure it so you know when you have gotten there?" By taking control over our lives, increasing and nurturing our connections to others, taking care of our health, and developing lives that are meaningful, we can create an environment that helps us resist depression or recover from it more quickly when it occurs. When all of those are not enough, sometimes we must turn to antidepressant medications.

Depression is a common experience for gay men and women as they confront their same-sex attractions. Young LGBT men and women experience bullying, physical and verbal abuse, losses, and failed expectations. For a mature gay man who has passed as heterosexual for many years, the effects may seem more subtle, the most common themes being isolation and loneliness. Once I was at a holiday cocktail party and someone turned on the TV to a college basketball game. Most of the men immediately gravitated to the TV set, except for two of us who had little interest in the game but not much else in common. We remained staring at each other over the punch bowl. In that moment, as a mature gay man with same-sex attraction, despite being socially active and well liked in my heterosexual community, I felt I needed to isolate myself emotionally.

Many gay men experience similar instances, fearful that too much intimacy might expose their so-called abhorrent desires. In the novel *Blue Boy*, Rakesh Satyal wrote, "Nothing is more terrifying than knowing that one glance out of place could destroy my whole existence." For a closeted gay man whose life has been primarily interwoven in a heterosexual world, thinking of leaving the security of that known world can be paralyzing. Isolation and loneliness appear preferable to the unknown rejection from the community.

Am I Depressed, or Just Sad?

Feelings of loss can accompany loss of a loved one, a pet, a body function, a job, a home, or a community. A sense of loss also occurs when what we expect doesn't materialize. For a few months after my mother's death, I experienced waves of grief. At first the waves would nearly drown me or smash me against the rocks of loneliness and loss. Then they would subside but be followed by another wave, another crash, and then another period of calm. Over time, the waves lost amplitude and frequency, but an unexpected reminder of my mother would trigger an occasional staggering wave of grief.

Thanksgiving, Christmas, and Easter had belonged to my mother; holidays became somewhat shallow after her death. Oyster soup was a tradition on Christmas Eve at my mother's house. First she would boil plump, juicy oysters down to the size and moistness of a raisin. Then she dropped the essence of oyster into skim milk. That was our oyster soup. One year Doug said, "Let me make the oyster soup," and my mother reluctantly agreed. He started with heavy cream, added potatoes, seasoned it with a healthy amount of pepper, and added healthy amount of onions and celery. At the last moment, just before serving, he added oysters and scallops that remained plump and juicy when he served it. Concerned whispers drifted in from the next room: "Did you see what he's doing to the soup?" To our amazement, we loved his oyster stew. Doug had bested my mother. He still makes it for the two of us on Christmas Eve, but the absence of my mother detracts from some of its richness.

Depression spans a spectrum of disorders ranging from mild interference with daily function to a wish to die. Depressed people say that the pain of depression is far worse than the pain of cancer, kidney stones, and childbirth. Few who have not experienced depression can imagine what it is like. Depression is different from uncomplicated bereavement. Depression can occur unrelated to loss; sometimes it doesn't even include feelings of sadness. Emptiness or agitation is common. Something that psychiatrists call "neuro-vegetative" symptoms always accompany depression: difficulty sleeping, apathy, exaggerated guilt, low energy, difficulty concentrating, and changes in appetite. Thinking becomes like swimming in molasses. Indecision overwhelms the depressed person. One man told me he couldn't decide which way to walk around his truck. Another woman said she couldn't decide which button on her blouse to button first. These symptoms compromise functioning.

All depressed people seem to think in a similar way. Predictable distortions in their thinking occur. Their thoughts are more like the thoughts of other depressed people than they are like their own thoughts before they became depressed. The word "should" begins to dominate their thinking. They focus on the way they feel to the exclusion of the feelings of others. They see their situation as irreversible and all-encompassing. Depressive frameworks dominate their thinking and create overly harsh judgments about themselves.

Depression creates predictable distortions in thinking:
- Things are all good or all bad
- Everything is about me
- Conclusions are drawn that go beyond the evidence
- Details are taken out of context
- Positives are rejected; negatives are exaggerated

Depressed people have a certain kind of distorted logic that makes a great deal of sense to them but to almost no one else. Suicide begins to look like the only "rational" way to relieve the excruciating pain. I imagine my grandfather's thoughts prior to his suicide went something like this: "I am in more pain than I could have ever imagined. I can see no escape. Suicide is the only thing that will make the pain end. My death will be difficult for my family, but my life is toxic to them. My living will hurt them more than my dying." Depression twists logic; it minimizes the consequences of a stigmatized death and denies any hope of possible recovery.

Depression in the LGBT Community

Evidence exists of increased rates of diagnosable psychiatric disorders and substance abuse in the LGBT community. There is also an alarming rate of suicide, and rates of suicide are underreported. Suicide is one of the three leading causes of death for adolescents, and gay adolescents are four times more likely to commit suicide than their heterosexual peers. This has become a major public health crisis. In 2007, the suicide rate among middle-aged Americans reached its highest rate in twenty-five years. Prevention programs tend to focus on suicide among teenagers. Middle age is overlooked, and fewer resources are available for the LGBT community in midlife.

Population-based studies of suicide in the midlife and older LGBT community are virtually nonexistent. The possibility that sexual confusion and conflict about sexual identity might be a contributing factor to suicide among middle-aged LGBT people is rarely, if ever, considered. Even within the gay community, the subject of gay suicide is resisted because of fear that talking about suicide will undermine efforts to remove the idea that homosexuality is a form of pathology. Many of the suicides in the gay community occur while a person is contemplating the public disclosure of sexual orientation and gender-identity issues.

Psychiatrists cannot predict who will commit suicide, but there are established criteria used to assess risks. Risks include being male, being depressed and lonely, and abusing drugs and alcohol. Unresolved sexual-identity issues heighten anxiety, loneliness, and isolation. This creates a fear that life is not going to turn out as planned. The mature man may no longer have parents as a source of support, and early signs of medical problems may accelerate fears of aging. Because of a fear of exposing his secret, he frequently resists seeking help.

Risk factors for suicide that may be higher in gay men:
1. Depression and anxiety
2. History of alcohol and substance abuse
3. Loss and/or failure to meet expectations
4. Feelings of hopelessness and isolation
5. Lack of social and spiritual support
6. Unwillingness to access treatment

Late stages of life reflect all the stages that came before and can have long-lasting effects. We live our older years in much the same way as we lived our younger years. Prior life experiences such as education, occupations, and social class influence how people experience their declining years. We all prefer to be part of a community that accepts and supports us, but for some, isolation makes that very difficult. Even when they live alone, elderly gay men often continue to have emotionally intimate relationships with others. In their 2000 study of gay and bisexual men and women over the age of sixty, Arnold Grossman, Anthony Augelli, and Scott Hershberger found that when a person is part of a stigmatized minority, being in the presence of others like you has a positive effect on self-esteem. Those who are isolated may have as much as 65 percent more depressive symptoms. Becoming a part of a community where you don't have to always censor your speech or edit your behavior is remarkably liberating. It creates a feeling of finally coming home again. Grossman and colleagues reported that within their networks of friends and family of choice, the sexual orientation of their companions was less important to gay members than the freedom to be open about sexual orientation. But the community will not seek out a mature man who finally chooses to come out. Finding that community will be up to him.

Secret Identities

I once had an abscessed tooth, and in the absence of a dentist, I seriously considered trying to pull it myself to end the horrible pain. Each of us seeks to maintain a sense of internal integrity, while still making a positive impression on others. We are driven by a fear of being discredited. Sometimes that means keeping secrets, especially when the concealed information is sensitive—a history of abortion, a positive HIV status, or sexual attractions.

Secrets are like abscesses. They are painful; they hurt when we touch them, but we can't stop touching them. A secret that is at the center of our integrity creates excruciating pain. Secrets produce symptoms of worry, anxiety, and anger that pressure us to disclose them for relief. We long for the momentary intense pain that comes with rupturing it to release the pressure. We know that once it ruptures, most of the pain will disappear.

Concealment of sexual orientation may occur consciously or unconsciously. Monitoring the secret against societal norms requires considerable effort, constant vigilance, and behavioral self-editing. Although there is a wish to disclose the secret, the need to make a favorable impression on others often overpowers the need to disclose. When we consider revealing that we are gay, we sense it will create a vacuum in our self-esteem and we fear that it will be filled by all of the shameful, stereotypical characteristics of what it means to be gay that we have internalized.

A study by Roger Schindhelm and Harm Hospers in 2004, reported in the *Archives of Sexual Behavior*, compared risk-taking behavior in Dutch gay and bisexual men as it related to the timing of coming out. The study found that 68 percent of respondents had their first homosexual experience before revealing their homosexuality. Concealment correlated with age; the older the person, the greater the concealment. Concealing sexual orientation also correlated with more lifetime sex partners and more casual sex. Concealers engaged more frequently in anal intercourse with casual partners. They also had more unprotected anal sex compared to those who came out before their first same-sex experience.

"Coming out" is an intimate disclosure that has the power to strengthen or destroy relationships. It defines oneself in a way that acknowledges and integrates feelings and desires that previously were unacceptable, thought to be immoral, and never revealed to anyone. For me, it was a process that began with a life of guilt, fear, and hiding, followed by a period of intense self-examination, and ended with the development of a positive gay self-identity. Although some would say a person cannot be "self-actualized" until he assumes a complete and open gay identity, many men who have sex exclusively with men say that goes too far. They believe that while disclosure is important, people can still feel actualized without disclosing their sexual identity in every aspect of their lives.

In my interviews I commonly found that even though it may have taken decades for a man to come to his own acceptance of his sexuality, he often mistakenly expected his family to embrace it immediately. Families initially may be overwhelmed and unsupportive, but in my experience many learn to modify their own internal value system to incorporate acceptance of their family member's sexuality. Sadly, some gay men and women have found their families completely unwilling to accept them. Their only alternative is to walk away and find a "family of choice."

The Stages of Coming Out

Several theoretical models for the "stages of coming out" have been described. One of the most widely referenced is in the paper "Homosexual Identity Formation: A Theoretical Model," written by Vivienne Cass in 1979. Cass suggested that gay men and women are raised as non-homosexual children in an anti-homosexual society. This development creates a sense of "internal incongruence" between how these individuals perceive themselves and how they are perceived by others. According to Cass's model, a need for internal integrity propels people forward through the various stages, and choosing to live with a discrepancy between one's personal and public identities prematurely halts developmental progression.

The stages of homosexual identity formation as described by Cass:

Stage 1. Identity Confusion	Information about homosexuality assumes greater validity in an attempt to answer the question, "Why am I different?"
Stage 2. Identity Comparison	Behavioral guidelines for heterosexuality lose their relevancy as one considers, "I may be gay, but I feel so alone."
Stage 3. Identity Tolerance	Accepting the possibility of being gay, one asks, "Where are other gay people?"
Stage 4. Identity Acceptance	Telling a few other people becomes acceptable since "I may be gay, but I am still OK."

Stage 5. Identity Pride	"If the world must be divided into homosexuals and heterosexuals, I am gay and I don't want to pass for straight."
Stage 6. Identity Synthesis	The anger subsides and homosexuals and heterosexuals are seen as neither all good nor all evil. "I am OK, but just happen to be gay."

Many coming-out models, including Cass's, suggest that openly identifying as gay is a linear developmental process. It begins with an awareness of same-sex attraction emerging in early childhood, followed by typical timing and sequencing of certain milestones, and eventually reaching the final end point of completely coming out. These models have similar, distinct themes: tell yourself, tell your mother (who probably has already figured it out), and then tell the world. Another common theme: coming out occurs only in a climate of alienation and shame, surrounded by forces that seek to suppress the truth. Often little support exists.

Earlier models imply that one size fits all, and that "self-actualization" only occurs when you move through the stages in a regular and progressive way until reaching the point of living an openly gay life. In these linear models sexual development typically ends in the twenties, but always by age forty. There is an orderly series of ideal or typical stages that are posited as the exclusive paths to recognizing, making sense of, and giving a name to emerging sexuality.

These models are useful as a heuristic device that simplifies a complicated process, but they tend to collapse individual stories into common feelings, common thoughts, and common events. They are problematic because they do not provide alternatives—something that I struggled with as a man who came out in midlife. Since my life did not comply with these theoretical models, I began to question whether or not I was gay rather than question the universality of the models.

As one example of how limiting these models are, many men I interviewed who have sex with men object to Cass's fifth stage, "I am gay and I don't want to pass for straight." Whether they are primarily gay- or straight-identified, many men disclose their sexuality to varying degrees depending upon their situation. They may be completely out with gay friends, out to a few close friends and family, but not at all out to other family members or at work.

The study by Schindhelm and Hospers suggests that those who have an early initial awareness and acceptance of their homosexuality progress through homosexual development before having much same-sex experience. They self-identified early on as gay, and they completed their sexual development as young men. For of a wide variety of historical, economic, and social circumstances, other men come to acceptance of their homosexuality later, sometimes much later, in their lives. Men who choose to come out when they are more mature develop their homosexual identity

Men who conceal their sexual orientation until they are older expose themselves to greater health risks.

later. When gay men have not resolved their internal homophobia, they experience low self-esteem, greater social isolation, and greater health risks.

The New Coming-Out Model: A Trajectory

Because earlier models for coming out underemphasize sociocultural factors, this stage-sequential framework for gay identity development is being discredited in favor of a hypothesis that there are multiple trajectories for gay self-definition. A trajectory describes how a projectile moves through space, a rocket in flight. Objects moving through space have both individual characteristics and properties in common, but they must obey the laws of physics; they require energy to move them, and their environment influences the progression of their flight. Each object is unique in itself and in its pathway.

Rockets are launched only after their propellant is fired; until then, they are governed by the laws of inertia. People tend to maintain the status quo unless compelled to alter it. Future options and outcomes are fuzzy and ill defined. Some choose not to come out because they suspect that they might lose much more than they will gain in a more legitimate future that they can only vaguely visualize.

Some men say they have "always known" they were gay. Because the world is a different place now, some young people appear to blast right past all of the milestones and are completely out in early adolescence.

Others who have an early knowledge of their sexual orientation withhold disclosure, delay homosexual experiences, and remain closeted until they are older and have detached from their families. Some younger men may find it easier to come out when they are further along in their education and career. Financial independence provides greater access to a wider range of social options. They may reach coming-out milestones in a more sequential way. Others postpone dealing with their same-sex attractions until midlife or beyond often because they have been unable to resolve questions about who might be hurt by revealing their secret as opposed to who might be hurt if they continue to conceal it.

Each stage of the earlier models of coming out has a benchmark. Some gay activists insist that those who move through the stages grudgingly or stall before the end point are defective. When I was in my thirties I read about the stages of coming out, and I discovered that the suggested age for completing all stages was somewhere in the mid-twenties. I thought, "I can't be gay. I'm over thirty-five and I'm only in stage 2." Although I "just went gay all of a sudden," I didn't exactly throw open the closet door, jump out, and shout, "I'm GAY!" My progress toward a public and personal gay identity was halting and tortuous. I didn't come out, I inched out—backward—often waiting to be asked if I was gay rather than confronting the issue head-on.

The trajectory for coming out, and the associated milestones, is highly variable. And as I learned firsthand, it doesn't occur sequentially. Some milestones may never be reached, some may happen more than once, and there is no end point where all of the work of coming out is finished. Most people, including my patients, for example, presume that I am heterosexual. The more men I spoke with who came out in midlife, the more my own story was repeated back to me. Decisions about when and to whom to come out is a process that never ends. Several factors can affect the timing of coming out:

- Parents and closeness of family structure
- Age, gender, and level of maturity
- Socioeconomic group, profession, and education
- Race, religion, geography, and culture
- Evolution of societal values
- Bisexuality

- Idiosyncratic life experiences

My own process of coming out certainly did not fit the molds I'd found while exploring my own inner conflicts. It is difficult for me to say at what point my marriage began to fail. I fell rather easily into my professional identity. The head of my psychiatric training program told me that I had more maturity as a physician at the beginning of my residency than many other residents had when they finished. I was living out the dictates of my culture: a man is the protector and provider. But long before I began to question my sexual orientation, I had doubts about my skills as a husband and father.

In the spring of 1985, as I was rushing down a corridor in the hospital where I worked, a woman I hardly knew cheerily asked me, "Is it true that you're getting a divorce?" I knew her just well enough to feel that she was the last person I would want to know anything about my personal life. "Bitch," I thought, but without any change of expression, I dodged her question with a question. "Where did you hear that?" Sometimes being a psychiatrist comes in handy. "Your daughter Krista announced it to the fifth-grade class yesterday, and my son came home and told me. I just wanted to help stop the rumors—if they're not true." Her excitement clearly revealed her hope that the rumors were true, and her delight about knowing the dirt trumped any empathy she might have felt for me or my wife, Lynn.

The openness with my wife, and my daughter Krista's intuition, which I'd only learned about secondhand at the hospital, jolted me into recognizing that I needed to speak with my thirteen-year-old, Whitney. My daughters have always been very close, and I assumed that what one knew, the other also knew. But at thirteen Whitney was preoccupied with becoming a teenager. After a movie with her friends, I took her for a drive and told her, "Your mother and I are having some serious problems, and there is a possibility we might get a divorce." She screamed and sobbed, completely blindsided by my announcement. It was the most painful moment in our relationship, at least up to that point.

As Lynn and I agonized about the possibility of divorce and breaking the most important commitment either of us had ever made, we searched to reconcile the asymmetries of our potential losses. Neither of us came from a family where anyone had ever been divorced. Every person in our small Nebraska hometowns—about twenty-five miles apart—could have disapprovingly named every couple in town who had been divorced. As a child, I had a younger friend whose parents were divorced and whose father was detached. I could not understand how that could happen. My mother was a single parent because my father had died, but I wondered how anyone could ever lose his father because of a stupid decision his parents had made.

My expectation was that Lynn would adapt as easily to the role of "doctor's wife" as I had to being a physician. It was a role that never suited her. In 1969, we were stationed in Florida with the Navy. Lynn joined a bridge club of other doctors' wives; all were raised in the South and all had "help." Lynn commented to them that we had very few African Americans in rural Nebraska. One asked her, "Well, who does your work, then?" Lynn must have sputtered as she responded, "Well . . . *we* do!"

Although I don't think Lynn had read it, at least not yet, the opening words of Betty Friedan's *The Feminine Mystique* defined her life at the beginning of our marriage:

> The problem lay buried, unspoken, for many years in the minds of American women. It was a strange stirring, a sense of dissatisfaction, a yearning that women suffered in the middle of the twentieth century in the United States. Each suburban wife struggled with it alone. As she made the beds, shopped for groceries, matched slipcover material, ate peanut butter sandwiches with her children, chauffeured Cub Scouts and Brownies, lay beside her husband at night—she was afraid to ask even of herself the silent question—"Is this all?"

Rather than either of us recognizing that what Lynn was experiencing was shared by a large part of the women in our society, she felt like a failure because baking chocolate chip cookies wasn't enough for her. And just because I always blame myself for other people's unhappiness, I felt responsible for hers. Both of us blamed ourselves for not being able to make the other happy because of a failure at being what we thought we were supposed to be. Eventually, we began to blame each other.

When we were living in Maine, one day I came home after thirty-six hours of working at Maine Medical Center, where I did my psychiatric training; I metaphorically expected her to bring me my pipe and slippers. Our daughters were one and four years old at the time. Her response was, "I suppose you think I've been having a *blast* around here for the past two days!" Why wasn't this working? Hadn't we done everything right up to that point?

Lynn found work as a receptionist in a law office. Although I had difficulty understanding why our children needed to be in childcare for a job that wouldn't even pay the bills for it, Lynn obviously was feeling better about herself. I even commented to one of my best friends who knew of our difficulty, "I think she may have a crush on her boss, but I don't care. Her mood is so much better."

After ten years in Maine, we moved back to Iowa. Lynn decided to go to law school. Her studying and my work moved us further apart. I remember taking Whitney and Krista to church one Sunday by myself as she studied for an exam, and I thought, "Is this why I got married?" They say that medicine is a jealous mistress; law school is as well. Whether law school pulled us further apart or was simply a rationalization that we used to legitimatize our increasing emotional distance is an unanswerable question.

I remember one day sitting alone in our kitchen thinking, "I cannot live like this, feeling this alone in a marriage." Against all that I believed in, I decided, "I am going to have an affair." It never occurred to me that it would be with a man. I met Alfredo a short time later.

Each Christmas the studio where my daughters studied dance put on performances of *The Nutcracker*. They always needed men for the first scene where the Stahlbaums host a lavish party around a tall Christmas tree. Shortly after meeting Alfredo, and long before considering my divorce, I decided to audition and was given the role. At a post-rehearsal party for all of the adults in the cast, I stalled until all of the other guests had left. I wanted to talk with the rather effeminate younger man who had hosted the party. As we sat with a glass of wine, I told him I wanted to talk to him because I thought I might be gay. He seemed surprised and responded, "I don't know why you would want to talk with me about that. I'm not gay." I hadn't yet joined the gay fathers' support group, and my gaydar was still in training.

Prior to meeting Alfredo, I had encouraged Lynn to see a counselor with me to see if we could rediscover some meaning in our relationship. What we had was not enough for me, and it didn't seem to be working very well for her either. After I fell in love with Alfredo, I discovered I could have something more. Then one evening Lynn brought me some pages she'd printed off my computer. She had discovered some of my writing that journaled details of my relationship with Alfredo. She said nothing, just handed the papers to me. A very big abscess was about to be drained.

I felt relieved that my secret was out, but confused about what to do. I knew that I wanted to leave the marriage. How would I tell my mother, who loved Lynn as much as she loved her own daughters? How could I tell the kids that I'd failed at being a father and I was leaving them when I knew how painful it had been for me not to have a father? Was I putting everyone through all of this pain just for sex? What I had discovered was that I would never be like those other men I was pretending to be. Somehow a barrier had been erected between those other men and me; they were one kind of man and I was another. But now it no longer mattered. I began to mourn everything that had given my life definition up to that point.

I wanted to put some distance between me and my former wife, so I interviewed for and was offered a job in Minneapolis. I took my younger daughter, Krista, with me when I returned to Minneapolis to look for a place to live. On the long, silent trip back to Iowa, she finally said, "Dad, if you move up there, we'll never see you." I hadn't wanted to believe that, but I knew she was right. I turned down the job I had just accepted and searched for one in Des Moines, about thirty miles away from where my two daughters would be living with their mother.

I loved my wife as much as I was capable of, yet I knew through no fault of hers that it wasn't enough. I wondered if she knew it, too. I love my children more than I ever thought it possible to love another person. I had always promised to give them the father I didn't have, and I had participated in every aspect of their lives, from dirty diapers to practicing Suzuki violin and piano lessons. I suffered through every dance recital.

But being a good father and a good "noncustodial parent" are not equivalent. My children were the center of my life. How could I just set aside the commitment I had to my children, just because I had discovered I was capable of loving a man in a whole different dimension than I had loved their mother?

While I was seeing Alfredo during the last months of my marriage, his wife gave birth to a son. One day when she was away, I went to see them. When he brought his infant son to me and I saw the way he looked at him, I knew that our relationship would end. I could see that he loved his son like I loved my daughters, and I loved that about him. But I understood immediately that his

> **Being a good father and a good "noncustodial parent" are not equivalent.**

relationship with his son would always be a higher priority than his relationship with me. Although I had decided to end my marriage, he was a long way from making that decision. I was still so over the moon about him that I was ignoring the early signs of his jealousy that would later become a far bigger issue in our relationship than the birth of his son was.

On the day I moved out, Lynn had arranged to be away with Whitney and Krista. It didn't take long to pack. Lynn and I had independently made a list of the twenty-five things we most wanted that were acquired during our marriage. We agreed that we would accept as equal the total value of all the items on each of our lists. Of all the things on each of our lists, only a restored gilded mirror found in our barn in Maine was common to both of our lists. I easily loaded all twenty-five of my things along with my clothes into the little red Corolla that sat in front of the new home we'd just designed and built. This was our dream home, one we had expected to occupy at least for the duration of the thirty-year mortgage.

As I packed the Toyota, one of the doctors I worked with arrived unexpected and uninvited. He followed me in and out of the house with each load I carried. He asked me the most inane questions. He'd never been to our house before, and he gave no reason why he'd come. I thought, "If you've come to save my marriage, you're a little late." I needed to be alone in my grief, but he clung to me like a wet swimsuit. My increasing anger with him at least distracted me from my extraordinary sorrow. As I closed the front door, I knew that I was closing the door to a part of my history. I could never again enter that house—a house that still felt like my house—unless I was invited, and being invited didn't seem even a remote possibility.

I worked seven days a week for the entire first year of my new job, partly because the work demanded it, but mostly because I needed something to fill the void in my life. I picked up my kids on Wednesday nights and returned them to school on Thursday mornings. They visited every other weekend, an inconvenient disruption in their lives. I had difficulty trying to recapture the feeling that I was still their father. We were all grieving. I still had to confront telling them that this disruption in our lives was the result of discoveries about my sexuality, and I needed to do this before they had even more than a rudimentary understanding of adult sexuality. My empty condo didn't feel like home to any of us. I tried to learn to cook. One Wednesday when I arrived home with the girls, I found that I had forgotten to put the roast beef in the slow cooker, so we had a meal of just vegetables that had cooked for twelve hours.

I didn't tell my mother I was gay; she asked me. Shortly after I moved to Des Moines she visited me, and before her visit Alfredo and I made a plan to test her out by having him drop by my condo. After she went home, she wrote me a brief note, "After our visit, I got to wondering if you might be gay. Love, Mom." The abscess of my hidden sexuality was lanced. In an eight-page letter to my mother that I copied and sent to my brother and sisters, I confessed much more than they needed to know.

I was frightened and uncertain about coming out, but with each step I began to feel more relieved, exhilarated, and validated. I anticipated that some friends, family, and colleagues would be shocked, confused, and even hostile. I was certain some would accuse me of exploiting my wife and destroying my family. Those were accusations I was prepared for—I had already had them. My trajectory had progressed through telling myself I was gay, confessing it to a few others, and finally telling my family. It hadn't gone as badly as I'd expected it to. But I was only beginning to make a new way for myself professionally, and I thoroughly believed that being out professionally would undermine my position of leadership in my new job as medical director of psychiatry at one of Iowa's leading hospitals.

One of the causalities of being the "noncustodial" parent is the inability to participate in your children's lives on a day-to-day basis. I missed those thirty-second conversations with my daughters over a glass of orange juice as we all rushed out the door to begin our days. When you're divorced, almost every interaction with the children lacks the spontaneity available to intact families. One of the few exceptions was a night I took my daughters to a movie. On the way, I stopped to buy sugar-free Gummy Bears. We shared them through the trailers and film credits, when suddenly we all began to experience gas. At first, we tried to discretely sneak out our farts, but the gas was so intense it simply became impossible. Nothing bonds a family together like a shared fart. Soon we were farting without reservation, laughing and just acting like a father and his daughters. For several years those moments of relaxed abandon were rare.

My wife sold the house we'd built. Although I understood that financially she couldn't maintain it, I wasn't ready to let go of the symbol of the dream we'd created together. We fought frequently, and our arguments were usually triggered by money. One day when I arrived to pick up Whitney and Krista, she was wearing a sweatshirt I'd bought for Whitney. I exploded with an uncharacteristic rage that went well beyond the limits of a borrowed sweatshirt.

All of life's important decisions are made without enough information, and coming out is no exception. We make our decisions based upon predictions about how our lives will be affected by the possible outcomes. A decision to change must carry with it a substantial chance of achieving something considerably greater than what might be lost, an economic principle called "loss aversion." Those of us who have waited to come out until later in life typically have done so because of our fears of losing something very important in our lives, but the things we value—the things we most fear losing—are uniquely our own.

"Those Fucking Queers"

Jason McGee is a twenty-seven-year-old man who lives in rural Tennessee. He describes himself as a black American rather than an African American. He said, "The South expects certain things of you as a man, and being gay ain't one of them. Down here, people like me ain't gay or homosexual; we are 'queers' and 'fags.' For a Southern black man, being called sissy, fag, queer, or homo is one of the biggest disgraces ever." According to McGee, it brings shame to your family and you are isolated because of it. He went on to say, "People would talk you into nonexistence." He believes that being "black and queer" would almost certainly make him the victim of a hate crime. He said, "I'm masculine, so no one knows who I don't want to know."

McGee comes from a loving and intact family. His father is his friend as well as his dad, and he is not treated differently within the family. His parents accept his excuse that he doesn't date because he's busy with school and a job. His brothers are in long-term relationships with women and have given his parents grandchildren. He regrets that he will not be able to. McGee has several cousins who are gay, although only one of them is out, and he lives far away. Starting at age eleven he began experiencing sexual play with one of them. It began by wrestling with him, and one day he ejaculated but didn't know what it was. They continued to have sexual play, but it always began with wrestling. Sometimes they were naked. Later they began to masturbate each other.

McGee is a Baptist who says he loves God and loves his church; he belongs to a congregation comprised mostly of white people. Although he sees himself as gay, he is out to no one except his brothers, and he is out to them only because they confronted him when they discovered some gay porn on his computer. They asked him if he could change, and when he said that he couldn't, they accepted him. He has no intention of coming out to the rest of his family. He believes coming out would mean "letting go of so many I love," both in the family and in his church. He said that he does not come out because, "I don't want to bring pain to myself, but even more important to my family and friends. It would hurt them to learn the truth. I am not hiding it from them, but it is none of their business. But I don't ignore my feelings because that would cause me inner damage."

At times he struggles in his church because, "It hurts to hear (homosexuality) preached so hard against." He says some of his church can't see past what their eyes show them, but he said he's not perfect so he doesn't expect them to be perfect either. McGee reconciles the issue for himself, quoting Romans 3:23: "For all are sinners and fall short of the Glory of God." Then he said, "ALL are sinners. All. Everyone, not just gays. ALL. In God's eyes, no one's sin is worse than another man's sin. People are born in sin, so you can be born gay, as I believe I was."

McGee works full-time in a laboring job while he attends college. He said that he talks country because "I am country." He prefers bluegrass music to rap, and some of his friends have called him an "Oreo," meaning they think of him as black on the outside and white on the inside. He said, "Black is who I am, not who I'm trying to be, but I refuse to dress, talk, or act like society thinks I should. I am my own man. I like what I like. I don't care about the majority."

He describes his sexuality as "complicated," especially because he is primarily attracted to white men over the age of forty-five, which he discovered through an attraction to his male teachers. He has had a limited number of sexual partners as an adult and is not looking for a relationship, but neither is he avoiding it. "I don't act out my sexuality," McGee explained, "except maybe online, and even then, I am not feminine by any means." He said that his sexuality doesn't define him or what he does because he doesn't let it rule his life.

When asked if he felt he had to choose between his ethnicity and sexuality, he said that a lot of people think you can't be both, "But I refuse to do anything less. I can't choose between the two; it's not even a choice. I am a gay black man." He is cautious about how he acts around "certain minority groups." Although he has come to peace with his sexuality internally, he is uncertain of what it means for his future. He wants a relationship and children. "I look around and I see the type of man I like everywhere, and yet I can't have any one of them," he said. "I see my friends with wives and girlfriends and I just go back home to my closet."

McGee remains uncertain how to handle the issue of coming out. He doesn't see coming out to his parents as a possibility right now, although he has talked with other black men who felt that they had more freedom and more options after coming out, but for him it isn't a priority right now. "I need to get myself figured out. I'm still in the closet because I can't see what good coming out will do in this area. I hear about the free feeling you feel once you're out, but hell, I don't want to be alienated or hated either. There ain't no big gay community for support here. It's every man for himself," McGee continued. "I get along fine, but it is still a challenge when you realize you're alone."

A few years ago I met another African American man at the gym. We often worked out at the same time and frequently ran into each other in the dressing room or sauna. Over several months we talked about a lot of things and were in agreement about most political and social issues. Since only about 3 percent of the population of Iowa is African American, I had not had many opportunities to develop a friendship with a black man. Then one day he said to me, "We've got to do something about the fucking queers in this place." Although we'd never talked about it, I had assumed he knew that I was gay. I was devastated, and I went to talk with one of my gay friends who was there. I told him what had happened and also about my experience in the Lutheran Church. He said, "You know, it isn't like that everywhere," and he invited me to his church, where all are welcome.

Getting to Know Gay

Coming out means running the risk of losing friendships developed in the heterosexual world, social status, heterosexual gender role advantages, and ideals associated with marriage. Men who haven't come out have hidden a fundamental part of themselves because of a fear of losing love and respect and of being abandoned and alone. Some simply fear exposing an imperfect masculinity. Although such negative outcomes can be quite painful, psychologists tell us that typically we overestimate the intensity of our feelings of loss and how long those feelings will last. Psychology tells us that we fail to learn from prior experience that the repercussions from revealing our secrets are almost always less than we anticipate. We underestimate the psychological power we have to transform negative experiences into positive ones.

Ultimately, the strength of a person's support system is the most significant influence in how coming out unfolds. Although the net impact of revealing secrets is typically more positive than negative, and is usually more positive than anticipated, the benefits of revealing sexual identity certainly are not guaranteed. Personal revelations are significantly influenced by the response we receive from others. In considering whether or not to come out or how and when to disclose sexual orientation, it is important to develop strategies that are likely to result in positive responses from a network of supportive friends.

Nonsequential milestones of gay self-identity formation:
1. Awareness of same-sex attraction
2. Consensual sex with someone of the opposite sex
3. Consensual sex with a same-sex partner
4. Thinking of oneself as bisexual
5. Thinking of oneself as gay or lesbian

6. Telling mother
7. Telling father
8. Telling someone other than parents

Fix It, Put Up with It, or Get Out

As I got older, I felt an increasing sense of urgency to deal with my hidden same-sex orientation. The same was true of the men I interviewed who came out in middle age; time is passing quickly, and life begins to seem too short to start over again.

As a psychiatrist, I have learned to tell my patients who are dealing with significant life conflicts to simplify the decision-making process by pointing out that there are basically only three options: change it, put up with it, or get out of it. In most cases one of those three options can be eliminated immediately. Since attraction to someone of the same sex is not going to change, a married man is left only with suffering through it or getting out. Acceptance generally evolves in a positive direction, even when the initial responses to coming out are unfavorable. Change does occur, albeit slowly. Many relationships—once thought lost—improve over time as family and friends begin to reconcile their homo-negativism with their positive feelings for the gay man.

However, let me be clear in saying that sometimes things really are as bad as they seem. Some of my closest friends from my "heterosexual past" disappeared from my life completely. For them, change felt impossible, and they reacted by getting out. While it is easy to be critical of them for being homophobic and judgmental, the truth is that I had never really let them know me completely.

Age significantly affects how a person comes out. The age at which a man finally becomes consciously aware of same-sex attractions will significantly impact the course of his coming-out process. Most men can remember the precise moment in the locker room when they first noticed one of their peers had sprouted a pubic hair. However, the significance of maturational events differs for homosexual and heterosexual men.

In the process of interviewing for this book, I discovered that many, if not most, mature gay men experienced homosexual attraction as adolescents. But for some, the significance of those early homosexual feelings was not recognized until later; sometimes only after coming out were those attractions really understood. I have also discovered, however, that many heterosexual men have also had very similar sexual attractions as adolescents, although they were reticent to acknowledge them or, in fact, interpreted them differently. Both homosexual and heterosexual men spin those past experiences, attaching significance as suits their current sexual identity.

The earliest moments of sexual attraction occur when adolescent identity is just forming, most often while teenagers are still under parental authority. Some gay men develop a "full out" status as an adolescent, while others may self-identify as gay but delay same-sex experience and coming out. Then there are those like me who come out as mature men. For them, the milestones of the coming-out process can be quite protracted; their homosexual identity is formed much later in life. Some others may never be comfortable accepting a gay identity.

"But at some point, all of that changes. In our weariness we begin to sense the truth, that more doors have closed behind us than remain ahead," writes Richard Russo in *Bridge of Sighs*. Almost nothing is written on the subject of coming-out milestones for mature men who delay dealing with their homosexual attractions. When I reached midlife, I was confronted by a series of complicated and interlocking doors. There were doors for my spouse, my parents, my kids, my siblings, my coworkers, my friends, and my religious community. I would knock through one door, only to find a solid wall. Other doors I could only peek in, and then realize I must not go inside. Some doors I knocked on over and over again. The nature of the closet walls can be difficult to define. We move through those doors through a process of negotiation.

When I first came out to my heterosexual friends, nearly all of them rejected me. My best friend for thirty-five years was completely unable to deal with it, and although his wife secretly sent me a note from time to time, he cut off all ties. My best friend during my psychiatric residency disappeared from my life as well, and most of the mutual friends during my marriage initially aligned with my former wife. Although not having them as a part of my life comes as a great loss to me, I must accept that our friendship was partially based on a lie. I wasn't honest with them or with myself about who I am.

Geography figures significantly in coming out, especially for middle-aged men who have already established communities for themselves, albeit in their heterosexual roles. Contrary to the stereotype, not all gay men wish to live in urban areas. In an older (1987) but still relevant study, Frederick Lynch described gay men living in suburbia as individualistic and strongly oriented toward work and career building, valuing homeownership and long-term relationships. They are not much different from their heterosexual suburban peers, and certainly not the hedonistic gay men of the lascivious stereotype. For some gay men in rural and suburban areas, their homosexual activity has been primarily a weekend, leisure activity, rather than a full-time identity. Some research describes gay men living outside of urban areas as more frequently passing as heterosexual, being more fearful of exposure, anticipating more intolerance and discrimination, and having fewer homosexual friendships and sexual encounters.

Coming out professionally remains a significant issue for many gay men. The reality is that being gay can compromise professional advancement. Alexandra Levit, writing in the *Wall Street Journal*, reported that a Harris poll found that 44 percent of LGBT participants feel unable to talk freely to their coworkers about their partners, and up to 78 percent don't feel comfortable bringing their partners to corporate social functions. Since federal laws do not safeguard against being fired because of sexual orientation, gay people must balance the stress of bearing a secret with the risk of losing their job.

When I relocated to Des Moines after my divorce, I moved only thirty miles away, but it was an entire world apart from where I'd been while I was married. I knew no one and for a while couldn't even remember my own phone number or the names of any streets, save the one I lived on. I was starting a job as medical director of psychiatry at one of Iowa's largest hospitals, despite having no experience as a medical executive. When I was introduced as medical director at the first psychiatry section meeting, no one said anything. Instead, their eyes rolled toward the ceiling as if to say, "Who the hell are you, and what do you think you're doing here?" I felt as if I was about to be waterboarded.

During those first few months on the job I often wondered myself, "Who the hell am I, and what do I think I am doing here?" I had never served in an administrative medical position, and once I moved into management I was no longer just one of the guys. I had no one to bitch to. I felt adrift between hospital administrators with one agenda and psychiatric physicians with another. My grasp on my role as medical director felt very tenuous. I was still attempting to conceal my sexual orientation professionally. Coming out as gay to the other psychiatrists seemed as if it would release my grip altogether. I threw myself into the job, working seventy hours a week. It also proved to be a great escape from my feelings of failure as a husband and father, and left me little time to think about my loneliness and how much I missed my kids. As Justin Spring wrote in *Secret Historian*, "Normal men do not often have to choose between love and a career. . . . But the homosexual, it seems to me, often finds himself in a place where the choice between a career and love seems inevitable."

About six months into my job as medical director, I was met at the door of the psychiatric unit by Marsha, one of the hospital's social workers. One of the psychiatrists, "Dr. Brown," had been a constant problem for me, and Marsha said to me, "Dr. Olson! Dr. Brown is planning to go over to hospital administration to tell them you're gay." Fearing that my life was about to collapse, I went immediately to my boss and said, "I have something to tell you. I'm gay." "Loren," she responded reassuringly, "we knew that before we hired you."

"How could you know that? The only person who knew was my ex-wife."

"Apparently not," she said with a sly smile, and then, "can I ask you a question?"

"Sure." My confession had weakened any power I had to negotiate.

"Why is it that there are so many middle-aged men coming out these days?"

I didn't know the answer or even if what she said was true. So, again using my powers of psychiatry to deflect uncomfortable questions, I asked her how she knew I was gay. She wouldn't tell me exactly, but said one of her secretaries raised the issue when I first came in to meet with her because Alfredo had accompanied me when I arrived for my interview. Obviously, I was less successful in guarding my secret than I had thought!

I definitely had overestimated the consequences of being out professionally, and was fortunate to have experienced very little in the way of outward discrimination. Only once did my sexual identity seem to be an issue professionally. I had interviewed for a medical director position at a major health system in Indiana. We had completed negotiating the contract, and I was all set to sign. Out of the blue the recruiter called and said the hospital had decided to stop all negotiations and discussions about hiring me. No explanation was given, and in my opinion, none was necessary.

When I first arrived in Des Moines I barricaded my personal life from my professional life. I decided I would never deny being gay, but neither would I march in the Pride Parade waving a rainbow flag in anyone's face. However, it wasn't long after my move that I met Doug, and our relationship turned serious very quickly. One July morning, we awakened to a flawless, sunny day. The ten thousand bicyclists on RAGBRAI, the *Des Moines Register*'s Annual Great Bicycle Ride Across Iowa, were scheduled to be going through Des Moines. The temptation was too great. I called the hospital and told them I had food poisoning and couldn't possibly make it to work that day. Doug and I spent the day chasing the bicycle race in my Jeep Wrangler with the top removed. Early the following morning, Doug and I received a phone call from one of his friends asking if we'd seen the *Des Moines Register*. There, on the front page, was a picture several columns wide of the two of us sitting at a traffic light watching the bicyclists ride through downtown Des Moines. I should never lie. I always get busted in a very big way.

General theories about psychological development do not include differences for gay people, and although it is useful to consider the various models for coming out, they typically lack any emphasis on self-development and often ignore factors about individual life paths such as age, location, and religion. Individuals must direct their own advancement through the course of their life.

Heterosexuals don't have to declare their sexual orientation. Men who are "undetectably gay" often encounter the "heterosexual presumption." I am frequently asked, for example, "How's your wife?" Until recently most of my patients didn't know much about my personal life, and for a long time that made it easy to pass as heterosexual, something I welcomed. At what points, I have asked myself, and to what degree, should I make a commitment to publicly declare my sexuality? As I became more comfortable as a gay man, I began to ask myself, "Does social justice require that I correct everyone when they make that mistake?"

Being gay does not really tell us much about who we are because there is no single gay identity and no final step in a developmental process. For many it is a non-issue, and as one matures, sex drive diminishes as the central organizing force of one's life. As men become older, I found in my interviews, they begin to distance themselves from an all-encompassing gay identity and say, "I'm just me." Gay identity is integrated with all other aspects of life, including relationships with family and employers, involvement with church, community, and political organizations, and committed romantic relationships.

Mature gay men refuse to be molded into a universal gay identity, just as they once struggled to be free of the stamp of heterosexual identity. Unlike a rocket, each of us has the capacity to choose our own destination and the trajectory that gets us there. The models for development of sexual identity—or timelines for coming out—are flawed in that they often end at twenty or the latest at forty years of age. No matter when we confront our sexual identity—whether as a teenager or in our last decades—we all evolve throughout our lifetimes.

Harold Kooden, in *Golden Men: The Power of Gay Midlife*, wrote that each man must direct his own advancement through the sexual development process. By taking more responsibility for one's own history, a gay man has a deepening sense of active participation in his life that reduces his feeling overwhelmed and out of control. Kooden was critical of the traditional models of coming out because they lacked emphasis on self-development. He states that older gay men who are self-accepting and psychologically well adjusted adapt well to the aging process. He says that satisfaction with being gay correlates with better adjustment in midlife and greater life satisfaction. Kooden also believes that involvement in the gay community leads to higher overall life satisfaction.

Being gay is not something anyone plans. In most cases we would have wanted something we thought of as "better," that is, until we accept that what we have is pretty damn good. We are individuals. We are launched into this world with a presumed heterosexual flight path, but the course our lives take is influenced as much by our own composition as that of the world around us. Eight of the respondents to my survey of mature men who have sex with men were over eighty years old. Four of them either came out or were outed in their eighth decade of life. Their life stories defy the universality of stage-sequenced coming out. Our lives evolve as the deniable becomes undeniable. There is no single identity, no single trajectory. No one else can live our lives.

Chapter 5
Are You Shooting at the Wrong Target?
Detox and Rehab for Addiction to Approval

Therefore the sage is guided by what he feels. And not by what he sees.
He lets go of that and chooses this.

—*Daodejing,*
Laozi

"Ken's dead." Bruce's call jolted me from my recovering-from-Saturday-night's sleep on Valentine's Day, 1988.

"What?" I screamed into the phone.

"He was murdered last night. The cops were here early this morning and questioned me," Bruce said, with a mixture of anger, fear, and sadness. On Saturday night, we had all spent time together at the Brass Garden, Des Moines's only gay disco.

"What happened?" I had an eerie feeling that perhaps I wasn't really awake. "Who? . . . What? . . . Where? . . ." I couldn't even formulate the questions.

"Nobody knows anything yet. Turn on your TV. That's about as much as I know. It happened at his apartment. I guess someone stabbed him. Jennifer was home, too, but she's okay."

"She was there the whole time? Oh my God!"

I sat there alone on the Ikea-like trundle bed I had purchased for my daughters to use when they visited me. The only other furniture I had in my condo in downtown Des Moines was a battered old oak library table that held my computer, four 1950s red leatherette bar stools, and a picnic cooler for a refrigerator. I had an air mattress on the floor for my bed, and whenever I sat down on it to go to bed, the contour sheet would pop loose from every corner. During the divorce, I'd asked my lawyer if I could buy the small condo, and she responded, "You've got to live somewhere." I had just begun a new psychiatric practice. I had child support, alimony, and a new mortgage, too. I had no money left to create the gay love nest

79

that I had envisioned during the preceding months as I considered leaving my wife and kids to pursue life as a newly single gay man.

As I watched the Sunday morning news, the reality of Ken's murder gradually wedged its way into my brain. It was an odd feeling to see a place where I'd been many times for dinner parties suddenly surrounded by yellow crime scene tape. But I also realized that given different circumstances, I might have been the one who was being autopsied. It was also the beginning of the AIDS crisis, and I began to wonder what kind of world I had just joined. Perhaps all the losses I'd feared were going to materialize, and in an even bigger way than I'd imagined.

I had met both Ken and Bruce at a gay fathers' support group that had been formed to help gay fathers deal with the unique personal issues related to coming out as a married man with children. The group provided a lifeline for several of us who'd been in heterosexual relationships, some of us still married, and all of us with children. Confused, questioning, and working our way through the questions about our sexuality, we were mentored by others who were further along in the process.

Ken, Bruce, and I were about the same age, each of us had two kids of similar ages, and all of us had divorced after coming out to our wives. The first few times I went accompanied by Alfredo, the married Argentinean man I had secretly been seeing during the last months of my marriage. The group consisted of several men who were all very committed to maintaining their roles as fathers. We were all concerned about finding ways to help our kids deal with the confusion and loss thrust upon them by our sexual declaration. Had it not been for this small group of men, I would have felt entirely alone after I left my family.

One Saturday night after a bitter fight with Lynn, I stormed out of the house and went to Des Moines to a gay bar. I met a man there (who I later learned was a friend of Bruce and Ken), and I went back to his apartment with him to spend the night. In the morning before I left, he told me about the fathers' group. When I got home in the morning, I was met by my angry yet relieved wife and one of my psychiatric colleagues. Lynn had called him to come over because she was afraid that I had killed myself.

Ken, Bruce, and this group of formerly "heterosexual" gay men comprised my entire circle of friends, gay or straight, and the only people other than my wife whom I had told about my increasingly unmanageable sexual attraction to men. Medicine had taught me to be thoughtful, rational, and deliberate. I never formed impulsive conclusions. Now my reason and emotion were like two wrestlers locked in a combat embrace, each trying to pin the other. I remember wishing that my wife might become an alcoholic so that I could justify leaving her with the world on my side. Deep down I knew, but it was entirely up to me to break the strangle stalemate.

Ken had been out longer than either Bruce or I had, and when I met him he had a "longtime companion," the euphemistic code words used for gay lovers in all the AIDS obituaries at that time. Ken's relationship with his partner was one I admired and longed for in my own life. When their partnership ended, it underscored my concerns that gay men were only capable of riding one bus until the next one came along. Many straight people, but also quite a few gay people, believe that stereotype. One of my interviewees, who has sex exclusively with men, refuses to refer to himself as gay because he believes transitory relationships based solely on sexual attraction are the hallmark of being gay. Ken and Bruce both valued long-term relationships, but both struggled to find them. What I admired most about both of them was their total commitment to being a father to their children.

Ken was my gay coach. He knew how to be gay, at least as I understood it from the stereotype. He loved to dance, drank a lot, spent too much money, and had a quick wit and a sharp tongue. He was a smart dresser, and he once said to me, "Loren, if you blouse your shirt when you tuck it in, you won't look so fat around your waist." Far from being offended, I listened eagerly, with the same intensity I had earlier in my life when I had tried to learn to be a heterosexual man. Now that I knew that my sense of difference was the result of being gay, I wanted to learn everything I could to become a part of this new brotherhood.

Ken was a devoted father, and his older daughter, Jennifer, lived with him. First she lived with him and his partner, and after Ken's relationship ended, it was just the two of them. Jennifer was a teenager, a good student and a hard worker. She appeared unblemished by her father's homosexuality and all of his gay friends. I had hoped she would help my daughters get through this transition successfully.

Bruce was more like me, and our lives were remarkably parallel. We came from small towns, had been in the military, and were divorced with two kids. He was very social, frequently entertained friends, and seemed to know every gay man in Des Moines. His home was always filled with friends and activity, and he always included me like an old friend instead of one he'd just recently met. He is one of those friends that no matter how long you've been apart, each new conversation is a continuation of previous ones.

After establishing such a close bond with these men, I was shattered to hear that one of them had been murdered. Slowly, a few facts about Ken's death began to trickle in. After going to the theater on Saturday night with a friend, Ken had gone to the Brass Garden. After last call he dropped his friend at home, and then went to the "gay loop," a cruising area where the search for Mr. Right evolves into the search for Mr. Right Now. Ken met two young men there and took them back to his apartment. No one except James Michael "Billy" Green and Gary Titus knows exactly what happened after that, and a search for the facts revealed contradictory stories.

Green said that they were underage and had been searching for someone to buy alcohol for them. Titus claimed they had pretended to be gay to get Ken to pick them up. Ken invited them back to his apartment to drink. He said that when they arrived, Ken put a gay porn movie in the video player. Green said that he thought Titus might have agreed to have sex with Ken, but instead the two decided to rob him. When Ken resisted, Green stabbed him. Some believe that the robbery was an afterthought designed to cover up their intent to kill a gay man.

After killing Ken, Titus and Green entered Jennifer's bedroom; they hadn't realized that she was there, but they left her unharmed. Jennifer discovered Ken's body when she woke in the morning, having slept through the grisly murder that had unfolded only a few steps away from her bedroom. On Green's twenty-first birthday, both men were convicted of first-degree murder and sentenced to life in prison without parole.

At his trial Titus testified, "All gay people should be dead." In 2010, on his Web site Titus admitted that both he and Green had a pattern of assaulting gay men for no reason other than that they were gay. (Did you know prisoners have Web sites?) He now professes to have become a born-again Christian. He said he found Christ after accompanying another prisoner, ironically another one of his former bashing victims, to a prison revival. He has since become a jailhouse preacher. While in prison his brother wrote him a letter saying, "Gary, I want you to know I'm gay. . . . What if you ran into me at the Gay Loop?" His brother later died of AIDS. Titus has married since entering prison.

Titus says that preying upon gay men brought power to his "otherwise powerless existence," as if he were the real victim of this heinous event. He writes, "I thought myself superior to them due only to their sexual preference. I looked upon their sexuality as a weakness to capitalize on for personal gain." Tragically, for those who seek this kind of affirmation, it is short-lived, and the gay bashing must be repeated over and over to recapture that feeling of strength. Rejecting any responsibility for this despicable act, Titus went on to put the entire blame for the murder upon Green.

Green also met a former bashing victim while in prison, and, like Titus, also credits the victim with helping him find his commitment to Christ. Green appeared with Jennifer on the *Oprah Winfrey Show* in a program about victims confronting perpetrators. A young woman who saw him on the show wrote to him and subsequently married him while in prison. Parole boards probably create more born-again Christians than prison revivals do.

The Chemicals of Pain and Pleasure

Serotonin is the chemical messenger in the brain that is critical in regulating emotions. Too much serotonin will inhibit sexual behavior, and low levels of it correlate with depression, angry and aggressive behavior, irritability, and impulsivity. Many of the newer antidepressant agents, used for both depression and anxiety, are called specific serotonin reuptake inhibitors (SSRIs). Their net effect is to increase serotonin at the junctions between neurons in the parts of the brain associated with regulating emotion.

Dopamine is the pleasure molecule, unloaded into the brain in massive doses just before a person receives the payoff for some winning behavior. It also is associated with controlling movement, emotional responses, and pain. Dopamine rewards can come naturally through eating chocolate and other comfort foods, sexual activity, and approval from others. The dividends of dopamine also come through the use of caffeine, alcohol, cocaine and methamphetamine, nicotine and marijuana, and gambling and other risk-taking behaviors, like anonymous sex in airport bathrooms. Dopamine neurons take in data we don't consciously comprehend, and too much dopamine can make you crazy.

Grandfathers may not know much about dopamine, but we do seem to know instinctively that you can't tickle your grandchildren unless you raise their anticipation of the tickle attack by playing the "I'm-gonna-get-you" game. Timing and unpredictability are critical. The heightened apprehension must be managed carefully or it will pass by quickly. Dopamine is dumped in the child's brain during the anticipatory phase of the attack, not during the tickle assault itself. Adults also instinctively play the sexual I'm-gonna-get-you game, although with much different stakes in mind. My friend Ken played that game when he put the porn video in the machine, with unfortunate consequences.

Dopamine is the pleasure molecule, and too much dopamine can make you crazy.

When I was in the Navy, I proudly wore the wings of a flight surgeon. As the drug czar for the squadron, I was responsible for the men's drug education. The early 1970s were a difficult time in our country's history. Young men and women protested the Vietnam War and confronted the establishment. They advocated for drugs and free sex. No one envied my assignment to do the sexually transmitted diseases and drug lectures before we were deployed.

I stood before a crowd of young sailors with their arms folded across their chests, staring at the floor. The senior men—there were no women in the squadrons in those days—both officers and enlisted, were adamantly opposed to drug use. Most of the younger men had been drafted into the military and resented the disruption in their lives. Drug use proved to be the perfect way to rebel. Alcohol abuse was almost requisite for career advancement of military men. The young men finally sat up and smiled when I turned on alcohol abuse as just another form of drug abuse.

Several of the corpsmen, the Navy's medical support personnel, spoke in guarded but rather transparent ways about their use of marijuana. The more they talked about it, the more it intrigued me. I decided I wanted to try it. I asked one of the corpsmen I trusted if he would help me. One evening, when my wife was visiting her family in Nebraska, I invited the corpsman to come to my house and to bring some marijuana with him. The stakes were high for me. Officers were forbidden to fraternize with enlisted men, and I could have been severely reprimanded just for asking him over. To invite him over to do drugs with me at a minimum would have brought me before the captain, and could have led to being dishonorably discharged from the Navy.

Since I planned for this to be a one-time event, I was determined to make the most of it. The sailor and I sat in our living room and he instructed me in how to roll a joint. As I began smoking mine, I inhaled cautiously, briefly holding the smoke in my lungs. I could see that he was getting mellow, but I felt nothing. I wasn't sure what to expect, but I didn't seem to be experiencing the same thing he was. I decided I wasn't inhaling deeply enough. I began to take deep drags on the joint, doing as he'd instructed and holding my breath as long as I could. Still I felt nothing, and so I smoked the entire joint before I stopped.

All at once, I was high, very high. I got up and began to pace around the room, trying to ground myself in some reality I couldn't find. I was hit with a very powerful urge to try to have sex with the young sailor. That's when I started to panic. Rumors had circulated around the Navy clinic that he was gay, but he had never discussed it with me. Although I was still homosexually innocent, the effects of the marijuana threatened to unbridle my unconscious desire. Now I can see that I may have wanted him more than the marijuana.

Then the paranoia struck. I began to believe that the Naval Intelligence Service was spying on us through the closed draperies. They would charge me with fraternization with an enlisted man, lascivious acts, and the use of illegal drugs. I would be dishonorably discharged from the Navy and lose my license to practice medicine. Once this was exposed, I would also lose my wife and family. Every ambition I had about my future was about to go up in a cloud of cannabis smoke. I was desperate for my rational mind to return and rescue me from the dopamine haze, the NIS, and my homosexual psychotic thoughts.

Feelings are the summation of information we can't or don't want to comprehend consciously. Very little of our brain is involved in rational thought, while the vast majority of it is constantly processing information in its unconscious circuitry. Rational thought is a lion tamer in a cage filled with hungry wild animals. The brain abhors the contest between feelings and rational thought and consumes immeasurable energy containing information we really don't want to access.

Anticipating rewards is pleasurable, and the anticipation enhances the dopamine effects. But if it goes on too long, the dopamine effect grows stressful. Once I took my kids to a carnival and we rode the Turbo Force, a one-hundred-foot-tall tower with tubs that flip over as the tower spins. The ride went on far too long, and I was desperate to get out of that cage. Our screams were being amplified to the crowd and it only encouraged the sadistic carny to prolong the ride. Our pleadings raised the collective dopamine level of the crowd long after ours were depleted. Maturity is knowing that not every dopamine rush must be gratified.

> **Maturity is knowing that not every dopamine rush must be gratified.**

The Insurgency of Feelings

Successful decision making relies on a balance between deliberate thought and instinctive assumptions. Jonah Lehrer, in *How We Decide*, writes that we have two kinds of thinking: intuition and reasoning. Intuition makes up the large majority of all thought processes; it is fast, easy, and indefatigable. Intuition is connected to the brain's centers involved in motivation and reward, while reasoning is not. According to Lehrer, reasoning is slow, arduous, and demanding. He likens our rational decision-making process to training an elephant, where change comes slowly and each incremental change receives immediate rewards.

Most of the work of the brain does not occur at a logical level. When buying a new car, I read all about the cars recommended in *Consumer Reports*, but in the end, I always buy the one that I fall in love with. Often we believe we are making a rational decision when we are really making an emotional decision and then searching for justifications to make our decision appear rational. Lehrer states, "If it weren't for our emotions, reason wouldn't exist at all." As our brains collect bits of experiences, our rational minds quickly create "rational" explanations for things that can't be explained or are simply untrue. As Benjamin Franklin said, "So convenient a thing it is to be a reasonable creature, since it enables one to find or make a reason for everything one has a mind to do."

86

Our minds are engaged in a continuous conflict that operates outside of our awareness. The most important thing we can do is to listen to what every part of our brain is telling us. We must consciously search for the facts we need, but then allow our brains to incubate those facts together with our feelings before making a decision.

According to the prospect theory of economists Daniel Kahneman and Amos Tversky, "In human decision making, losses loom larger than gains." Because we undervalue the future, they argue, our decisions are impacted more by a fear of losses in our present life than the prospect of potential gains. Therefore, we opt for the status quo, often making uninformed decisions based on fear. This principle seems to govern many men's decisions to remain in the closet, and, as was my case, in their heterosexual relationships long after they've begun to have sexual relationships with other men.

Our brains carry a "negativity bias," meaning criticism has more impact than compliments do. Bad is stronger than good. As political campaigns demonstrate, nastiness, in the form of mudslinging, can be extremely effective. Researchers have demonstrated that there is a very definite ratio between positive and negative interaction that is necessary in personal relationships. John Gottman, PhD, author of *The Seven Principles for Making Marriage Work*, wrote that as long as there are five positive interactions for each negative interaction, a satisfying balance in the marriage can be achieved, conflict will diminish, and marriages can become more successful.

Various parts of our brains have been identified as serving different functions. The bottom of the frontal lobes integrates visceral emotion into decision making, connecting feelings to higher, more rational thought. But the engine of this part of the brain can become flooded with too many facts, causing a person to no longer be able to make sense of a situation. Other parts of the brain generate negative emotions like fear, anxiety, and acrimony, which impact decision making. Small wonder that often mature men make the decision to come out only after they have been confronted by a situation that forces them to do so.

A part of our temporal lobe helps us theorize what others are feeling and allows us to empathize with them. Individuals vary in their capacity for empathy from far too much to almost none. The world is full of impulsive people, who, like Titus and Green, appear to have a major functional deficiency in their capacity for empathy. Empathy helps us with moral decision making. We treat others well because we know what it is like to be treated unfairly and we can conceive of what we would feel like in their situation. The dopamine reward system of the brain responds to being treated fairly in the same way it responds to hitting a jackpot or eating a hot fudge sundae. Those with lower levels of serotonin are more sensitive to unfair treatment.

Some people seem to have a particularly heightened sensitivity for empathy, often caring more about others' feelings than they care about their own. One gay man told me that the primary pleasure in his relationships with men comes from pleasing his partners. When I asked him how he received his own sexual pleasure, he said, "I can always take care of that myself." He went on to say that his attractions are bittersweet because he is only attracted to older men, and he has lost five different partners through death.

Made-Up Memories

Neuroscientists tell us there are two kinds of memories, conscious and nonconscious; each is processed by two distinct networks in the brain. All memories are distortions of actual experiences, and in some cases they may be entirely imagined. Memories can be confusing mixtures of fragments of real and dreamed events, a montage of happenings from different times and places that are remembered as if they were one.

All memories are reconstructions, filled with factual errors. Memories before the age of five are doubtful. I have only wisps of memories of my father, and because he died when I was only three, many of these memories almost certainly can't be real. But I need them to be true. I have an image, unchanged since I was a child, of riding on a horse with my father, sitting on the saddle in front of him as we rode out to the pasture one cold evening to check the cattle. I see him as a handsome man in rugged clothing, wearing a brown felt broad-brimmed hat, as ubiquitous in the 1940s as the ball cap is today. I can still feel the chill in the air, see the dried-up stalks of corn, and smell the leather of the saddle. As we got to the field, a sudden gust of wind blew the hat from his head and sent it rolling down the cornrows. He gave a "whoa" to the horse to retrieve it. When he got down, I remained alone on the horse until he returned with his hat.

I imagine him saying to me, "Be a big man and stay here on the horse while I get my hat." Although the image is hazy, the feeling I have when I recall that memory is of being vulnerable, my strength and experience clearly not a match for that powerful horse. But, at the same time, I feel trusted by the most important man in my life. That feeling of being the master over a difficult task was implanted in the deepest parts of my mind, and it continues to impact my understanding of what it feels like to be a man. It is a feeling I have always sought to recapture. This image penetrates every corner of my self-esteem, yet the feeling eluded me for most of my first forty years.

We are just now learning where memories of social interactions can be located within the anatomical structures of the brain. Emotions attached to memories intensify memories. At three years old, my brain was not yet well formed. Perhaps, but only perhaps, this experience with my father was the beginning of the networks in my brain that would control how I would relate to other men throughout the rest of my life.

Insiders and Outsiders

I was drawn to psychiatry because of its complexity; it is a profession where nuance and ambiguity coexist with the gelatinous facts of the science of the brain. When I told my mother I wanted to be a psychiatrist, she said, "Why do you want to stop being a doctor?" For her, psychiatrists were physician outsiders. In the late 1960s, her only reference was small-town Nebraska, where if someone went to see a psychiatrist, he or she never returned.

Categorization is a useful tool our brains develop to reduce the complexity of the world; it can also be destructive. Labels are often static, arbitrary, and far too restrictive. Although people and societies evolve over time, labels, once assigned, resist change. Sexuality is far too complex to divide into just two categories, "gay" and "straight," with "bisexual" thrown in as a default category for those who don't fit easily into the other two. Historically, the word "queer" was used to describe men who felt a sense of difference and saw themselves as outsiders, marginalized by society.

In the Antebellum South, just "one drop of blood" was enough to brand someone as black. The primary purpose of the "One Drop Rule" was to expand the slave population. Today, an extremely diverse group of people is called "Hispanic," even if the only thing they have in common is that their first language is Spanish.

The Cherokee tribe was one of several tribes of Native Americans who once owned slaves, and when they freed their slaves, they made them members of the Cherokee Nation. In 1906, under the Dawes Rolls census, all descendants of the slaves were labeled "freedmen," even if they were equal parts Cherokee and African American. In 2007, the Cherokee Nation amended their constitution and limited citizenship only to those listed as "Cherokee by blood," expelling descendants of the black slaves they once owned, and all tribal citizenship rights that the freedmen descendants had held for more than 140 years were removed.

For a pamphlet arguing against Prussian anti-sodomy laws in 1869, Karl-Maria Kertbeny coined the word "homosexual" by combining a Greek and a Latin root. He hoped that by labeling homosexuality a medical problem, homosexual men who were being blackmailed would find compassion. The word "homosexual" stuck, but so did the idea that homosexuality was a form of pathology.

In 1871, Paragraph 175 was added to the Reich Penal Code: "[Homosexuality is] an unnatural act committed between persons of the same sex or by humans with animals," and this behavior was to be punishable by imprisonment and loss of civil rights. Eventually it was used to justify the extermination of homosexuals during the Holocaust.

The Law of Small Numbers forms the basis of all stereotypes and prejudices. Simply put, it states that what is true for some must be true for all. If some homosexuals are sissies, all must be. Applying this principle, societies describe groups of people by isolating one or two easily recognizable characteristics, elevating those traits to the highest level, and then generalizing those characteristics to everyone in the group. Once this is done, the search for any invalidating evidence stops, and stereotypes become fixed.

Sociologists tell us that all groups of people behave in similar ways, and they define the behavior in terms of "in-groups" and "out-groups." They suggest that these principles hold true whether we examine behavior in religion, politics, social relationships, or sexuality. I joined a college fraternity because I was trying to satisfy a need for connectedness. I believed membership would confer on me some positive feelings of acceptability. Sociologists call this "basking in reflected glory," but, as I found, borrowed respect vanishes quickly.

In all groups, individual interests are sacrificed and merged with the interests of the whole, the most extreme example being the military, where the esprit de corps exists to inspire devotion, honor, and obedience. Members of units within the military speak about the intense love each has for the others even though their relationships may be quite brief.

People who identify most strongly with a group see themselves as typical of all group members. They become outspoken and begin to believe they speak for everyone. These guardians protect the group from problematic or contradictory information that interferes with group cohesiveness. This behavior is apparent when we consider conservative talk show hosts like Glenn Beck and Rush Limbaugh, who exalt their norms and thinking as if they were universal truths.

But this is also true of some of the most outspoken gay activists. In the documentary movie *Outrage*, in speaking about Senator Larry Craig, Elizabeth Birch, former executive director of the Human Rights Campaign, said, "We don't want him anyway." It created a great laugh line for what appeared to be the largely gay audience.

Powerful leaders like Senator Craig who are hypocritical about their sexuality are in a position to do great damage to a large number of people. Many of us have lied about our sexual orientation, particularly while we were in a state of confused transition. For some, that state of confusion lasts a very long time, and in the process, we hurt others. That holds true for Senator Craig just as it holds true for me.

I have a great deal of respect for Ms. Birch and the HRC; however, where does one go for group membership when you're not wanted by the Human Rights Campaign, the nation's largest lesbian and gay political organization? I believe that Ms. Birch's remarks were motivated by her strong loyalty and commitment toward the HRC rather than any particular hostility toward Senator Craig. Because I can identify with some of Senator Craig's motivations for concealing his secret life, perhaps I felt stung by her remark. I may have thought, "I've been a hypocrite. Maybe they wouldn't want me either." But gay men and women are subject to the same principles of sociology as everyone else, and we must guard against the possibility that loyalty to our own community might also create for us a sense of moral superiority.

Half of the more than thirty thousand deaths from suicide occur in people between the ages of forty and sixty-four, and the numbers are climbing. Four out of five of those deaths are men, and one of the leading risk factors for suicide is feeling alone. Inclusion, particularly for those struggling with coming out in middle age, is key. Coming out in midlife is frightening enough but would be terrifying if there were no community to become a part of.

Sociologists explain that as we become members of a group, we begin to know other members well, eventually seeing ourselves as similar to them. However, we satisfy our need for individuality by recognizing there is also diversity within the group. We are connected emotionally to them, we hurt when they hurt, and we experience joy when they do. We also begin to exaggerate the positive characteristics of our group and may begin to see ourselves as having a higher moral authority than other groups. Marilynn Brewer wrote that many discriminatory behaviors are not motivated primarily by antagonism toward the out-group but rather by a desire to promote and maintain positive relationships in our own group. However, the very factors that make allegiance to our own group important create fertile ground for distrust of those outside. The need to justify the values of the in-group creates a sense of moral superiority. Loyalty to our own group then conspires to create disdain and hostility toward the out-group.

Because we associate primarily with members of our own group, we don't really know other groups, and we see them as more homogeneous and generic than they actually are. Some who have little or no experience with gay people feel confident that they can define us. They believe that gay people are unrestrained and disregard all laws or morality, as demonstrated in this exchange of e-mails I had with "George":

> **George:** [You do] not think that homosexuality is wrong. Homosexuals fit the description of Nietzsche's Übermensch, the man above other men. He stands above other men because he does not submit to a moral law that he did not himself devise. That is to say, his behavior is not restrained by any law. Pederasty, homosexuality, the corruption of the clergy, the devolution of society into paganism, it all hangs together.

Loren: You don't know me.

George: Oh, but I do know you! You have identified yourself as a homosexual, an immoralist. If a person can define for himself that homosexuality is perfectly good, there is nothing in the world to stop him from defining pederasty as perfectly good. Nothing binds his conscience. Morality is a matter of taste. Homosexual-, fornication-, and abortion-embracing churches are literally dying before our eyes.

Loren: You are as unable to see the evil in yourself as you are to see the good in me. You have attributed to me stereotypical characteristics of being gay with no attempt to know me as a Christian or a human being. You don't know me.

We assign negative characteristics to the other group and begin to see them as more evil than they are. Conflict escalates from name-calling to discrimination to attacks, hate crimes, and genocide. Propaganda that characterized all Jews, Gypsies, and homosexuals as subhuman and a threat to the Aryan race allowed the Nazis to exterminate those they felt threatened by. The Germans hated the Jews for a reason, but the reason was fear-based and founded on a distortion of facts. American history is replete with crimes of hatred and prejudice, from lynching to cross burnings, to vandalism of churches and synagogues, to murders of gay men and women.

The term "hate crime" did not become a part of the nation's vocabulary until the 1980s during a wave of bias-related crimes that included Ken's murder. Perhaps Titus and Green's brain chemistries or their family environments led them to kill Ken, but by their own statements it is more likely that they felt threatened by homosexuals. Their hatred caused them to make preemptive attacks on gay men, making themselves self-appointed warriors for all homophobes out there—the Law of Small Numbers in its most brutal form.

The dominant heterosexual community has at times blamed gay men and women for having brought hatred upon themselves. When those in the out-group feel morally excluded, threatened, and vulnerable, they begin to exalt themselves, claiming higher moral authority, and they degrade, hate, and attack the opposition.

Following Stonewall, gay people became a more powerful group. No longer hidden, they became bolder and more unified, even making their own preemptive attacks on the powerful, through groups like ACT UP, as described by Jason DeParle in an article in the *New York Times* on January 3, 1990:

> To the businesses, bishops and bureaucrats that they accuse of slowing the fight against AIDS, [members of ACT UP] often seem rude, rash and paranoid, and virtually impossible to please. And they are . . . members of ACT UP, the AIDS Coalition to Unleash Power, refer to themselves as a despised minority, literally fighting for their lives. And that they are as well. Another word helps describe ACT UP: effective.

Contact between a dominant majority group and a racial, ethnic, religious, or other minority group reduces prejudice. Psychologists call this "the contact hypothesis." Research has demonstrated that heterosexuals' attitudes about homosexuality are changed most significantly when a homo-negative person has an open discussion about homosexuality with two or more close friends or family members who are gay. From a global perspective, it is easy to suggest that social justice demands that each of us who is gay must share our sexual orientation with others, but when it comes down to how these decisions impact the people we love, coming out becomes far more difficult.

Early in my years of coming out, the extent to which I took up the task of implementing "the contact hypothesis" by coming out was limited. In 1992 I participated in the March on Washington for Lesbian, Gay, and Bi Equal Rights and Liberation. Organizers estimated one million attended the march, but the National Park Service estimated attendance at 300,000. Either way, my presence didn't make a large, tangible difference, but experiencing the great diversity of men and women there had a tremendous impact on me. The march was organized to bring attention to the government's lack of response to the AIDS epidemic.

There was an incredible sense of camaraderie and common cause. At our hotel, Bruce, my partner Doug, and I, who had traveled to the march together, were shouting across the courtyard at the other marchers. One room, directly across from us and a floor below, had its sheer curtains drawn, but in the dimming light of evening we could just make out the figures.

We watched as the two became more and more passionate, our own sexual tension rising. Suddenly, one of them stood up. We all realized at the same time that she had breasts and almost in unison we exclaimed, "We've been watching two women!" Discovering that we unknowingly had been watching two women have sex drained away our sexual excitement. Being at the march had made us feel part of a group—a large and powerful group—but in that moment we learned that our group was much more diverse than we had realized.

Being in the presence of so many other gay men and women revealed to me the sheer size of our out-group, but also proved the great diversity within it. It also confronted me with the stark reality of how many of our group had died from AIDS. During the march, the last display of the AIDS Memorial Quilt covered the entire National Mall. Bruce, Doug, and I located the panel of our friend Jim, who had died of AIDS. I was filled with grief for the tens of thousands of people who were victims of this devastating disease, and I experienced a great compassion for those many men my age who searched for quilt panel after quilt panel of the many people they had loved and watched die. As I looked at the dates on the quilt panels, I realized if I had come out earlier, my name could easily have been among them. I felt a great sense of connectedness to those who had died and the enormous guilt so often felt by those who escape the consequences of terrible tragedies.

Drag Is a Drag

I've only dressed as a woman twice in my life, once as a fourth grader, and once just after I came out. Neither was very successful. As a fourth grader, it was fun getting ready to go to school to participate in the Halloween parade through town, putting on makeup and some of my sister's clothes. But immediately after leaving the house, I knew I had made a bad choice. In choosing Halloween costumes we adopt alter egos, and as a boy, your alter ego is supposed to be a superhero or an athlete, not a woman. I quickly realized that my choice separated me from the other boys in my class. Instead of enthusiasm and confidence, what I felt was a sense of shame.

Just after we started dating, Doug and I, Bruce and Ken, and some other friends decided to "dress" for Halloween. Doug found a little sequined dance recital outfit at a Salvation Army store, and he decided to go as a majorette, an ostrich feather in his headband and tassels on his cowboy boots. I'm a large man, and all I could find at the Salvation Army store that came even close to fitting was a long, washed-out blue dress that most likely had never looked good on anyone. I put on a cheap platinum wig. After we got the false fingernails on, I looked in the mirror, and there was my mother staring back at me. Although my mother was not an unattractive woman, the last thing I wanted was to go to the Halloween party, my first quintessential gay party, looking like her!

Doug had no idea how to twirl a baton, but he was in the bar, leaping as high as he could while throwing his baton high in the air. The baton fell wherever and on whomever, and no one in the intoxicated crowd seemed to give a damn. I hated the dress and couldn't keep my false fingernails on. How does anyone ever pee when they're wearing false fingernails? Doug had a great time, but I was miserable. If doing drag was an essential requirement for being gay—as the stereotype implies—it was clear I might not fit in there either.

Being Gay and Feeling Good

Believing that we are competent, attractive, well liked, and morally good are the touchstones of self-esteem. I often worry too much about whether I am liked by others, and I expect rejection to the point that I look for evidence even when it doesn't exist. During the first year of my relationship with Doug, he was unable to decide whether or not to remain in Iowa to be with me. Because of my inflated fears of loss, I kept pressuring him to make a commitment. Doug was frustrated by my anxiety and reminded me to live in the moment of our relationship.

In describing their motivations, Titus and Green, who murdered my friend Ken, perceived that acting on their hatred for gay people would compensate for their feelings of powerlessness and finally give them some self-respect. They, like me—albeit in a completely different, violent, and ineffective way—were seeking self-esteem.

Our "ideal self," the person we wish to be, is the sum of all traits, values, and issues we consider to be important. This is the main organizing principle of self-esteem, the nucleus formed early in life. It enlarges and becomes more complex with maturity. For example, having perfection as an ideal creates a chronic gap between what is expected and what is achieved; when perfection and failure are the only two options, a sense of failure is inevitable because perfection is not achievable. Each new experience is filtered through these negative constructs, resulting in a broad range of negative generalizations about yourself and a growing tendency to personalize everything. Self-criticism and self-blame begin to dominate the thinking. Events are polarized into good and bad, and because we seem to have a bias for it, we selectively focus on things that are negative. This negative thinking is generalized to the assessment of the world, leading to isolation and loss of motivation, and resulting in the physical signs and symptoms of depression.

> **Self-esteem comes from believing that one is competent, attractive, liked by others, and morally good.**

Andrew Tobias, in *The Best Little Boy in the World*, describes how many gay men try to compensate for what they feel are their deficiencies by going to extremes to please others. I had believed that because gay was bad, I couldn't be bad. So I was going to be good, and I'd be the best at being good that I could be. This was a very common theme in the interviews that I conducted. But my measure for being good had been being what others expected me to be. Choosing to be a psychiatrist rather than a family care doctor became the touchstone for my evolving decision-making process; I didn't need my mother's approval of my professional choice. If I wanted to be a psychiatrist, I would be a psychiatrist. If I wanted to be gay, I would be gay, too. I could be gay and still be good, but it would mean giving up an expectation of approval from others.

One day when my daughters were quite young, I was in charge of their care for the day. After hearing, "Daaad-deeee" far too many times, I thought, "I have not had one complete thought all day without it being interrupted." I felt guilty about having such a thought. I was failing in my commitment to be the best father ever. I now believe that I have the capability of being a good parent a maximum of six hours per day—on a good day—and the rest of the time I must settle for just good enough. My best effort will have to suffice. It was with some relief that I read Dr. Bruno Bettelheim's book *A Good Enough Parent*, in which he wrote that being a perfect parent and having perfect children is far less important than having a good relationship with them and understanding their emotional needs. Choosing "good enough" over perfection as a standard makes the goal far more likely to be achieved.

Several years ago at a meeting in Arizona for medical executives, I heard Dr. Harry Levinson, emeritus professor of psychology in the Department of Psychiatry at Harvard, discuss a model for self-esteem:

$$\text{Self-esteem} = \frac{1}{(\text{Ideal self - Actual self})}$$

The rules of reciprocal numbers suggest that the closer the person we think we are ("actual self") moves toward the person we want to be ("ideal self"), the more self-esteem is increased. I tried using Professor Levinson's formula on some of my patients, but many people responded to me with a glassy-eyed math-anxiety look. I began to use the following diagram to explain this to my patients, and almost immediately they began to understand the issue.

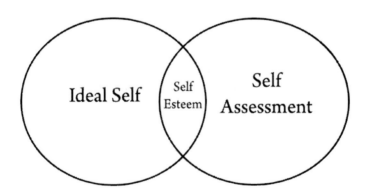

Professor Levinson suggested that we have the power to modify the "ideal self," the person we wish to be. Often the "actual self," the person we think we are, is based less on facts than on a negative bias in our brains. In other words, we tend to be overly harsh in our self-criticism. The formula, he points out, does not contain anything about approval from others; lasting self-esteem, Dr. Levinson insists, can never be achieved by seeking approval from others.

Using this diagram, my patients began to see, as I had, that energies directed at pleasing others would never lead to a predictable and lasting feeling of satisfaction with oneself. Always seeking approval drives us to become what William Sloane Coffin, a Presbyterian minister and peace activist, calls "quivering masses of availability." Anna Freud had the same insight when she said, "I was always looking outside myself for strength and confidence, but it comes from within. It is there all the time."

Three steps toward improving self-esteem
1. Take control of the "ideal self" and make it your own, not something you inherited.
2. Learn to see yourself as you are; avoid exaggerated self-criticism.
3. Look inside yourself for strength and confidence; approval from others is fleeting.

This was a dramatic revelation in my own life. If I wanted to feel good about myself, I had to analyze all the things I had been told I must be, and then asses which of those things I wanted to commit myself to being. I felt a new sense of freedom as I took complete control of this ideal. I realized that seeking approval from others is nothing more than a form of addiction. A "hit" of approval creates a rush of good feelings that lasts but a moment. The search for the next "hit" begins immediately. To achieve a lasting sense of self-esteem, I had to choose for myself a high but achievable standard, work hard to reach it, and be objective in measuring my progress. Getting to know other gay men whom I admired and respected was an important step in deconstructing the old and reconstructing that new ideal.

It was after I came out that I realized that I needed to be fair and accurate with my self-appraisals. I recognized that seeking approval for being someone I didn't really want to be undermined my self-esteem. The remarkable thing is that often when we choose outside of what is expected, others approve of us as much as if we had chosen according to expectations.

Typical, inherited societal ideal self values (in order to be happy, I must):

- Not make mistakes
- Be successful (usually measured by income)
- Be accepted by all people all of the time
- Have a wife/husband and a family to complete myself

Cognitive therapists talk about "automatic thinking," and the cascade of those thoughts goes something like this:

I cannot start my lawn mower.
→ Every man should be able to start a lawn mower.
→ In fact, I can never do anything most men should be able to do.
→ I am worthless as a man.
→ I am a drag on my family and society.
→ I may as well kill myself.

These negative pathways are practiced so frequently and successfully that a depressed person can instantly shift from something as banal as mechanical trouble to extreme existential angst, a response that goes far beyond anything justified by the circumstances.

The basic principles of cognitive therapy suggest that these thoughts have their origins in early life, incorporated through role models, feedback, and culture. Although these thoughts, especially the earliest ones, are difficult to change, they are subject to modification, meaning distortions in our thinking can be corrected. Cognitive therapy does not question the existence of unconscious thinking, but it does suggest that looking entirely at the roots of these distortions, as in more traditional psychodynamic psychotherapy, is unfruitful.

Automatic thoughts:
- Are habitual, learned, and practiced
- Are global and generalized ("always" or "never")
- Are specific and discrete (e.g., "I'm fat")
- Appear to be plausible, intuitive, and factual
- Lead to negative events being taken out of context and magnified

Men who struggle with their same-sex attractions can feel as if they are being dragged by a strange new force. Desire and reason—I should be attracted to women because that is "normal"—are pulling in two different directions. While this turmoil may initially appear during the emotional upheavals of adolescence, it can persist, as in my case, throughout adulthood. The cultural values of masculinity, femininity, and sexuality are incorporated into our "ideal self" in often unrealistic and unattainable ways. This gap in expectations and outcomes creates the sense of "difference" that gay men feel. It creates additional distortions in thinking, and "shoulds" dominate our thoughts: I *should* like women, I *should* be able to fix a lawn mower, and I *should* have known not to have dressed as a girl for Halloween. These are things we believe a boy should instinctively know. Failure to attain the "shoulds" can create a sense of shame that translates into the rage that some gay people feel toward a homophobic culture. Although anger toward an unjust society is appropriate and actions directed at changing that culture are admirable, unfortunately, it will not help anyone feel better.

When I was in eighth grade, I was in the drum line for our school's marching band. Our band, along with many others from across the state of Nebraska, was invited to participate in a parade on Band Day at the University of Nebraska. We were relaxing after we'd changed out of our band uniforms and visiting with members from other schools. One of the baton twirlers from another band was showing off a little, and my best friend, Fred, said to her, "My friend Loren here can twirl a baton better than you can." I was horrified, but he kept insisting that I perform to prove his point.

Although when I was younger I had spent hours alone practicing, with Sousa marches blasting from the 45 rpm record player I'd put in a window, I never imagined performing publicly. It was one more part of my life that I had compartmentalized, a part of myself I kept invisible from the outside world. When I practiced twirling in private, I felt freer than I felt during most of my childhood, but during that moment, I realized how truly strange my baton twirling was in the eyes of everyone else. I took her baton, performed every skill I knew, and easily surpassed her best efforts. My victory was empty of any pride and filled with a great sense of shame.

The first step in improving the way we feel about ourselves is to take a good look at the childhood ideal self and begin to modify it into something that is more representative of our own personal values and gifts. One important way to do that is to seek out others whose values are more consistent with our own. The isolation of many men who have sex with men perpetuates their stereotypical beliefs about "faggots," "twinks," and "the scene." Joining the fathers' support group changed all of my preconceived ideas about gay men. I met gay men whom I loved, admired, and respected. I learned to recognize alternatives to the prescribed values I had obtained as a child. The "shoulds" melted away and the "want to be's" began to dominate.

"There is nothing either good or bad, but thinking makes it so," Hamlet says to Rosencrantz and Guildenstern in Shakespeare's *Hamlet*. One of my patients continues to be tormented by a long-term homosexual relationship he had with a classmate in high school. He cannot set the incident aside, and he is constantly plagued by his memories of it. Although he is married, he lives a lonely life, never speaking to anyone other than me about these thoughts. In our sessions I am reminded of another line from *Hamlet*, where Queen Gertrude says, "The lady doth protest too much, methinks." And even in our sessions, he is unable to accept that he stayed in the relationship because he wanted it as badly as his sexual partner did. The thought that he might be gay is far too unimaginable to him that he has never come to the point of making a decision about leaving the only life he knows, and the possibility of a different future is too elusive for him to imagine.

"Moral integrity," in psychiatric terms, is the formal relation each of us has to ourselves. Integrity includes knowing your desires, not deceiving yourself about those desires, and acting upon them. It means resolving the ambivalence and inconsistency in conflicting feelings. Some may have compelling reasons to avoid neatly resolving incompatible desires, but the cost of not resolving them can be great. Searching for this authenticity, this wholeheartedness, is never ending—life is very complex and multifaceted. But achieving integrity includes the incorporating of all parts of our personalities into a harmonious, uncorrupted, and intact whole.

Chapter 6
Ain't Nobody's Business: Tricks of the Trade

*An individual life is the accidental coincidence of but one life cycle
with but one segment of history.*
—*Identity and the Life Cycle*,
Erik Erikson

A headline stretching across the entire front page of the *Idaho Evening Statesman* on November 1, 1955, announced to the citizens of Boise, Idaho, "Boiseans Held on Moral Count." Two days later, the paper ran an editorial headlined "Crush the Monster," in which the editors called homosexuality everything from a moral perversion to a cancerous growth. With the arrest of three men in October 1955, an investigation began into allegations that more than one hundred young men and teenage boys had been involved in sexual acts with a ring of adult homosexual men. The newspaper editors demanded that the entire situation be "completely cleared up, and the premises [city] thoroughly disinfected." Anonymous calls flooded the Boise Police Department switchboard as people turned in the name of any man who was suspected of paying too much attention to any young boy. Parents hovered over their children like a hen over baby chicks, and the city's gay residents realized that a witch hunt was in full swing.

At least twelve men from Boise were arrested for "infamous crimes against nature." The national news media goaded the public with headlines like "Male Pervert Ring Seduces 1,000 Boys." By the time the investigation wound down in January 1957, some 1,500 people had been questioned, 16 men faced charges, and 15 of them were sentenced to terms ranging from probation to life in prison.

On November 20, 1955, the *Idaho Statesman* abruptly softened its position, noting that homosexuality existed in every community and had existed "as long as the weaknesses of the human mind have been evident." The *Statesman* declared that homosexuals were not criminals and incarceration was not an appropriate response. It claimed that as long as the focus was on punishing the adult men, the involved boys, now "infected" by the homosexual men, would eventually "travel the same path and carry the identical threat to the next generation of youth." The scandal limited the debate to seeing homosexuality as a mental illness requiring treatment or as a criminal act that should be punished.

Coercive sex with anyone, and in particular with children, is wrong. Although the investigation was framed in terms of protecting children from adult predators, the probe was not confined to investigating charges of men having coercive sex with underage boys. Some of those convicted and sentenced to prison were found guilty only of sexual encounters with other consenting adults, their previously private sexual identity accidentally colliding with a short but tumultuous segment of Idaho's history. There is little doubt in my mind that the events in Boise shaped the developing consciences of young boys who were just becoming aware of their sexual urges. Perhaps former Idaho senator Larry Craig, ten years old at the time, absorbed a lesson that sexual indiscretion (or the perception of it) could ruin a man's reputation.

The same cultural wind was blowing over Nebraska, where I grew up. A few years earlier, when I was about seven, Nebraska's Republican senator Wherry was quoted in the *New York Post*: "You can't hardly separate homosexuals from subversives. . . . Mind you, I don't say that every homosexual is a subversive, and I don't say every subversive is a homosexual. But [people] of low morality are a menace in the government, whatever [they are], and they are all tied up together." Senator Wherry, quoting "reliable police sources," said that there were 3,750 homosexuals holding federal jobs. It was the height of the Cold War and people feared that foreign infiltrators abetted by homegrown subversives were preparing attacks against the United States. These fears penetrated our minds as children, and our games morphed from cowboys and Indians into soldiers fighting Stalin and foreign terrorists. Homosexuals were lumped into the category of subversives, not that they were considered communists, but because they were thought to be susceptible to blackmail and could be coerced into revealing government secrets.

When someone fell under suspicion of government agencies, the question they feared the most was, "Are you now or have you ever been a member of the Communist Party?" However, a close second was, "Information has come to the attention of the Civil Service Commission that you are a homosexual. What comment do you care to make?" The term "McCarthyism," named for Republican senator Joseph McCarthy of Wisconsin, was applied to attempts to expunge Communists and homosexuals from American public life. It has since come to signify all political extremism and civic hysteria.

Many conservative Americans were fearful that the country was in a state of moral decline, and gay and lesbian civil servants were demonized as part of the Washington bureaucracy. In June 1950, the Senate authorized an official investigation, the first of its type in the history of the United States, popularly referred to as the "pervert inquiry." The report accused the Truman administration of indifference toward the danger of homosexuals in government, explicitly mentioning a "lack of emotional stability" and "weakness of . . . moral fiber" as defining characteristics of homosexuals. Dismissals from the federal government and the military increased dramatically. Thousands of homosexuals were harassed by police, arrested, dismissed from jobs, and even imprisoned. The term "pinko fag" became the era's worst slur.

Presidential candidate Adlai Stevenson was described as feminine, dainty, and weak—not a tough-talking man's man. Rumors were spread that he was gay. J. Edgar Hoover, director of the Federal Bureau of Investigation for nearly fifty years and considered by some to be the most powerful person in the United States, was said to have been a cross-dresser. Hoover hated Stevenson's liberal politics and attempted to brand him as "queer."

Presidential candidate Dwight D. Eisenhower and his running mate, Richard Nixon, were portrayed as regular guys in favor of morality. In 1952 the incumbent Democratic administration was alleged to be engaged in immoral behavior, and the Republicans finally won the White House, campaigning under the slogan "Let's Clean House." These issues were debated across the tables in the coffee shop in my hometown in Nebraska, and while they were intentionally shielded from my ears and those of my peers, the fears of communism and homosexuality certainly leaked into our developing unconscious minds.

Despite the mainstream fear, there were early gay activist groups. In the early 1950s, one of the earliest American gay movement organizations, the Mattachine Society, began to challenge some of society's ideas about homosexuality. Given the fearful political climate,

Mattachine Society meetings often took place in secret with members using aliases. A poll taken at that time suggested that 95 percent of homosexuals would not be willing to take a pill, if one existed, to become heterosexual. They also responded that they would not wish their own brother or son to be brought into a society that scorned them. The Mattachine Society asserted that one should have no more guilt about being homosexual than one should have about his or her skin color. They took the following positions:

1. Any laws designed to protect the young were appropriate, including laws that forbade force or unfair advantage.
2. Laws should be maintained against overt public sexuality between men.
3. Laws should protect same-sex behavior between consenting adults when done in private.
4. Laws should be based on whether or not there was coercion and force rather than against specific sexual behaviors.

Despite the Mattachine Society's efforts, as I was finishing college in the late 1950s, three thousand men were arrested by the Los Angeles Police Department for lewd acts in public places. The police alleged that homosexual sex was occurring more and more conspicuously in public places and therefore was justifiably punishable by the law. The LAPD said their goal was to reduce immoral sexual behavior.

In March 1967, by the time I was just completing my third year of medical school, I heard the national broadcast of "CBS Reports: The Homosexuals." For most of an hour, Mike Wallace, a familiar figure from *60 Minutes*, provided his audience with some of the most disturbing anti-homosexual propaganda ever heard. Wallace's report, which followed the general mentality of the time, reminded viewers:

This much is certain. Male homosexuals in America number in the millions. And their number is growing. They are attracted mostly to the anonymity that a big city gives them. . . . The average homosexual, if there be such, is promiscuous. He is not interested in or capable of a lasting relationship like that of a heterosexual marriage. His sex life, his love life, consists of a series of chance encounters at the clubs and bars he inhabits, and even on the streets of the city. The one-night stand is a characteristic of the homosexual relationship. . . .

Airing to many thousands of viewers, the report spread an inaccurate and exaggerated portrayal of gay men. I don't remember exactly what impact Mike Wallace's report on homosexuality had on me at that time, but in retrospect I am sure that I tried, somewhat unsuccessfully, to believe it really didn't apply to me except as evidence that I really wasn't gay. I was still a part of that large majority of Americans who looked upon homosexuality with discomfort, disgust, and fear. Ignorance surrounding homosexuality was the norm in the 1960s; Wallace later admitted his nescience and regretted his involvement in the report's creation.

Movies, too, added to widespread misconceptions of gay people in the 1960s and '70s. According to Vito Russo in *The Celluloid Closet: Homosexuality in the Movies*, in about four out of five films with gay subtexts, gay characters either committed suicide or fell victim to violent death. The movies suggested that being gay was so dramatic, unpleasant, and frightening that it would drive even an otherwise well-adjusted person to self-destruction. Even the gay characters who lived had little in their cinematic representations to be admired.

The first movie that portrayed coming out in a nonsensationalistic way was *Making Love*, a 1982 movie starring Michael Ontkean as a happily married doctor who falls in love with "Bart," played by Harry Hamlin. In 1982, at the beginning of the Reagan era and before the explosion of AIDS, this film lacked some of the edge it would have had if it were made today, but it took many people outside of their comfort zones. It also profoundly touched the lives of many gay baby boomers by portraying homosexuals as men who did not have to be victims or victimizers with tragic but inevitable outcomes. In the movie, two gay men were shown as normal and capable of an emotionally rewarding relationship—living a life others might aspire to.

I remember watching *Making Love* on TV. My wife had it on in the living room and I carefully positioned myself in the dining room behind her so that I could watch over her shoulder, not letting her know how intensely interested I was. We didn't speak. Looking back, I believe this was the place in my own history where my unconscious mind was beginning to rail against the culture I'd grown up in, a culture filled with hostile mischaracterizations of homosexuality. In that moment I began to recognize that my marriage could not be resuscitated. I began to entertain the idea of having an affair, something that until then I never would have considered. Even as I began to think about being unfaithful to my wife, the thought never occurred to me that it would be with a man. Shortly after, I met Alfredo.

> The movie *Making Love*, released in 1982, was the first movie to depict gay men as normal and capable of loving each other in healthy, emotionally rewarding ways.

Senator Craig, Ted Haggard, and others like them believed they were just straight men who were having sex with other men. When asked if they were gay, they said no because they did not see themselves as "infected" with the immorality, emotional instability, and untrustworthiness of gay people. They were patriots, capable of tough talk with their masculinity intact. In their mind's eye they were not traitors, feminine, or weak. They were men's men who just wanted a blow job, and it was so much easier to find a man who was willing to do that. I know that's what they were thinking, because that's what I thought, too.

Why is it that it took a movie in the 1980s to awaken me? Why is it that some gay men who, like me, grew to adulthood during Stonewall believed the propaganda about homosexuality while others rebelled against it? Were some of us more predisposed to buy into stereotypes as a result of some inherited personality traits? Was it perhaps related to our relationships to our fathers, or the influences of our social community? Were our fears for loss of job, friends, and family more easily fanned? Or did a high need to please and a low tolerance for conflict make us more susceptible to accepting the values handed to us?

As discussed in the previous chapters, men choose not to come out for a variety of reasons. For those of us who were born in the 1940s and '50s, the hetero-normative culture was the only one imaginable, and homosex was not even seen as *real* sex. It is no wonder that someone like me couldn't confront his sexual identity—an identity essentially denied by the dominant culture—until middle age. However, later in my life I came to understand that each of us is unique as an individual, living in discrete cultures with different value systems that are impacted by the forces of a particular time in history. I now see that there can be no universal explanations for how each person chooses to deal with the conflicts about sexual orientation, but understanding the social context of the time of our sexual development offers some clarity into my life and the lives of my contemporaries.

The Loneliest Years

When I was in medical school, I made and cancelled three separate appointments to see a counselor at the University of Nebraska Medical Center. I was very lonely and unhappy. I remember thinking how much I would welcome some chronic, minimally painful, yet terminal illness so I could die a heroic death and not have to live the next part of my life. Although I had some very good friends, I always felt outside the social fabric of my class. I wanted someone to share my life with me, but I seemed to have difficulty connecting with women on an intimate level. I dated some very bright, articulate, and beautiful women. I was aware that some of their mothers wanted them to fall in love with me, although I never believed their fathers felt the same way.

The only logical reason I could think of to explain why I was still single was my own father's absence; I lacked a husband/father role model and I needed someone to mentor me through the relationship process. Once my sister told me that she also had some confusion about just what a father's role is in a family; her confusion validated my own misguided perspective. I hoped my life would come together when I got married and had a regular, acceptable sexual partner, but I was having doubts about finding someone. Undoubtedly there were gay bars in Omaha while I was in medical school, and it would have been a perfect time to explore them. But I wasn't aware of them, nor do I know anyone from my class who would have admitted to having gone to any of them. Even if I had known about the bars, I would have found it impossible to admit that I wanted to go, and fear would have overwhelmed me.

The Vietnam War was in full force as I approached the end of medical school—it was a reality I couldn't ignore. Military recruiters assured us graduating med students that unless we were women, veterans, or disabled, we were not likely to escape the draft. In my junior year of medical school, I signed up for the Navy, also taking on the extra commitment of flight surgeon training.

I had a year between medical school and the Navy, and I decided to interview for medical internships in Chicago, New York, St. Louis, and New Orleans. Although unaware of it at the time, I now can see that the unconscious forces of my mind were pushing me toward the anonymity and permissiveness of the big city. However, around the same time, I met my future wife. "Rational thought" captured my mind, overpowering whatever unconscious motivations I had. We decided to stay in Lincoln, Nebraska.

Absent Father, Close Binding Mother

The psychiatric literature I read in medical school did nothing to challenge the cultural values I had acquired in my youth. No defense of homosexuality could be found in the earliest edition of the *Diagnostic and Statistical Manual of the American Psychiatric Association*, which listed homosexuality as a pathologic deviancy.

Two psychiatrists, Dr. Irving Bieber and Dr. Charles Socarides, wrote in the mid-twentieth century that homosexuality develops because a child who is barely able to function as a heterosexual seeks to extract masculinity from his male sex partner. This theory, like the one discussed earlier about the homosexual man's craving for the "encircling arms of his father" resonated with me because of my fears that I was not masculine enough to be a real man. In hindsight, I am shocked that I could ever have believed either of their theories. It just makes no logical sense that two men, supposedly both deficient in masculinity, could expect to extract masculinity from each other. And yet there are still those who believe it.

In 1962, Dr. Irving Bieber headed a nine-year study of 106 gay men, at the time the largest of its kind. Bieber concluded, "A constructive, supportive, warmly related father precludes the possibility of a homosexual son; he acts as a neutralizing, protective agent should the mother make seductive or close-binding attempts." Male homosexuality, according to Bieber, is an adaptation to a disorder in one's relationship to other men. Homosexuality develops, in Bieber's view, because an overly protective mother senses her son is vulnerable, and fearing he will be injured, pulls the child close to her. She isolates him from his peer group and siblings and develops an overly intimate relationship with him as her favored child. Bieber believed that the child becomes closer to her than her own husband, and the father, resenting it, pulls away even further. According to Bieber, a good father will reassert himself and take control away from the mother. His intervention rescues the child from the undesirable future of homosexuality. Although discredited by his professional peers, Dr. Bieber remained steadfastly committed to his controversial theories. Even late in his life Dr. Bieber defended his work: his obituary in the *New York Times* stated that in 1973 Dr. Bieber told an interviewer, "A homosexual is a person whose heterosexual function is crippled, like the legs of a polio victim."

Dr. Charles Socarides, another leading psychiatrist writing about gay men whose work I was exposed to in medical school, was featured in Mike Wallace's report on homosexuality. He, too, argued that homosexuality was a "neurotic adaptation" that, in men, stemmed from absent fathers and overly doting mothers. Dr. Socarides was one of the cofounders of the National Association for Research and Therapy of Homosexuality (NARTH). To this day, NARTH focuses on promoting "reparative therapy for homosexuals," and propagates the conservative perspective many in the United States seek to redraw American culture by making homosexuality the equivalent of heterosexuality. NARTH holds Drs. Bieber and Socarides up as two of its leading prophets. Their writings, while discredited by peers in their own profession, are treated like scripture.

Throughout his life, Dr. Socarides continued to maintain his position that homosexuality is not a normal variation, despite the fact that his son, Richard, is openly gay and has been nationally active as a gay rights advocate. When asked about his relationship with his father for Dr. Socarides's obituary in the *New York Times*, Richard was quoted, "It was complex. We tried to relate to each other as father and son." Dr. Socarides may well have known a great deal about absentee fathers, having divorced the first three of his four wives, a fact never mentioned by family values conservatives.

In the mid-twentieth century, homosexuality was not seen as a crime in most of Europe; England was one of the last countries to change its laws. Societies were beginning to question whether or not the interests of the public were being served by prison sentences of up to sixty years for consensual man-on-man sex. Were homosexuals really twice as dangerous to society as second-degree murderers? Prison sentences for homosexual behavior were six times as long as for abortionists, more than twice as long as for bank robbers, and more than seven hundred times longer than for public drunks.

Integrating Genetics, Development, and Culture

My training in psychiatry—emerging from the homophobic world of the 1950s and developing in the rapidly changing 1960s—followed a rather classical Freudian tradition. Sigmund Freud proposed a structural theory of the brain that said that much of our mental life is unconscious and our feelings are a consequence of underlying conflicts. Freud's theory hinges on the id, the ego, and the superego. The id is the unconscious cauldron of raw drives, particularly sexual and aggressive ones. The ego is both conscious and unconscious, containing the elements of rationality and reasonableness plus the responsibility for maintaining contact with the external world. The superego also contains both conscious and unconscious elements; it develops early and is learned from parents, teachers, and others in positions of authority. The ego mediates in conflicts between the primitive forces of the id and the restraints of conscience of the superego. According to Freud, a person achieves optimum mental health when the id, the ego, and the superego are brought into equilibrium.

By the time I entered my psychiatric training, Ivan Pavlov's classical conditioning theory and B. F. Skinner's operant conditioning theories were beginning to weaken the hold Freud's psychodynamic theories had on psychiatry. The focus of psychology moved from the theoretical unconscious to observable behaviors—although it appears we may now be moving back toward a rediscovery of the unconscious.

In order to understand the complexities of how the mind works in cases of both mental illness and mental health, I have found most helpful the "biopsychosocial" model described by George Engel. This model looks at all of the known, broad forces that affect us: biological, psychological, and sociocultural elements. One single factor might weigh heavily or not at all. This model, in my professional experience, can be used to gain insight into how homosexuality manifests itself within each individual as well as in larger societies.

Previously I discussed the genetic basis for homosexuality. A growing consensus of scientists believes that a biological predisposition to homosexuality exists but is not a sufficient explanation for the expression of homosexuality. Arguments that homosexuality cannot be genetic because it is "nonprocreative," and therefore would eventually be extinguished, have been countered by the study of other species in the animal kingdom in which there exist nonprocreative individuals. What has been discovered is that these individuals may contribute significantly to the overall success of the biological community.

The brain and behavior are inextricably linked, and although the balance in psychiatry has shifted to a more biologic orientation, we are once again realizing that all behavior cannot be understood only through an expanding knowledge of synapses, receptors, and the circuitry of the brain. The biopsychosocial approach helps us capture the dynamic complexity of each individual by taking the biological evidence and combining that data with the unique concerns of each individual, his values, and his life context. Whatever the cause of homosexuality, the coming-out process must be approached in a person-centered way and conflicts related to decision making must be worked out on an individual basis.

All of this discussion of psychological theory matters because each of us must live our own lives. Although you may struggle to discover what is right for you about your sexual identity, trust yourself to know where and how your experiences intersect with the lives of others and how your life connects you to the culture around you. You are the only one who can weigh the potential price you will pay for coming out against the possible gains. The benefit of understanding that your sexual identity is uniquely tied to a combination of biology, psychology, and your environment should allow you to recognize that you are not limited only to the binary choices of gay and straight, out or closeted. Alternatives related to your specific life and personal makeup do exist.

Not One but Many Closets

Cultural context and differences across discrete social groups and historical events greatly impact perceptions of homosexuality. Plato said the following in the fourth century:

> Homosexuality is regarded as shameful by barbarians and by those who live under despotic governments, just as philosophy is regarded as shameful by them, because it is apparently not in the interest of such rulers to have great ideas engendered in their subjects, or powerful friendships or passionate love—all of which homosexuality is particularly apt to produce.

Years later, another philosopher, Plutarch, whose homeland of Greece had been conquered by the Romans, wrote, "The intelligent lover of beauty will be attracted to beauty in whichever gender he finds it." Romans were largely indifferent to gender and gender orientation, and Roman laws made absolutely no restrictions on the basis of gender.

Some Native American tribes were also rather indifferent to gender. In those tribes, homosexuals were described as having two spirits and were considered to have special gifts. In these tribes, gay people served as shamans, and in some cases had a same-sex spouse. Joe Medicine Crow is quoted by Walter Williams in *The Spirit and the Flesh: Sexual Diversity in American Indian Culture*: "We don't waste people the way white society does. Every person has their gift." Of course, acceptance of homosexuality was not universal in all tribes, and now gay Native Americans are discriminated against in some of their communities.

> **Joe Medicine Crow said that Native American societies don't waste people the way white society does.**

In some cultures, homosexual behaviors are part of a coming-of-age ceremonial rite, and help men cultivate spirituality and personal bearing in relationship to other men. Shirley Oliver-Miller of the Kinsey Institute wrote about anthropological reports of the Sambians of Papua New Guinea. These reports described a culture of "ritualized masculinization," where young men fellated their elders in order to receive the "masculinizing force" of semen. When the boys grew up, they married and then became the recipients of fellation by younger boys. All males participated in their adolescence, but as adults, they were expected to marry. At the same time, some Sambian males were described as homosexual in the Western, sexual-erotic sense of that term, and they existed in the same proportions as estimates of homosexuality in Western cultures.

The examples given—Greek, Roman, Native American, and Sambian cultures—illustrate that alternatives to contemporary Western interpretations of homosexuality exist. The idea that homosexuality is unnatural, something at odds with dominant norms, only persists because a portion of our society has judged it disgraceful, creating a culture of secret sexual expression.

That culture, in my experience, can only be harmful to individuals. The rich are said to be able to afford their indiscretions because they have the power and money to conceal them. Gay professional athletes, actors, wealthy businessmen, and politicians are notable examples. In the end, money wasn't enough to help Lord Browne of Madingley, the chief executive of British Petroleum (BP) who was forced to resign in 2007 when he perjured himself about the nature of his relationship with Jeff Chevalier, a gay escort he'd met on a site called Suited and Booted.

Lord Browne had allegedly misused BP resources by making substantial payments to Chevalier, establishing him in luxury accommodations, taking him on holidays, purchasing clothes for him, and setting him up in a business. The House of Lords rejected Lord Browne's attempt to keep his relationship with Chevalier secret and exposed Lord Browne as a liar, humiliating him in the process.

Lord Browne, reportedly unaware of a gay subculture when he was young, began frequenting gay bars for the first time in New York City after Stonewall. He relied on the discretion of others to keep his secret. For several years, even though his homosexuality was something of an open secret, Lord Browne steadfastly denied his gay identity, a victim of the culture of secrecy. Ginny Dougary quoted him in the London *Times*: "It was obvious to me that it was simply unacceptable to be gay in business, and most definitely the oil business." He is now in a relationship with a man, and said, "I'm happier than I've ever been. I feel amazingly fortunate. Amazingly."

The closet Lord Browne inhabited is quite different from that of a twenty-one-year-old man from the South who posted this "personals" ad early in 2010: "Are there any other bi/closeted/gay rednecks like me around?" He went on to describe wanting someone who would hunt, fish, and chew tobacco, but he also required that if his friends came around "no one would be able to tell. I ain't out and I don't wanna be!"

The size of a closet and the thickness of its walls vary from one person to the next. Sometimes it resembles a bomb shelter. Living a hidden life is far more complex for those in rural America, for many immigrant populations, and for those practicing fundamentalist religions, where the key institutions are home, church, and school. For many of them, homosexuality is seen by the community as an otherworldly decadence, and homosex is seen as an act that one does, not an identity, something one is.

Non-Western and Immigrant Perceptions of Homosexuality

In some of the most extremely fundamentalist societies, heterosexuality is compulsory. In September 2007, while speaking before an audience at Columbia University in New York City, Iranian president Mahmoud Ahmadinejad was asked about the alleged execution of two hundred homosexuals in Iran earlier that year. He responded by saying, "In Iran, we don't have homosexuals like in your country. In Iran, we do not have this phenomenon. I don't know who has told you that we have it." Homosexuality serves as evidence of the degradation of American society.

Early in 2010, the Ugandan Parliament debated a law threatening the death sentence for serial homosexual offenders or active homosexuals living with HIV. Under the law, anyone convicted of homosexual acts could face life imprisonment. Family and friends who failed to report them, and landlords who rented to them, would face up to seven years in jail. People working in public health agencies counseling homosexual men on HIV prevention would also face the possibility of imprisonment. This final piece of the law is ironic given that Uganda made incredible strides in HIV prevention. In 1993, its people had the highest HIV infection rates in the world. However, a structured response from the government in collaboration with international organizations and nongovernmental organizations has resulted in a reversal of rates of infection.

118

Some believe that this law was encouraged by Christian fundamentalists from the United States. Ugandan talk radio was filled with scandals and outings. Because the culture in Uganda defines all sex as heterosex, there is no separate "gay identity." Those who do identify as "homosexual" are ostracized, seen as a subclass, and disempowered or discriminated against. According to a post on the blog GayUganda, openly gay Ugandans have begun to push others considering coming out to remain unseen and voiceless for their own protection.

David Kuria, director of the Gay and Lesbian Coalition of Kenya, in an interview with the *Equal Rights Review* in 2010, described life for a homosexual in Kenya. Kuria explained that most countries in Africa have compulsory, legally enforced heterosexuality. Anyone wishing to engage in same-sex practices must live two lives; according to Kuria, 60 percent of men who engage in same-sex practices also engage in heterosexual activity. "Concurrency" is the word he used to describe ongoing parallel heterosexual and homosexual practices, often with multiple current partners. Homosexual activity is largely concentrated in networks, mostly urban and interconnected. The concentration, and "concurrency," from Kuria's point of view, is thought to be largely responsible for the large incidence of HIV transmission in Africa. The basis for negative attitudes about homosexuality, from Kuria's perspective, is not that homosexuality is "un-African," but rather that being gay is somehow un-biblical. Even though other behaviors like fornication and adultery are considered by the Scriptures to be serious offenses, they are treated differently.

According to Kuria, Africans generally believe that changing from a homosexual orientation to a heterosexual one is possible, and can even be instantaneous. Same-sex sexuality is criminalized as "crimes against the order of nature," a colonial inheritance from English law. Homosexuals are indistinguishable from the general population and they often engage in heterosexual relationships, including marriage. Kuria described the feeling for many gay men as being "imprisoned" in their marriages. However, he also identified that many married gay men love their spouses, and most cannot see themselves living in societies where anything other than a heterosexual family relationship is the norm.

In rural areas of Africa, as well as many rural areas throughout the world, there is an even greater requirement for hetero-normativity. The rural masculinity model means not only being heterosexually partnered but often includes having multiple partners. Some of the men I spoke with who engaged in homosex practices felt a need to overcompensate, and they felt driven to have even more partners, particularly heterosexual partners. I received this letter from a man from India: "I am a thirty-year-old Indian, married and have one son. I am sexually attracted to older men, but I love my wife and do have sex with her. How can I make this stop?" The criminalization of homosexuality in India dates back to 1860, when the country was still under British rule, but in 2009, the New Delhi High Court repealed Section 377, decriminalizing consensual sex between LGBT adults. Although homosexuality appears in old scriptures and paintings, today it is a taboo and a highly stigmatized subject. Historically in India, same-sex behavior was hidden and led to harassment by police. Recently, some more progressive laws have been implemented.

In some Indian literature, homosexuals are characterized as Kothi and Panthi. Kothi are more feminine and act as passive partners, have had an earlier sexual debut, may be much younger than their sexual partners, and have a greater number of sexual partners, sometimes with the exchange of money. Panthi generally prefer to have anonymous sex with strangers and more easily pass as heterosexual. Most have had their sexual debut with a woman. More commonly they are the active partner. Most Panthi adhere to social norms, and most have yielded to an arranged marriage. For them, anonymous sex rarely interferes with other matters and is hidden from family and friends.

The Japanese live by the rule, "If it smells, put a lid on it." According to one interviewee who had spent considerable time in Japan, same-sex activity is compartmentalized and the Japanese are more comfortable than Americans in living with contradictions, as long as order is maintained. For Japanese men, there must always be a respectable life on the surface. The gay community in Japan is less public than in the United States, but it is not difficult to find bars and saunas that serve as gathering places for men of all ages. Not all of the clientele are gay, and many of them are looking for a quick sexual release.

Gay characters appear on Japanese TV, but the rule is that no matter how entertaining, it is still perverse. Gay men are often seen in the same category as prostitutes, bar girls, and the criminal underground. Civil unions are not permitted, and there are basically no out politicians or businesspeople.

Asian immigrants are noted for a strong work ethic, humility, and strong family ties, but this also may contribute to their difficulty in coming out. I received this correspondence from a thirty-five-year-old man who immigrated to the United States from Vietnam with his family when he was nine years old:

> I am out to my friends as bisexual, but as for my family, it's "Don't ask, don't tell," since I don't want to create drama and tensions. Basically I am prioritizing one battle at a time. I did tell my father that I am bisexual and he was somewhat supportive and hoping that I will like girls more than guys. Growing up being discriminated [against] and coming to the USA, it's harder for me to speak out about [being a part of a] sexual minority because of fearing that I, too, will get discriminated against. So I hide in the closet until the time is right. We waste too much time and energy on sexual orientation and shame. Too many people get depressed because of sexual conflicts and discrimination. I did mention about my sexual orientation during a speech a couple of years ago; it was a small conference and it was safe to talk to my peers. They're progressive people and are supportive, not prejudiced, toward sexual minorities. The good thing about sharing our experiences is that it provides wisdom and experience to others so they don't have to suffer the shame and bad feelings of being different.

In analyzing cross-cultural notions of heterosexuality, some commonalities arise: In many countries the homosexual male who is more feminine and acts the passive sexual partner is typically devalued, just as many women in those cultures are. The sins of those who are more like "real men" are more easily forgiven or overlooked. As in the United States, some men simply opt out when adult expectations force heterosexual dating and marriage after an age where same-sex play may have been ignored or tolerated. Other men engage in "trade," hiring male partners for sex in which they are almost exclusively the penetrative partner, an acceptable "masculine" behavior. Most do not discuss it with others. Some men will seek out anonymous sexual partners in public venues. The culture of secrecy exists worldwide.

Gay immigrants experience a kind of double jeopardy by having difficulty establishing an authentic sexual identity that is not only different from the mainstream American culture but also different from the family values and ancient cultural traditions of their parents. This exposes them to the possibility of multiple oppressions: racism, sexism, generational clashes, and stigmatization from both outside and within their immigrant communities. Because of this, they may resist being labeled gay and struggle with a decision about whether or not to come out.

Immigrant families are frequently tied together much more tightly than other families in America. Homosexuality is seen as deviant and bringing dishonor and shame to the family. Coming out can mean rejection from their families as well as from the entire community of friends who have immigrated to the United States. Male children have strong obligations to marry, create families, and sacrifice their own interests for the benefit and tranquility of the family.

For many ethnic minorities, coming out involves putting aside mandates from the community, often having to decide whether their ethnic identity or their sexual identity will take precedence. If they choose their ethnic group, they will surround themselves with homo-negativism; if they choose a gay identity, they lose the social support of their primary ethnic group and have no buffer against racism.

Closets Can Be Dangerous

Closets are dangerous places when it comes to issues of public health. Criminalization of homosexuality generally creates an underground of sexual activity. Andrew Francis and Hugo Mialon, assistant professors of economics at Emory University, report that where tolerance of gays is higher, HIV rates are lower, and that where tolerance is low, there is a higher rate of men having sex with other men in underground cruising areas, such as parks, beaches, and restrooms. Their findings were thought to have so much potential impact on policy decisions that in 2009, Emory University published the report on their Web site prior to its publication in a peer-reviewed journal.

The culture of secrecy often can lead gay men to live a life of pretense, engaging in illicit sex in sleazy, clandestine venues like public

122

parks and public restrooms. The risk of exposing themselves and their partners to disease is high, not to mention the risks of public humiliation. Living a secret can only reinforce a sense of shame and guilt. But that isn't to say that these encounters are purely anonymous. In those societies where heterosexual expression is mandatory and oppression is extreme, gay men and women create underground *communitas*, invisible gay spaces.

Sometimes we believe that we have made great progress in our understanding and acceptance of homosexuality over the past decades. After seeing Mike Wallace's 1967 CBS report, I never could have imagined that I would one day live in a place where Doug and I could be legally married. That said, many of the same social forces that caused me to delay coming out until midlife continue to operate, and in some places those forces are more severe than anything I had to encounter. However, as my personal experience attests, life-changing societal evolution does happen. If it didn't, women would still be waiting to vote and we might all still be either slaves or slave holders. American culture for gay men is far from perfect, but things are moving forward.

Here's how I see living authentically as a mature gay man:

1. Your value as a human being depends on things far more important than your choice of sexual partner.
2. Right and wrong are nuanced, complex concepts, not absolutes.
3. Maturity gives you the wisdom to examine values and dogma and decide for yourself what you believe.
4. Work out the best compromise that allows you to feel good about yourself in the context of your own life experience and spiritual needs.
5. Live life according to your own rather than someone else's expectations, and hope that those you love will come around to support you.

Chapter 7
How to Have Sex in a Tree

I'm supposed to sit around and love him while he decides what to do with his fucking wife and daughter.

—Evan, in the play *Out Late*,
Tim Turner

"Hey, Loren, I wanna show ya somethin'." My friend greeted me almost immediately after I jumped out of our car at his parents' farm in Nebraska. I was about ten and he was a couple of years older. We ran off to the barn, where he took off his denim jeans—back then only sissies wore shorts—and in less than a minute, he masturbated to the point of ejaculation, likely not his first time that day. He launched my education in sex as he announced, "I just shot my wad." Farm boys knew more about sex and at an earlier age than town boys like me, but their knowledge wasn't much more nuanced than "It takes a bull and a cow to have a calf." At that time I still believed that to make a baby a man must pee on a woman's crotch.

Discovering ejaculation introduces most boys to sex, and their education builds slowly throughout adolescence and young adulthood. Ejaculation is what men do that women can't. It is a man's role in reproduction. For a young boy, it is the essence of becoming a man. Fortunately, it is immensely pleasurable. But education encompasses both information and disinformation, and it is shaped by cultural attitudes. When a man discovers his homosexuality, his education must begin all over again.

Discovering our sexuality is much like observing the night sky. One evening, my younger daughter and I were returning from a family reunion in Wyoming. It was August, and at dusk we lay down on the asphalt in a parking lot in the Badlands of South Dakota to watch the stars. The setting sun introduced the earliest and brightest stars. As night unfolded, more and more stars appeared as darkness lay over us like a blanket. The constellations and the Milky Way began to interrupt the darkness that then exploded with so many shooting stars we didn't have enough wishes for all of them. When a boy first discovers ejaculation, it is like the first visible star, but it is only a tiny hint of a world that will unfold.

Young boys are sexual beings, and erections and erotic dreams begin long before boys know their significance and well before they can ejaculate. During this period of sexual discovery in early adolescence, group sexual play is not uncommon. After dark, on our Boy Scout camping trips, we would strip off our clothes and run around naked. Although often accompanied by erections, being naked created a sense of excitement that was far too amorphous to call it "sexual." Sexual exploration with other boys was accepted, up to a point, and if my sexual attraction to other boys surpassed that of my friends, I wasn't aware of it.

During my childhood summers, I spent time on my friends' and relatives' farms, and we couldn't wait to get to the hayloft and shed our clothes. No one discussed masturbation, although the Boy Scout manual mentioned something about "unhealthy behavior." I masturbated a lot, sometimes several times a day, but probably no more than most of my friends. I would promise myself that I would touch myself only briefly and then stop, but I never could. Sometimes I thought, "That was fun. Whatever it is, I want to do it again. I think I will do it again now." Tissues were a luxury, so my mother, without comment or censure, washed a lot of handkerchiefs.

The adults who supervised us never seemed particularly concerned about our nakedness and exploration. Looking back, it seems as if their attitude was just "boys will be boys." If there had ever been any concern that these activities might have made homosexuals out of us, the adults certainly would have intervened. But as we grew older, I felt there seemed to be some growing sense of disconnection from what other boys might have been experiencing, but no one ever talked about it. It was as if there were a wall being gradually built, with me on one side and all of the other boys on the opposite.

Emotional Networks

Our brains are hardwired for several different emotional systems, each with its own anatomical location: fear, attachment, maternal nurturance, anger, anticipation, play, and sex. These primitive structures in the brain remain constant in all humans from one culture to the next. As our brains mature, these centers progressively interconnect in ways that are unique to each individual. Early on, scientists pinpointed the limbic system as the seat of emotions and motivation.

As the secrets of the brain are revealed, neuroscientists have seized upon a portion of the limbic system called the amygdala as the brain's emotional control center. The amygdala allows us to respond quickly to danger; through the experience of fear, we appraise a situation and choose a protective response. The amygdala assigns emotional significance to events and modifies how experiential memories are recorded in another part of the limbic system called the hippocampus. Although some emotion enhances detail in our memories, when emotions run too high, the amount of detail recorded in the memory of the hippocampus may be reduced. Memories stored in the hippocampus modify our thinking whenever we encounter an emotional situation, and through a series of feedback loops they also influence the emotions recorded in the amygdala.

The brain functions through these networks of multiple, integrated centers, and these networks change dramatically through our learning. The brain undergoes enormous changes between the ages of nine and seventeen. These changes result in significant refinements in the way we function physically and emotionally. In a young child, not all connections are yet formed. During adolescence a person gradually shifts from characteristically childlike emotional reactions to greater self-regulation, social awareness, and emotional control. Later on, the amygdala relinquishes control over emotions to the prefrontal cortex of the brain (which develops later). The onset of hormone production in remote parts of the body of the adolescent complicates all of this even more, as anyone who has been around a teenager knows.

An intricate series of networks connect and integrate the emotional centers of the brain.

My first real awareness of being in the presence of something that might have been homosex—although I didn't recognize it as such at the time—came when I was about nine years old during a rare family vacation to Chicago. As we visited the shore of Lake Michigan, just east of downtown, I darted barefoot across the hot sand to change into my swimsuit in the men's bathroom. In a concrete block building that was open to the sky, naked old men crowded around driftwood-colored wooden benches that lined the perimeter of the changing area. The men were more distressed by the presence of their young, unwelcome guest than by their nakedness.

When I walked into the room, all activity—if there was any—froze. Perhaps my discomfort came just from being in the presence of naked men. With no men in our household, it was the first time I had ever been in the presence of a totally naked man. And here was a room full of them. No one looked at me in a sinister way, no one talked to me, and no one touched me. I didn't see anything overtly sexual (but until I was nearly forty, everything relating to homosexuality went unnoticed). In fact, I really have absolutely no evidence that anything sexual was happening. But when I remember the incident, the emotional memory it creates is similar to the feelings I have had as an adult when I have been in a highly sexually charged environment. The circuitry of my brain wasn't wired enough to assess the situation and plan an appropriate response. I changed quickly and ran back to the beach and the security of my mother.

The first girl in our class to have her period was the first person to help me connect some of the centers in my brain. She happily shared the details she remembered from the movie shown to the girls in the fifth grade. We boys never saw it. A new scheme preoccupied me: if I could just have sex with a girl, I would finally feel like a man. In the seventh grade, I pinched a girl's breasts while we were roller-skating to see if she might want to have sex with me, but she angrily skated off. I was disappointed, not that she rejected my primitive attempt at seduction, but because I felt nothing when I did it.

Wanking to Yang

Although our brains are all similarly hardwired for several emotions, the way the networks interconnect those little pieces of each of our brains where emotions are centered varies considerably from person to person. Our different life experiences create unique, fine structural areas in our brains. These connections evolve and expand throughout our lifetimes as new learning adds complexity. Rakesh Satyal, in the novel *Blue Boy*, says, "Only now am I able to fully understand what being called gay means. . . . It means that you are wired for a different life entirely. It means that your body, your feelings, your responses toward all other people are different. You do not look at men the same, you do not make love to them the same way."

128

Emotions change how we think, and thinking alters our behavior. A young physician related to me his struggle to figure out his sexuality. I said to him something about struggling with his yin and yang, and he responded, "Recently, I've been spending a lot more time with my yang." He fantasizes about both men and women when he masturbates, but he feels increasingly anxious about his indecision. "I feel so ill at ease talking with women. Nothing seems to come naturally. I could never chat with them on the Internet because I wouldn't know what to say. Talking with men is easier. I'm not gay, but I don't understand the difference." Although we used to believe that our brains were fully developed when we were quite young, our brains and our thinking continue to evolve throughout our lifetime.

People who masturbate have more sex and more satisfying sex. In "Sex, Romance, and Relationships: AARP Survey of Midlife and Older Adults," it was reported that of all men in their fifties, 42 percent masturbate to ejaculation at least once a week. Men masturbate for all sorts of reasons. Masturbating helps men learn what sensations arouse their bodies and how to control their orgasms so they may have more satisfying sex lives. Men masturbate as a stress reliever or a "pick-me-up." Masturbation satisfies sexual needs in the absence of a partner. Prolonged absence from sexual activity can impede a return to satisfying sex, and 90 percent of men over the age of eighty still fantasize about sex. It becomes an acceptable substitute for hidden or forbidden wishes. When you masturbate, you control all the variables.

Whether or not the Bible prohibits homosexuality hinges a lot on the interpretation of the Greek word *malakos*, which has been translated as both "homosexuality" and "masturbation." I am neither a biblical nor a Greek scholar, but I bet that when that committee met to decide whether *malakos* meant that masturbation or homosexuality was the *real* abomination, there weren't many men who were going to say that it meant masturbation. The homosexuals on the committee were going to lose either way.

Individuals differ tremendously in how much they masturbate. Some folks masturbate two or three times in their lives and others two or three times in a day. Although some people feel that those in monogamous relationships should feel no need to masturbate, most men continue to masturbate even if their partnership is completely satisfying. Unless masturbation in some ways compromises the sexual relationship with a partner, it is not problematic.

In the 1960s, Schachter and Singer developed the two factor theory. The theory proposed that emotion has two parts: physiological arousal and cognition. Emotion-provoking events induce physiological changes such as an accelerated heart rate and shallower breathing; those sensations make us aware of an emotion. This sends a message to the prefrontal brain, which plans and executes the appropriate response.

When I was a young Navy lieutenant flight surgeon, being gay in the military often led to a "general" rather than an "honorable" discharge. In 1971, the Navy stationed me in Sicily for a few months. One day a handsome, young, and single physician who worked with me at the Navy clinic asked me to go with him into Catania, a city in Sicily at the base of Mount Etna, for dinner and a concert. In the officers' quarters people whispered that he might be "a little light in his sneakers." After dinner, he asked me if I wanted to see his apartment. A few drinks later, he told me it was too late and he'd had too much to drink to drive me back to the Navy base.

When we were getting ready for bed, he told me the guest bed was not made up and invited me to sleep with him. He undressed, got into bed naked, and lay on his back with his arms over his head. I could feel my heart racing and I started to sweat as I anxiously undressed and got into bed with him. I also lay on my back, but my arms were on top of the covers, pressed firmly against the mattress, confining me as if I were in a straitjacket. At that moment I began to accept that I was signaling to gay men that I was attracted to them, but I still had no idea how. My racing heart and this new self-awareness were solid evidence in support of the two factor theory.

Alone Am I

Although the basic elements of all our brains are similar, the intricate networks connecting these elements do not all develop in the same way for everyone. Children have been characterized as either "inhibited" or "uninhibited." Inhibited children hover near their mothers, are quiet, and avoid strangers. Most children fall on a continuum between the two. As adults, some who were more inhibited continue to have difficulty separating from their families. They have not connected with others in

130

intimate ways. Throughout their lives their primary emotional commitments are to their families of origin. Coming out for them can be especially difficult. The death of their parents represents a huge loss. Although they may long for a meaningful relationship, they continue to isolate themselves, preferring no attachments. Their relationships are more instrumental than emotional. Uninhibited children spend less time with Mom and embrace new activities. Because they are less sensitive to the judgments of others, coming out for them may be less difficult.

A thirty-seven-year-old gay man from Canada is trapped in a life from which he can see no escape. He is a school administrator in a small town where living as an openly gay man would be extremely difficult. Being an experienced teacher with a master's degree reduces the possibility of any professional mobility. As an only child he feels a responsibility to care for his parents. His father has developed Alzheimer's disease and requires full-time care, and the family has few resources to pay for it. It became financially expedient for his mother to live with him, destroying his last boundary for privacy. His only escape was watching gay pornography or chatting in sexually explicit chat rooms, but he could not masturbate without fearing his mother would discover him. Consequently, he began to stay awake far into the night, compromising his performance in school the next day. He is losing hope that he can ever have someone to share his life with, and he has no one he can discuss his frustration and disappointments with. Although loneliness is imposed upon him by his role as a caregiver, he is more fearful that the loneliness will become worse once his role as a caregiver to his parents has ended.

Meeting someone involves taking risks, and one of the biggest risks is facing rejection. As one man said, "Gay partners don't just fall in your lap." Many men are shy about meeting others and waste evenings wanting to talk with someone but being unable to do so. Knowing what to say is only half the battle; knowing how to listen and ask questions is equally important. In more urban areas, there are often a variety of gay men's groups that center on hobbies like books, politics, sports activities, potluck suppers, and coming-out issues. These can serve as vehicles for developing a network of friendships. Putting a notice on Craigslist about a fathers' support group could be a good method for finding other men who have families. Gay bars, arts events, fundraisers, and an LGBT resource center can also expand networks of friends as well as people to date.

We seek intimacy, pleasure, affirmation, and approval from our partners and peers. The brain is the most complex organ in our biology and we want to understand it because we care about how we behave. Our DNA determines how the emotional centers of the brain are established, but each of us builds an intricate and evolving structure in our brains as we interact with our own changing environments. Life cannot be defined by a genetic code. We do not connect with humanity purely on a biological level. Developmental and cultural differences exist, and these experiences are what make us unique.

Pulling the Pin on a Hand Grenade

If discussing sexuality places a target on your back, a discussion of pedophilia, pederasty, and age of consent is like picking up a hand grenade without a pin. Ignoring the topic does nothing to defuse its explosive potential. Gay men have wrongly and frequently been accused of molesting children and recruiting children to homosexuality. So much distorted information has been produced by those who condemn homosexuality that the topic begs for comment. First of all, let me make it clear that I am not advocating for pedophilia, lowering the age of consent, or sex with animals.

After reading an essay online that alleged that homosexuals are responsible for the sex abuse scandals in the Roman Catholic clergy, I posted this response: "I am a sixty-seven-year-old gay psychiatrist and almost nothing you have written fits with my own personal experience or with the experience of any gay men that I know." Here is the e-mail response I received from the author of the essay:

> Homosexuality is just wrong: Did you read the quotes by gay rights leaders acknowledging that pederasty is at the core of the gay rights movement? One thing has baffled me for years. The question is: Why on earth would gay leaders speak about this connection so plainly, when they had to have known that such admissions would cause great damage to the gay rights movement? This is something I would truly like to understand, and I can think of no person better to answer it than a gay psychiatrist.

I corresponded with him because I believe that stereotypes are only shattered when our antagonists have a personal relationship with someone who is gay. I told him that most gay men I know had no idea what pederasty means. He replied that his job was to defend the papacy of the Roman Catholic Church—something that seems to me to be increasingly difficult, as the Catholic Church continues to come under attack over a series of scandals exposing widespread abuse of children, many of which date back several decades. I subsequently learned that the man I was corresponding with has a PhD in electrical engineering. If that makes him qualified to comment on the psychology of being gay, perhaps I am qualified to design a computer.

Shortly after the essay appeared in the Catholic press in 2010, CNN World reported on its Web site the outrage displayed by gay rights groups over comments made by a senior Vatican official linking homosexuality to pedophilia. Cardinal Tarcisio Bertone, the Vatican's secretary of state, made this comment during a news conference while on an official visit to Chile: "Many psychologists, many psychiatrists, have demonstrated that there is no relationship between celibacy and pedophilia, but many others have demonstrated, I was told recently, that there is a relationship between homosexuality and pedophilia." Bertone added, "That is true. This is the problem." (I wondered if Cardinal Bertone was told about "this relationship" by an electrical engineer.)

CNN further reported, "A Vatican spokesman said Wednesday that just 10 percent of the abuse cases against priests that were reviewed by the Vatican constituted 'pedophilia in the strict sense.'" In the same CNN report, James Cantor, editor-in-chief of *Sexual Abuse: A Journal of Research and Treatment,* and the head of the Law and Mental Health Research Section of the Centre for Addiction and Mental Health in Toronto, rejected suggestions of a link between homosexuality and pedophilia. "It's quite solidly shown in the scientific literature that there is absolutely no association between being a gay man and being a pedophile."

The *Diagnostic and Statistical Manual of Mental Disorders, Fourth Edition—Text Revision (DSM-IV-TR)* of the American Psychiatric Association defines a pedophile as one who has "recurrent, intense sexually arousing fantasies, sexual urges, or behaviors involving sexual activity with a prepubescent child or children." Pedophilic attraction is

133

sexual attraction in which it is *obligatory* that the partner is a prepubescent child who has not yet developed social awareness and emotional control. The *DSM-IV* states that the child is usually thirteen years of age or younger. It also specifies that the perpetrator must be age sixteen or over and at least five years older than the child.

Almost everyone agrees that a sexual relationship with a preadolescent, or when there is coercion, is wrong. Parents and governments have an obligation to protect vulnerable children from adults who disregard their interests and easily manipulate them. The few studies that suggest that pedophilia exists more commonly in homosexuals are often quoted, but under scrutiny are seriously flawed. I am a gay man, but I am also a father and a grandfather. How could anyone believe that any gay person, but particularly gay fathers, would accede to a gay rights movement that would sacrifice the sexual innocence of their children or grandchildren?

My correspondence with the engineer screeched to a halt when on May 5, 2010, the *Miami New Times* published a photograph of George Rekers, one of the leaders of the Christian conservatives, as he returned from Europe accompanied by a twenty-year-old male prostitute he had hired on a Web site called Rentboy.com. Rekers claimed his only mistake was to have hired the male prostitute "without properly vetting him." Rekers, a clinical psychologist and a Baptist minister, began his lucrative career by writing a book advising parents on how to raise their children so they would turn out straight. He promised that homosexuality could be "cured" and had been responsible for some of the most vicious assaults on homosexuality. Rekers has since been divorced by two of the organizations he helped found, the Family Research Council and the National Association for Research and Therapy of Homosexuality (NARTH). His damaging writings and public appearances tell us more about his fractured psyche than they do about homosexuality. Rekers's exposure was profoundly disappointing to my engineer correspondent.

I want to avoid sweeping generalizations about those who oppose homosexuality. History, however, has repeatedly shown that homosexual conflict often besieges the men who are caught up in rigid ideological judgments against homosexuality. Occasionally, their passion breaks free and they find release in clandestine homosexual contacts.

Prior to having received the initial correspondence from the engineer, I had never before read anything suggesting that pederasty "forms the core of the gay rights movement." In fact, the word "pederasty" rarely crosses the lips of anyone other than those who condemn homosexuality. In that context, it is frequently and incorrectly interchanged with the word "pedophilia."

There are several definitions for "pederasty." The different uses of the word are important. The definition that provides the least reproach to homosexuality describes pederasty as a nonspecific sexual activity where one of the two participants is a minor, i.e. between the ages of thirteen and nineteen. A more restrictive definition states that pederasty means anal intercourse between two men where the receptive partner is a minor, a definition that implies coercion. In contemporary American society, depending upon the jurisdiction that defines age of consent, an adult who has engaged in pederasty could be charged with felony sexual assault.

One of the gay leaders whom conservatives connect with pederasty is Harry Hay, who died in 2002 at age ninety. Stuart Timmons chronicled Hay's life in a book, *The Trouble with Harry Hay: Founder of the Modern Gay Rights Movement.* Hay had once been a member of the American Communist Party, and he had a brief marriage to conceal his homosexuality from the party. Prior to his death, Hay was considered an elder statesman of the gay rights movement. He was one of the founders of the Mattachine Society in the early 1950s. Hay reported that his first homosexual encounter occurred at age nine. At age fourteen, he discovered homosexual lovemaking with a twenty-five-year-old sailor. He described it as "the most beautiful gift that a fourteen-year-old ever got from his first love!" Hay's defense of his experience with the sailor disturbs many, and confounds our contemporary notions of adolescent sexual maturity.

Different cultures celebrate the transition from childhood to adulthood with various traditions. Quinceañera is a traditional Latin American celebration for girls when they turn age fifteen. Historically, it signified the young girl's eligibility for marriage. During the ceremony, adults present the honored teen with a pair of high heels as a sign of her ascent into womanhood. She, in turn, gives her younger sister a doll as a symbol of relinquishing childish interests. Bar mitzvah—bat mitzvah for girls—is a solemn ceremony held at age thirteen to admit a Jewish boy or girl into adult membership in the Jewish faith. This ritual communicates that a young Jewish person is entirely responsible for adhering to Jewish law.

But the brain does not mature in a day, and maturity varies from individual to individual and across cultures. Some adolescents are capable of thoughts and actions with unusually high levels of maturity, and some come from societies that demand it. I once had as a patient a twenty-five-year-old African man studying in the United States. I hospitalized him for his first episode of acute mania. He sent for his African wife, who was but fifteen years old and had infant twins. I told him I doubted her ability to travel thirty-six hours with two infants, and without being able to speak English. He said, "Dr. Olson, you don't understand our culture," and I didn't. It was an important lesson for me to learn: understand people in the context of their lives. My patient's culture demanded of his wife a high degree of emotional maturity, whether or not from my perspective she was capable of it.

K. D. Alston wrote the following for my blog, MagneticFire.com:

> The fact that urban children have to be aware of their environment and be savvy at dealing with whatever comes up demands of them a level of maturity that most outside of that situation cannot understand. [Perhaps demanding from them more than they are in fact capable.] The neighborhood I grew up in had many obstacles for children to overcome. Besides having a pervasive drug problem, Baltimore has an equally pervasive issue with violent crime. Dangerous situations are commonplace. Exposure to those issues forces children to mature quicker than most. Living in an urban environment, I was exposed to many things sexual. I was not a typical eleven-year-old, emotionally or physically. At age eleven, I was already 5 feet 10 inches and around 150 pounds. Physically I was mature and fully functional sexually.

Alston's life in the Baltimore ghetto and the world of the African wife of my patient are vastly different from the world of my youth. Although my life's circumstances dictated a high level of emotional maturity, I maintained a high degree of sexual innocence, perhaps even longer than I should have. An adolescent may reach physical and sexual maturity long before he reaches emotional maturity, but emotional maturity may also precede the loss of sexual innocence. These difficult transitions will be experienced differently by a child who is "inhibited" than by one who is "uninhibited"—whether in the Baltimore ghetto or in rural Nebraska. There is no universal age at which an adolescent becomes capable of giving consent for sexual activity, and those who cannot protect themselves must be protected from those who would exploit their innocence.

Strong emotions change how we think. Discussions of "age of consent" enrage some people beyond the point at which any sensible discourse can occur. People disagree passionately and vehemently over what age a boy has the emotional maturity to give consent for sexual activity, but particularly if it is sex with another boy. When I was in high school, freshman girls who dated boys out of high school were called "fast." Although I felt very sexual as an adolescent, the drive I experienced seemed to be diverted from its logical target. With a growing awareness that my friends were becoming more sexually active, I began to feel more and more disconnected from them, but I didn't know why.

Sexual maturity is a very complex issue from a genetic, cultural, and neurological development standpoint. Both heterosexual and homosexual adolescents usually do not have the capacity for commitment and permanence of adult relationships. The brains of adolescents have not developed sufficiently to be able to understand all of the consequences of their behavior. Today, even in our more liberal society, if two adolescent boys are engaged in sexual activity, the older one would be called a sexual predator, even if the younger adolescent initiated the activity. Other than the sex of the partner, these relationships are no different than comparable heterosexual ones, but because they are homosexual they come under far harsher scrutiny. Let me be very clear that I am not endorsing pedophilia, pederasty, or changes in our social definitions of age of consent. It is the responsibility of our society to protect the safety of children and adolescents and to ensure that sexual behaviors are not the result of coercion and manipulation. What I am suggesting is that there is blatant hypocrisy in the way our society approaches homosexual adolescent sexual behavior compared to the way it deals with the sexuality of heterosexual adolescents.

Is it not unjust for the age of consent to be different for homosexuals than it is for heterosexuals? In 2000, the Sexual Offenses Bill became law in the United Kingdom, equalizing the age of consent of heterosexual and homosexual relationships. Prior to the reign of Queen Victoria, gay sex was punishable by death. In 1967 homosexuality was legalized for those over age twenty-one. Homosexual consent was lowered to age eighteen under Tony Blair's administration. It was not until 1996 that it was alleged that the different ages of consent for homosexuals and heterosexuals breached human rights. Any change in the law was opposed by the House of Lords in the interests of "protecting children," leaving sixteen-year-old boys "prey" to older men.

When do the emotional networks in the brain become mature enough for sexual expression? Variations in development mean that the age of consent cannot be defined simply by a number representing age. Developing gay sexuality must be considered in the context of all adolescent sexuality. By the age of fifteen, 25 percent of all teens have had sexual intercourse for the first time. By the time adolescents reach the age of nineteen, 69 percent have had sexual intercourse. Gay or straight, sexuality emerges between the ages of fourteen and nineteen. By the late teens more than two-thirds of adolescents have had more than one sexual partner. Most adolescents, however, receive little advice on how to understand and explore their actualizing sexuality, making them more vulnerable to those who would exploit them.

Randy for Randy

When I entered high school in the late 1950s, I went out for football, as was expected of me. I was bigger than many of my classmates and I worked hard. As a sophomore, I started with varsity as a tackle and a linebacker. For the position I beat out another boy, Randy, who was a couple of years older than me. He had toughened his already muscular body by throwing bales of hay all summer. Taking his position on the varsity team really pissed him off. During football practice in the weeks that followed, he hit me harder and more often than necessary. He slugged me when the coach wasn't looking. Having no killer instincts to fight back, I caved.

I knew Randy's body well because a few years before, when I was about eleven and he was thirteen, I had explored it rather thoroughly. Our families were friends, and occasionally he would stay overnight. One night he said, "Let me show you something." He told me that "stuff" would come out of his penis accompanied by "a very good feeling." He proceeded to demonstrate with a performance that far surpassed the one I observed earlier with my friend.

I couldn't keep my hands away from Randy's body. Whenever we were alone, I touched him and he would get hard. He neither pressured me nor resisted as I would unzip his jeans and reach inside. I would watch as he masturbated and become frustrated when I couldn't duplicate his achievement. Even now, certain male smells will take me back to those experiences. Then one day it just stopped. We never did it again, although I still wanted to.

> **Sexual encounters that result from the use of coercive power of one over another are wrong, but they are wrong for *all* ages and for *all* sexual orientations.**

Those with strong feelings against homosexuality cannot see relationships like the one I had with Randy as anything but problematic. It would be scrutinized more harshly and considered to be far outside the realm of normal adolescent heterosexual experimentation. When it comes to adolescent homosexual experimentation, many fear the awakening of a sleeping giant, as if all adolescent same-sex activity is transformational. That issue is further complicated when age of consent comes into play—because he was older than me, a relationship like mine and Randy's is by default construed as predatory, even though I was always the initiator.

No matter how carefully I have written this part of the chapter—I have rewritten it several times—I am aware that some will misinterpret my words to mean that I am advocating for man-boy sex. There are those who are so horrified by the thought of homosex that their emotions will interfere with understanding. Let me be explicit: sexual encounters that result from the use of coercive power of one over another are wrong. Period. But they are wrong for *all* ages and for *all* sexual orientations. They are not more wrong or less wrong when the two are of the same sex.

One of the tasks of adolescence is to learn how to be a sexual person—a task that is no different for heterosexuals than for homosexuals. I have never spoken with a gay man who felt that he would have been heterosexual but for some adolescent same-sex exploration. Some men remember their adolescent sexual experiences with older males differently—as neither reciprocal nor voluntary, but rather based on an imbalance of power. An adolescent who wishes to refuse an adult's advances may be too intimidated by the power of authority to say no to a

> **Children must be protected from sexual practices where there is an imbalance of power; sexual exploration and sexual exploitation are *not* the same thing.**

priest, a coach, a youth leader or, even worse, a parent. A child's inability to say no must never be taken as consent.

Although I have no regrets or guilt about my experiences with Randy, sometimes I become anxious when I remember how I was unable to resist my attraction to him. I remember the relationship with Randy as being reciprocal, and I do not feel I was victimized or abused. We were both adolescents, incapable of understanding sexuality from a more mature perspective. Many of the men I interviewed for this book described very similar experiences. Even though I pursued Randy, today he might have been considered to be a sexual predator, put on a registry for sex offenders and given a legacy that would have followed him the rest of his life. The sexual activity that I had with Randy did not convert me into being gay. As I look back on that experience, I see it as an unfolding of my sexual orientation that began long before and continued long after my involvement with Randy.

Many boys, both homosexual and heterosexual, relate a history of sexual activity much like I had with Randy. If both are young, it may be ignored as "boys will be boys." But what of adolescent boys—and there are many—who like Hay had a relationship with an adult male? Apparently already aware of his homosexuality, Hay made it clear he had no intent to say no to the sailor. One of my gay friends has a gay son who late in adolescence had an ongoing sexual relationship with an adult man. My friend insists that the relationship was abusive, but his son, who is now an adult, continues to defend it as being reciprocal. Many but not all are harmed by these relationships, but none were converted into homosexuality by it. More than a few have told me they pursued the older man. Because of the differences in age, and presumably power, these are more complicated issues. But they should be no more complex for homosexual relationships than for heterosexual ones.

Kristijan is a mid-forties gay American man of Croatian descent whom I interviewed. Although currently inactive in the church, he was raised as a Roman Catholic, attended Catholic schools, and served as an altar boy. When he was thirteen, on a Friday night after an eighth-grade dance at his parochial junior high school, he waited for his brother under the lights on the front patio of the school. Although it was late, he was typically the last to be picked up and wasn't too concerned. As he stood there, someone started a car at the adjacent nuns' convent. The car slowly circled Kristijan and stopped near where he stood. The dome light came on and revealed the driver as the bishop.

The bishop waved Kristijan over to the car. Kristijan walked to the passenger side as the bishop lowered the window. He greeted the bishop, who asked why he was alone. Kristijan explained he was waiting for his brother. The bishop, a very handsome mid-fifties man with striking blue eyes, said, "I don't want you waiting alone." Kristijan responded that even though it was late, his ride was coming. Kristijan was aware that the bishop intended something more than keeping him safe, but the bishop was so insistent that Kristijan got into the car with him.

The bishop told Kristijan, "Don't worry about your ride. I will take care of you." As he reassured him, he reached over, put his hand on the inside of Kristijan's upper thigh, and snuggled his hand against Kristijan's crotch. Then the bishop said, "It's okay, you're with me now." Kristijan said his body was flooded by feelings of fear, mixed with sexual desire and excitement. He looked down at the bishop's hand and then into his face, which he described as warm and kind. The bishop nudged his hand into Kristijan's crotch again as he said, "It's okay. You can come with me." Although he very much wanted to go with the bishop, he thanked him and got out of the car. The bishop then said, "I'm sorry to see you go." Kristijan told me that he has no question that had they driven off together they would have gone to the bishop's house and had sex. Kristijan accepts that pedophilia is wrong, but he does not consider the bishop a pedophile or himself a victim. To this day, Kristijan regrets not leaving with the "incredibly sexy" bishop. His story indicates how complicated these issues are.

How can we explain the disparate experience of adolescents? Why are some crippled by their experience while others transcend it? The interpretation of these experiences does not rest on genital sex. The changes in the brain, the physical changes of the body and psychological maturity all come together in puberty, and the rate of change varies considerably from one teenager to the next. Chaotic and abusive families offer little support, and the effects of premature sexual activity are greater than for children in less dysfunctional families. Sexual abuse by a family member carries the greatest consequences. They are also greater if the activity was frequent and invasive and occurred earlier in adolescence.

Thinking holds power over emotion. For me, some of my experiences have taken on a new interpretation since I accepted my homosexuality; my brain was rewired to incorporate this new learning. Perhaps the difference between those with negative experiences and those of us who had more positive experiences is related to the way we have reconstructed the narratives.

Sexual exploration is vastly different than sexual exploitation. While sexual abuse is more common than once thought, in the 1980s the legitimate concern about abuse rapidly developed into mass hysteria. All memories are factually inaccurate, but these concerns produced an epidemic of false, "recovered" memories. Psychiatrist Joel Paris, in *Prescriptions for the Mind: A Critical View of Contemporary Psychiatry*, wrote, "Therapists, beginning with Freud, believed that everything that happens in one's life is recorded in the brain. . . . But that is not true. We do not remember most of what happens to us, and what we do remember is more a narrative than a recording." In society's attempts to deal with its collective guilt for ignoring sexual abuse of children for so long, we have in some cases created overly harsh penalties for sex between a young boy and an older one. For example, some very young adolescents have been labeled sexual perpetrators and incarcerated in sexual abuse treatment programs, yet there is limited evidence of the effectiveness of these programs. It is vital that we protect our children, but doing so in an informed way is critical. And our children must also be protected against overly harsh, ineffective, and in some cases, inappropriate "treatments."

The emotions of trust and fear recur frequently in stories like Kristijan's. When the Roman Catholic Church ordained pedophile priests, it gave them the mantel of trusted men of God. The Church offered sanctuary to troubled children who may not have been able to trust their families. When trust is destroyed by severe or repeated abuse, fear ignites the amygdala, incinerating the capacity to trust even when there is no danger. Children must be protected from sexual practices where there is an imbalance of power and an abuse of trust. What could induce greater fear than a breach in trust of those who proclaim to be our protectors?

Although sexual exploration that includes same-sex expression is forbidden, there is tremendous resistance to sexual education that would better equip a young boy to deal with his expanding sexuality. Many of those who feel the greatest need to protect the innocence of their children oppose sex education. They see it only as a subversive attempt to remove parental authority; they believe sex education undermines the values taught by parents.

Sex education should be so much more than a ten-minute discussion of "good touch" and "bad touch," ideas that are magically to be shed like the wedding clothes upon entering the honeymoon bed. Sex education could teach young boys that they have a choice, and that a failure to express their choice is not the same as giving consent. It could teach them about how to deal with an imbalance of power with someone in a position of authority. It could teach them about safer sex. Whenever children do not receive a healthy education about sex, they will seek to educate themselves. That sleeping giant is going to wake up.

Chapter 8
Hook-ups and Not-Quite-Sex

*If one does not want to suppress his nature and yet is afraid of expressing
it, what is he to do?*

—*Secret Historian:*
The Life and Times of Samuel Steward,
Professor, Tattoo Artist, and Sexual Renegade,
Justin Spring

I first explored the hook-up culture in 1976 in a movie theater around 57th
Street and Broadway in New York City. I was in the city with my wife;
she had other plans, so I decided to go to a movie. The marquee of the
theater revealed enough for me to know that I was entering a theater
playing gay porn. As I walked through the doors into the theater, I stopped
at the half-wall that separated the entrance from the seating area. I stood
there in the darkness and watched the screen, where for the first time in
my life I saw two men having sex.

As my eyes adjusted to the darkness, I could see that the theater
was filled only with men. Unlike most movie theaters, the men moved
constantly from one seat to the next. I chose my seat in the same way men
choose a urinal: always take the one that gives you the greatest possible
separation from another man. None of the other men obeyed that rule—
solitary viewing wasn't why they'd bought a ticket.

When I returned home to Maine, I continued to think about what I
had seen in the theater. I did not want to want what I was wanting, and yet
I could not stop from wanting it. The men in the theater validated the
stereotypes I held of a gay culture where the hallmarks are impersonal and
casual sex. The possibilities of losing my family, friends, and job had not
yet entered my mind. The harder I tried to ignore these feelings, the more
miserable I became. These desires began to boil over inside me and were
not going to be content simmering on a back burner. Not long after this
experience, I arranged another trip to New York, where I had my first
adult sexual experience with a man. I began to lay down some entirely
new interconnections in my brain.

Casual and impersonal sexual encounters are said to be the prized trademark of gay men's sexuality. The term "hook-up" was borrowed from the drug culture and is now used to describe casual, noncommitted sex. Hooking up is a subculture with its own rules and expectations. A person looking for a hook-up does not think about the other person; he only considers the moment and his own pleasure. I once asked a young Muslim how he reconciled his homosexuality with his religion and he responded, "This is only about pleasure. I am not gay."

One younger man, just beginning to explore his attraction to men, said he had received a "hand job" and a "blow job." He was shocked when I referred to it as having sex with a man. "These were 'hook-ups.' Not-quite-sex." He expressed concern about meeting a man he really cared about, knowing he might want to have anal sex. He considers anal sex to be the most intimate contact one man can have with another man; if it happened, it would erase any defenses he had built around being gay.

> **A "hook-up" is a casual sexual encounter that is based on pleasure without commitment.**

Pitchers and Catchers

For most of my early adult life I existed in a state of homo-naïveté. I could not imagine how two men could have homosex, at least beyond the limits of the most obvious ways. I only thought about man-on-man sex in sexual terms, not as an expression of love and commitment. No middle school movies enlighten men about how to have an intimate relationship with another man. In the weeks that followed my visit to the theater, the only man-on-man sex I would allow myself to think about was being the passive partner in oral sex. I had no fantasies about anal anything; that would have been taking the gay fixation way too far.

We categorize gay sex in the same black-and-white binary way we categorize everything else: "tops" and "bottoms" or "pitchers" and "catchers." Before I accepted being gay, I wondered how men negotiated their sexual roles. Perhaps after men established a relationship they begin to communicate about their sexual activity, but in the world of cruising I had observed in the movie theater, men expressed their attraction or availability in mostly nonverbal ways. With virtually no prior experience as a gay man, I had only a hetero-centric paradigm. As I later learned when I entered my homosexual adolescence, it is not that simple.

One gay man said, "If the anus was not meant to be a receptacle for the penis, they wouldn't fit so well together," but anal sex is not practiced strictly by homosexuals. It can be mutually pleasurable for heterosexual partners as well. Some men have a strong or even an exclusive preference for one role or the other. Other men describe themselves as "versatile," with no absolute preference for one role or the other; they say that their sexual role preference depends upon the man and the moment. In the bedroom, gay men simply do what they feel comfortable with and mutually agree to do.

A 2003 study published in the *Journal of Sexual Research* offered these findings regarding "tops," "bottoms," and "versatiles":

1. Self-labels are meaningfully correlated with actual sexual behavior (e.g., "tops" are more frequently attracted to and engage in insertive behaviors).
2. "Tops" are more likely than both "bottoms" and "versatiles" to reject a gay self-identity and also have a higher degree of self-loathing related to their homosexual desires.
3. "Tops" are more likely to have had sex with a woman in the past three months.
4. "Versatiles" enjoy better psychological health.

Hart found that men who live in cultures that are strongly opposed to homosexuality tend to be more highly invested in the role of being a top. Many of these cultures devalue women. Being a bottom is looked upon as abdicating masculine power and authority to become more like a weak and powerless woman.

Those men who are tops and also engaged in heterosexual behavior may serve as a bridge of transmission for HIV and other sexually transmitted diseases. The greatest risk of HIV transmission appears to come from men who only occasionally serve as a bottom because they perceive themselves to be at a lower risk for contracting HIV. Hart and colleagues found that the use of condoms does not correlate with men labeling themselves as a top or a bottom, but in general bottoms appeared to have a better understanding of their risk.

The Lowdown on the Down Low

"Everything you think you know about the down low is wrong," according to Keith Boykin, who wrote *Beyond the Down Low: Sex and Denial in Black America*. Before it was appropriated by a broader community, the term "down low" or "DL" was a term used primarily in the African American community to describe an underground society of men who secretly have sex with men while also regularly having sex with women. The word "gay" is considered a "white" term, filled with stereotypes, especially feminine connotations. Men who describe themselves as on the down low reject any term that might "emasculate" them and incorporate them into the gay community. They typically prefer to have sex with "straight-acting," masculine men. The men engaged in DL behaviors, Boykin explains, are often dedicated to wives and children, churches and communities. Like "hooking up," the DL attitude does not include a desire for any relationship beyond a physical one; it is simply about sex.

J. L. King, who wrote *On the Down Low: A Journey into the Lives of "Straight" Black Men Who Sleep with Men*, put a face on down low activities, but his broad and exaggerated generalizations about the African American community provoked a great deal of criticism. His expertise was not as a sociologist or health care provider but came primarily from many years of living a sexual double life. One of King's biggest errors was to suggest that the DL phenomenon was exclusively African American. Men and women of all ethnicities and sexual orientations regularly partake in sexual relations outside of committed relationships. There is no question, however, that his appearance on *The Oprah Winfrey Show* started a national conversation about men who have secret sex lives with both men and women.

According to Justin Spring in *Secret Historian*, Alfred Kinsey in his work in the mid-twentieth century discovered that there are significant class differences in sexual expression, particularly in attitudes toward premarital intercourse, prostitution, and homosexuality. Spring says:

Young men with only a grade school education experienced four or five times as many homosexual experiences as did young men who went to college. Moreover, lower-class males tended to be quite promiscuous in the early years of marriage, had a higher tolerance for homosexuality, and were much more direct, even blunt, in their approach to sexual acts of any sort.

The label "bisexual" parks controversy. Some insist that bisexuals are really gay men who haven't completed all of their rewiring. Some challenge the existence of the DL and insist that DL men are just a variation of being bisexual. Taken literally, "bisexuality" means there is an equal attraction to having sex with men and women, but the term has also been adopted by men who reject being called anything that they believe emasculates them.

According to a survey conducted by the Centers for Disease Control and Prevention, 1.8 percent of people between the ages of fifteen and forty-four self-label as bisexual. This likely represents an underreporting of the actual number. Men who consider themselves bisexual often feel caught between gay and straight societies. They feel neither group accepts them. Younger people seem to find it somewhat easier to talk about a fluid sexuality, where falling in love with a person's character exceeds the importance of the gender of the person. Those who do define themselves as bisexual face several stereotypes. They are described as promiscuous, going through "a phase," imagining it, or trying to camouflage their being gay.

> **Men and women of all ethnicities and sexual orientations regularly partake in sexual relations outside of committed relationships.**

In 2009, a group of Toronto researchers published a study in *Psychological Science* asserting, "Most bisexual men appeared homosexual with respect to genital arousal." They also found that bisexuality "appears primarily to represent a style of interpreting or reporting sexual arousal rather than a distinct pattern of genital sexual arousal." Controversy surrounded the publication, and both the gay and the bisexual communities attacked the findings.

At a regional meeting of Prime Timers, a group of mostly mature gay and bisexual men, one of the men stated he had never been to a "gay" event before. He announced to everyone he met in the hotel and casino that he was attending "a convention for bisexuals." He was in his mid- to late seventies, had been married for about forty years, and lived in a small rural town in a western state. He only began to come out following his wife's death. In the past, at times he would be drawn by powerful urges to have sex with a man. For many years, he lived a "down low" life.

He theorized that everyone is bisexual. He had parked his car in the bisexual parking lot, because accepting he was gay would have been driving too far and too fast in the gay lane. I briefly considered labeling myself as a bisexual, accepting that I had some attraction to men while clinging to hetero-normativity.

Gay Spaces

People outside of the LGBT community see gay culture as far more unified than it is, with common aspirations, common interests, similar lives, and even a shared "agenda." The truth is, few things bind gay men and women together. Oppression is one common element, but even that is not the same for everyone. Older gay men are likely to have experienced greater oppression because of their sexual orientation, or have chosen to remain so deeply closeted that they have suppressed their sexuality or lived in self-imposed celibacy.

Gay men often collect in gay spaces and often migrate to more urban areas to find acceptance and understanding. If a stigmatized condition is concealable, being in the presence of others who are similar has a positive effect on self-esteem, and those who felt they couldn't come out find a community that will coach them through the process. These micro-communities are frequently contingent upon gay affluence, and membership is often associated with conspicuous consumption. These gay spaces become places to see and be seen and a place to search for potential partners. The larger cultural effect of unified gay spaces is greater public awareness. The political and economic strength of these communities has grown and has brought about a gradual increase in civil rights protection and fewer repressive restraints.

While in earlier decades residents adopted a kind of uniformity that caused members to resemble one another, today the LGBT community is far more diverse and dispersed than most imagine. The gay community penetrates far beyond the confines of gay spaces into all areas of society. Gay men who hold more traditionally hetero-normative values have settled in suburban areas. In tolerant environments they integrate with the community; in others, where gay men must be circumspect about their identity, sexual activities are confined to weekend leisure activity.

Gay spaces typically emphasize a youthful culture, and attractiveness is a prerequisite for attaining and maintaining membership. Some gay friendships, much like their heterosexual counterparts, begin with sexual attraction, sometimes a one-night stand, perhaps followed by some dating. Some of these casual relationships lead to strong, long-lasting but platonic relationships. Older gay men may be excluded from these spaces because old is equated with being unattractive. Old people at times are considered to be politically conservative, senile, fanatically religious, and incapable of sexual interest. Loss of resources, incompetence, and dependency are all a part of the stereotype of aging. Older gay people experience a dual prejudice, one based on their sexual orientation and one on their age; both are founded on stereotypical descriptions. Combining the stereotypes of old people with those of older gay people paints a picture of the aging gay man who is poorly adjusted psychologically, sexless and yet preoccupied with sex. It's a stereotype that certainly doesn't relate to my life or the lives of my older gay peers. Although some of my friends have restricted, fixed incomes, they remain engaged in their lives, and socially and sexually active.

Gay spaces for older men do exist, with entrepreneurs just beginning to recognize potential markets for gay baby boomers. It's true that some gay men are childless and have large amounts of disposable income, but many gay men are now involved in parenting, whether biological children through arrangement, adoptive children by choice, or children from prior heterosexual relationships. I met Doug when I was a newly out gay man, with obligations for alimony, child support, and college expenses. He, more quietly than I, accepted how those obligations constrained our discretionary income.

Heterosexual men often depend upon their wives to negotiate their social involvements, and when I married my wife, I assumed that she would do that for us. Because I felt incompletely developed as a man, I felt inadequate to connect with other men. Among gay couples, roles are generally assigned on the basis of who does which better; nothing is assigned by societal definition of male or female spheres. Because there are no rigidly defined gender roles, masculine and feminine characteristics coexist comfortably, without examination or guilt.

Most Wanted Men

One older gay man I interviewed said about dating, "You eat, you laugh, and you cry. But mostly you just wait." The first task for many middle-age men who have been concealing their sexuality is to spend some time alone, deciding how far to take this newly discovered truth about their sexual orientation. Are you ready for a relationship? Are you ready to forsake the life of heterosexual privilege to become a part of a stigmatized minority? Do you believe that homosexual men are capable of long-term, monogamous relationships? Are you willing to give up a secret life of non-monogamous sex?

In the mid-1980s, while still exploring my own sexuality, I discovered a park near Des Moines where gay men were said to meet for sex. Although I knew little about cruising, I was eager to give it a try. I drove my open Jeep to the park and sat in it just observing. It was an afternoon in the middle of the week, so the park was rather empty. It was an uncommonly beautiful August day, sunny and mild with very little humidity. An athletic man of about forty was jogging around an open field. He would stop occasionally to stretch, always facing in my direction. He was a big man with a solid, slightly rugged body, the kind of man I find quite attractive, but in my apprehension I left the area to drive to another section of the park. A little later, his pickup pulled in behind me.

My heart began to pound and my breathing became shallow as he walked up to the Jeep and said, "How're ya doin'?"

"Fine."

He went on, "I'm from Oklahoma, here for the State Fair. Came out here to see if I could meet someone." We spoke in meaningless conversation for a while, and then he said, "I'd really like to suck your dick," shocking me with his directness. Not all sexual negotiations between gay men are nonverbal.

I was caught off guard. "No, I don't think so." His invitation intrigued me, but I had not yet learned the rules of cruising. My rational mind reminded me of the risks of public sex. He walked away, but I knew he hadn't given up. I repositioned myself and my running shorts, knowing that I had exposed myself, but only slightly.

He returned again to my Jeep and said, "I really want to suck your dick." I said no again, but with slightly less resistance. Then he said, "If you don't want to, why are you showing me your dick?"

I continued to refuse, and he walked away again. A short while later, I got out of the Jeep and walked deep into the woods, where I came to an old tree, partially rotting and leaning on its side. The woods were shaded and damp and smelled of composting leaves. I climbed about six feet up into the tree and sat there with my legs hanging over the leaning trunk of the tree. He followed me into the woods, as I was sure he would, walked up to me, and with his two large hands pulled down my shorts. This was more than "not-quite-sex."

Romantic love is based on sex and passion, and it changes over time. Most men who come out in midlife are beginning a gay sexual adolescence and they will spend much of their remaining life trying to integrate sex, romance, and love. Traditionally, men have met their partners through family and work associates, but this is impossible in a world where sexual orientation is concealed. My behavior in the tree in that park was far more adolescent than anything I'd actually done during my adolescence. But I was just learning how to be a sexual gay man.

Virtual Cruising and Virtual Sex

New opportunities for meeting now often begin without leaving home; about 60 percent of LGBT relationships begin online. The Internet has put millions of men in contact with gay culture in ways that were previously reserved only for those who lived in major urban areas. Although principally first used by those under thirty years old, social networking for people over the age of forty has recently grown at a fast rate.

> About 60 percent of LGBT relationships begin online, and the highest growth has been for people over the age of forty.

People are more likely to be drawn to use the Internet if they know others who have used it successfully. The Internet creates opportunities for men who have sex with men to skim profiles and anonymously meet new sex partners who have similar interests.

The Internet bears risk, however. Web sites often warn against sharing too much personal information and suggest that the first face-to-face meeting take place in a public place. One man I interviewed said that he will not consider sex with someone he meets online until he has visited with him for at least a year. In a 2001 study of gay men in London gyms, Jonathan Elford, Graham Bolding, and Lorraine Sherr found that most MSM who meet partners on the Internet are more likely to take sexual risks than are MSM who do not seek partners on the Internet. These men increase their risk of HIV and other sexually transmitted diseases if the sexual behaviors they seek are not consistent with safer sex.

Pornography is ubiquitous, and its use exploded with the onset of HIV/AIDS. About 90 percent of exposure to porn occurs via the Internet. The nearly universal use of the Internet means that even young children have been exposed to porn, either by choice or by chance. One Canadian research group wanted to compare people who had been exposed to pornography to those who had not, but they abandoned their study when they could not find a control group that had never seen pornography. Porn has distorted how we view normal sex; it does not substitute for good sex education. Sex does not always involve endless copulation and oral sex, nor does it always end with a star-spangled, explosive ejaculation.

Sex Addiction

Controversy surrounds the concept of sexual addiction. Its validity as a diagnosis is challenged not only by many psychiatrists and other mental health professionals but also by a majority of the general public. According to a 2010 survey by *Women's Health Magazine*, 63 percent of the public believes that sexual addiction is just another excuse for cheating.

Symptom checklists for sexual addiction abound in print and online. Questions typically include: Do you purchase pornography? Are you preoccupied with sex? Do you feel bad about your sexual behavior? Do you hide your sexual behavior from your partner? Has your sexual behavior interfered with your family life? Few men coming out in midlife could honestly answer no to any of those questions. Sex addiction treatment programs cast a very wide net.

Sexual behavior can become a problem and may be considered compulsive when it begins to interfere with normal daily activity.

154

Problems include multiple sexual partners, objectifying sexual partners, excessive masturbation, exposing yourself in public, and feeling compelled to have sex when stressed, anxious, or depressed. These behaviors become compulsive when you feel driven by sexuality and feel that you have no control. It is particularly problematic if you neglect your partner or become deceitful in your primary relationship.

The Internet has been referred to as the crack cocaine of sexual addiction. For some, sex is their only source of pleasure, soothing, and acceptance. Others use it to guard against loneliness, emptiness, and depression. Still, others are addicted to a constant flow of validation and approval from complete strangers. I once spoke with a man who said that he had masturbated thirteen times that day. Living in Pakistan and unable to explore his sexuality in a more personal way, he felt the Internet numbed and alleviated some of the pain of his loneliness and isolation. Other men ignore their needs for love and intimacy through constant sex.

> Some refer to the Internet as the crack cocaine of sexual addiction.

The science associated with sexual addiction is thin, although for some the pain of compulsive sex is real enough. Psychiatrists contend that the symptoms of compulsive sexuality might indicate any one of a number of psychiatric disorders. Most of the clinical descriptions of and treatment programs for sexual addiction are copied from the treatment programs for alcoholism and drug abuse. Treatments based on talk therapy and twelve-step programming continue to expand across the country; most are not reimbursed by insurance. That wide net catches many wealthy fish.

Dr. Jack Drescher, a New York psychiatrist who has treated many patients for sexual problems, says the research showing a correlation with chemical change and sexual addiction has not been determined. Paul Harasim quoted Dr. Drescher in the *Las Vegas Review-Journal* in 2010: "Sometimes an addiction model is a way to step out of the notion of personal responsibility. By medicalizing the problem, it makes for a more sympathetic figure." Psychiatrists generally believe that there are multiple psychiatric disorders that can display compulsive sexuality as one of the symptoms.

A diagnosis of hypersexuality disorder is being considered for inclusion in the *Diagnostic and Statistical Manual of the American*

Psychiatric Association in its fifth revision. The proposed wording is that it is a condition characterized by a progressive disorder of intimacy, compulsive sexual thoughts and acts, fixation on an unattainable partner, compulsive masturbation, and compulsive love relationships. The diagnosis would require that certain psychiatric conditions with hypersexuality as a symptom be considered and cast aside before the diagnosis of hypersexuality disorder is confirmed.

Till Death Do Us Part

In a list of the worst marriage proposals of all time, my proposal to Doug would rank well toward the top. I proposed to Doug in April 2009, shortly after the Iowa Supreme Court had unanimously ruled that within Iowa, marriage could no longer be limited to between one man and one woman. We were on our way to Lincoln, Nebraska, for a reunion with some of my closest friends from the University of Nebraska Medical School. I had never come out to these men. Doug had never met them, and I wanted to introduce him as my future husband. Only so much can be said about cornfields during a four-hour trip across Iowa. After we had exhausted all of the subjects that I really didn't want to talk about anyway, I introduced with trepidation the topic of the change in Iowa's marriage laws.

"Ya wanna?" I asked tentatively, doubting he would accept any proposal, let alone this half-assed one. We'd never had any serious discussions about marriage because in the twenty-three years we'd been together, there had been no reason to do so.

"I s'pose," he responded.

Neither of us was really sure of what had just happened, and I think we were both a little stunned. Grappling with a decision about whether or not to marry was a conversation Doug and I had never expected to have. We'd already resolved the essential precondition for the decision: "Are we willing to make a long-term commitment to this relationship?"

Doug and I can spend four hours choosing the color of paint for a bathroom, only to repeat the entire discussion the next day as if the first discussion had never occurred. But in the time it took to travel between two mile markers on the freeway, we had made a life-changing decision.

We quickly concluded that it would be in bad taste for two mature, previously married men to have an ostentatious affair. We immediately agreed that our wedding would be a very small, unpretentious gathering with only our families and a few close friends. All we wanted was a simple declaration of our love and continuing commitment to each other, an affirmation before our friends and family that we shared their values about marriage and family. We were not interested in making our marriage a conspicuous political statement, but as one gay friend said after his marriage, "Our same-sex marriages are historical and political whether or not we choose them to be." We were about to plow new prairie in Iowa.

September ushers in the most beautiful season in Iowa. Locusts announce with their singing that there are just six weeks to clean the gardens and tune up the snow blower. The crisp nights and clear skies replace the heat and humidity of August that drain our energy. It seemed the perfect time for our wedding, but planning any fall event in Iowa compels even the gayest celebrants to check the home football schedule of the Iowa Hawkeyes. They were scheduled to be out of town on our wedding date. The church and pastor were available.

> **In Iowa, same-sex weddings are like plowing new prairie.**

Doug and I love the Iowa State Fair, and the historical Agriculture Building, home of the butter cow, seemed like the perfect setting for two Iowa farm boys to have their wedding reception. The caterer was available and agreed to serve pomegranate martinis—probably the only time in Iowa they have been mixed in gallon jugs—and beef from our own farm. I hired the Blue Band because it was a tradition for Doug and me to listen to this group every year at the State Fair. The *New York Times* decided to print our wedding announcement, and the women at the Madison County Courthouse hugged us when we applied for our license. The clerks at the jewelry store fell over us to help us pick out rings. We kept the ceremony intimate, but the guest list for our reception quickly grew to more than three hundred people, and a flood of accepting RSVPs proved that we were in for a big celebration. Iowa has a long—but little-known—history of being on the cutting edge of issues of social justice, and we were richly blessed by the many people who celebrated with us in this new era of acceptance.

One relative asked, "Who will be the bride?" She had no experiential framework upon which to build an understanding of same-sex marriage, but just a few months earlier, neither did Doug or I. As we work through our coming out, those of us who are gay have resolved many of the issues regarding the nature of our relationships, but we often forget that others are just beginning to examine the essential meanings of same-sex partnerships. Our homo-naïve relative was just trying to understand us. Gay marriage can be legislated, but understanding, tolerance, and acceptance cannot be.

Doug had been a fundamental part of the lives of my grandchildren their entire lives, but thoughts about the potential impact on my granddaughters slowly eroded my wedding planning excitement. I worried they would be taunted when they returned to school in their small, conservative Ohio town, once their friends learned their grandpa had just married a man. I wanted to protect them from the pain I had felt when my coach told me I should be wearing a bra.

I called my daughter Krista to discuss my concerns. She responded, "Of course, we all want them to come to the wedding."

"What will you tell them?"

"We'll tell them that two people who love each other very much are getting married." I was embarrassed at how much I can underestimate my children.

Krista said to my granddaughter, "You know we're going to Iowa soon. We're going because Grandpa and Doug are getting married."

My granddaughter responded, "Oh? Who are they marrying?"

Krista answered, "They're marrying each other."

After a beat, my granddaughter said, "That's weird." She thought for a while longer, and then she asked, "Will there be cake?"

When I was thirty-two years old, my mother married my stepfather after having been a widow for nearly thirty years. As I lay in bed on their wedding night, I suddenly sat straight up and said, "Oh my God! Do you think they're doing it?" Until then, I had not thought of my mother as a sexual being.

The question about procreation did not escape my granddaughters. Just prior to the trip to Iowa for our wedding, Krista had "the talk" about sexuality with them. On the way to the wedding, it was all still very new to them. One of them asked, "Mom, you mean you have to do *that* every time you want to have a baby?" She assured her that you do. A long and dangerous silence followed. Then, the dreaded question, "Will Grandpa and Doug be doing *that*?"

Thinking quickly, my daughter responded, "No. They don't want children."

Married After a Twenty-three-Year Engagement

All of the wedding planning did not erase the fact that my marriage to Doug still encroached on my sense of reality. Long before the law approved same-sex marriage in Iowa, young gay men referred to their partners with bravado as their "husbands." Planning my own wedding made me realize that I continued to have anxieties about introducing Doug as my husband instead of my partner. Sometimes, with intentional ambiguity, I had introduced Doug to someone as my partner, hoping he or she might think I meant my business partner rather than sexual partner. The work inside my head was a long way from being finished.

Society imposes marriage as the standard by which all sexual and intimate relationships are judged. Eventually, 95 percent of all adults marry. "Hetero-normativity" implies that all people are part of a nuclear family and fall into only one of two distinct and complementary sexes, male and female, each having certain "natural" roles; heterosexuality is the only "normal" sexual orientation.

Gay men, for the most part, do not want to be alone any more than heterosexual men do. Random, casual sex becomes an unsatisfying substitute for what they feel is lacking in their lives. The majority of gay men, particularly those past the age of forty, want to have a loving and committed relationship with another man. They want to—need to—fall in love. American culture dictates that marriage is the quintessential characteristic of adult life. Adult intimacy and sexual intimacy are synonymous with heterosexual marriage. Gay men and women wish to marry for all the same reasons that heterosexuals want to marry—to make a public declaration of their choice of a person they wish to spend the rest of their lives with.

At the time I am writing this, Connecticut, Iowa, Massachusetts, Vermont, and New Hampshire have passed laws in support of marriage equality. Same-sex marriages are now approved in Belgium, Canada, the Netherlands, Norway, Spain, Sweden, and South Africa. Although support appears to be growing worldwide, in other countries same-sex couples can still be put to death.

Every time I tell someone that same-sex marriage is legal in Iowa, I hear the same response: "Iowa? Of all places! Who even knew Iowa had gay people?" On April 3, 2009, the Iowa Supreme Court held that "the Iowa statute limiting civil marriage to a union between a man and a woman violates the equal protection clause of the Iowa Constitution." Five objectives were advanced by the government: heterosexual marriage is a tradition; it promotes the optimal environment for raising children; it promotes procreation; it promotes stability in opposite-sex relationships; it preserves the state's resources. According to the Iowa Supreme Court, opponents of marriage equality failed to prove any of these objectives. The Supreme Court ruled that "religious objections to same-sex marriage cannot control the definition of marriage, which is a 'civil contract' under Iowa law."

> The Iowa Supreme Court held that "religious objections to same-sex marriage cannot control the definition of marriage, which is a 'civil contract' under Iowa law."

Many gay people as well as heterosexuals reject the idea of marriage, arguing that marriage is paternalistic and based on a need to control the behavior of the other. At the same time, however, gay culture is profoundly reactive to and conditioned by the traditions and values of present-day American heterosexuality. Some men who have sex with men find it difficult to let go of the heterosexual marriage paradigm. They resist the next step of forming a bond with another man. They are unwilling to forsake either the favored status of heterosexual privilege that accompanies having a family or the pleasures and freedoms of non-monogamous sex with men.

If there is anything fundamental to the social meaning of marriage, it's monogamy. As I previously discussed, the rules of fidelity in gay relationships are often said to be more relaxed. Heterosexuals may have a higher commitment to monogamy than do gay men, but Joan Atwood and Limor Schwartz in 2002 found that 55 percent of married women and 65 percent of married men report being unfaithful at some point in their marriage. Many people believe that an affair indicates there is something profoundly wrong in the marriage, but those who have affairs often report good sex with their partner and rewarding family lives. According to a 1999 AARP survey, "Sex, Romance, and Relationships," about 41 percent of the survey respondents said nonmarital sex was wrong. According to the same AARP survey, now only 22 percent give their thumbs-down vote to sex outside of marriage.

The default setting of an exclusive sexual and romantic relationship throughout a marriage is apparently difficult for most people, gay or straight, to maintain. What seems to render outside sexual relationships damaging is secrecy and lack of agreement. Pamela Druckerman, in *Lust in Translation: The Rules of Infidelity from Tokyo to Tennessee*, said that 80 percent of respondents indicated they thought infidelity was wrong, but most of those who got caught cheating didn't think of themselves as "the cheating kind." Only other people who committed infidelity were cheaters. Fidelity has more to do with your head than with your genitals.

Heterosexual couples are afforded nearly 1,200 federal rights and benefits that are denied to same-sex couples. Before we had the option to marry, Doug and I considered seeing a lawyer to try to resolve some of the concerns about the legal definition of our relationship, but the task seemed daunting. Domestic partnerships are contractual relationships that can be legally challenged, but the alternatives to marriage are clearly inferior. Through the years we recognized the financial disadvantages we had as an unmarried couple. According to estimates published in the *New York Times* in 2009, in the worst-case scenario, a couple's lifetime cost of being gay could be as high as $467,562.

But getting married is more than a consideration of finances. M. V. Lee Badgett, in *When Gay People Get Married*, wrote: "Marriage . . . has the power to define a relationship that others might not understand. Couples can use marriage to express to others what their relationship means and how it should be treated." Some research suggests that gay men have lower rates of sexually transmitted disease when in legally recognized same-sex partnerships. However, no research suggests that gay men and women will use gay marriage as a way to undermine monogamy in heterosexual marriage.

I had lunch with my agent, Linda Konner, before the wedding. She asked me, "Do you think your marriage will change your relationship with Doug?"

"Yes," I answered.

161

"How?"

"Well, the most obvious way is that it will resolve some of the legal complexities we face as an unmarried couple." I thought for a while, and then I went on. "But it's much more than that. We want to formally invite our families to accept each of us into the other's family as full members." Doug's brother, Todd, validated that for me when following the ceremony, he said, "Loren, welcome to the family." Following the wedding I received a note from my cousin Jerry, the family genealogist, that said, "I need all of Doug's information so I can get him included in our family history." A civil union will never be the same thing as same-sex marriage. That dotted line connecting us in the family tree was replaced by a very solid line.

Making a commitment that "this man is here for the rest of my life" changes the dimensions of a relationship. For Doug and me, it meant asking our family, friends, and colleagues to take a serious look at our relationship and to put it on an equal footing with heterosexual marriages. It also meant asking people to examine their own barriers to approval; it said, "You can no longer pretend we're just roommates who sleep in the same bed." I don't believe everyone needs to marry, but I do believe that every gay couple deserves the right to make their own choice about it.

> In the family tree, marriage changes the dotted line connecting two people of the same sex into a solid line; a civil union can never do the same thing.

Because both Doug and I come from fairly traditional backgrounds, marriage meant all of the things it does in the hetero-normative world: love, romance, a wish to express commitment to each other and to the community, and a public commitment to the continuity of the relationship. But even so, living in a relationship outside of tradition caused us to do more soul searching about getting married than if we'd been a heterosexual couple.

In theory, marriage commitment is lifelong. Some fear marriage will end in spite of the commitment; others fear that the commitment will keep it from ending when it should. Because both Doug and I were divorced, we knew firsthand that marriages often end. More than 50 percent of marriages end in divorce, but Massachusetts, where same-sex marriage is legal, has one of the lowest divorce rates in the country.

William Sloane Coffin wrote, "The argument that gays threaten to destroy heterosexual marriage is an assertion only, not an argument. If anyone destroys marriage, it's married people, not gays."

Attachment to others takes many forms. Passion is necessary in sexual attraction up to the point of choosing a mate; kindness and attachment are the more enduring and mature qualities necessary for a committed relationship. Because gay men have an expectation that their relationships will be short term, they sometimes fail to work on them. Doug and I had romance, passion, and great sex, and we felt at ease with each other from the start. We shared both a sexual intimacy and an emotional intimacy that sustained us as romance and passion dimmed. We laughed and cried together, shared our secrets with each other, and felt at ease with each other in ways we'd never felt before. I always felt like I was being myself. We learned to fight successfully, not by having to win but by finding compromise. We relinquished the need to try to impress the other.

In Tim Turner's play *Out Late*, Charles's wife, Eileen, says to him, "You're not gay if you're not doing it." Being gay is a social role as well as a sexual behavior. It is far more than genital sex. Homosexual desire is one thing, but living the life of an openly gay man in a relationship is quite a different matter. It often means living a life conditioned by the values of heterosexual sexuality and intimacy. One man who came out in his fifties insists, however, that he did not come out so he could trade his wife for a husband. He wrote, "Not all hook-ups are only about sexual pleasure but may involve a good deal of emotional intimacy as well. Many men find the variety of their relationships with other men, on various levels of intimacy, to give them fully satisfying lives. I'm not sure that all—or even most—gay men aspire to hetero-normative, monogamous lifestyles. Gay men are free to define or not define their relationships however they see fit."

Our sexual drive is a powerful, universal biological drive. In *Out Late*, Charles says to Eileen, "The point is, I am [gay]. Always have been. I see a woman. Nothing happens. I see a man. Something happens." We are born into a culture with identifiable norms and values about sexual expression and intimacy that are based almost entirely on a heterosexual paradigm. A stable expression of sexual identity depends upon a reassessment of those values and norms. It requires that we deconstruct those values and reconstruct a value system for how we express our sexuality and intimacy.

Fidelity, Cheating, and Polyamory

Gay men frequently have different expectations about monogamy in their relationships than heterosexual couples do. Some monogamous gay couples experience a relationship that feels too narrow, with no room even for platonic male friendships. A study of gay couples at San Francisco State University reported in the *New York Times* in 2010 that 50 percent of those surveyed have sex outside their relationships, with the knowledge and approval of their partners. Although statistics like these have been used as evidence that gay men are incapable of long-term, committed relationships, AARP's study removes some of the sting. As romance and passion diminish, love may live without desire, and ardor may abide without love. New attractions cause excitement to build, judgment to fail, and trouble to begin.

Our culture socializes men to be independent, and some male couples try to reduce their dependence upon each other by seeking sex outside the relationship. Some couples consider their relationships "open" but run into problems when there is a lack of agreement about how nonexclusiveness will be managed. Non-monogamous sex can interfere with sexual desire for the spouse, and if adventures become regular, they can become destructive to the relationship. Couples sometimes will introduce a third person into their sexual relationship to add excitement, but problems result if the primary spousal relationship is already strained and one of the pair feels left out.

Cheating can be an occasional indiscretion or it can become habitual. It leads to lying about sexual exclusivity and undermines trust in a relationship. Cheating can also become the preferred way of dealing with needs or acting out anger. Although gay male couples may be sexually non-monogamous, most will remain emotionally monogamous; the emotional commitment to their partner binds them together more than the nonexclusive sex pulls them apart.

While I was seeing Alfredo, we were both married. We both understood that we were cheating on our wives. We each justified our behavior with our own personal rationalizations, however weak. It is possible to attach oneself to more than one person emotionally, but loving more than one person is very difficult to do. The question, "Did you have sex with that person?" is what most people insist upon knowing, but emotional infidelity is far more damaging to a relationship than sexual infidelity is. Once loyalty shifts and trust is broken, it can be very difficult, though not impossible, to reestablish a solid relationship. In seeking resolution, the individuals in the relationship lock themselves into conflict if they focus only on how the other person could have betrayed them without asking what they might have done to contribute to the weakening of the relationship.

Some people are turning to what they call "responsible non-monogamy" or "polyamory." Polyamory literally means "many loves." No statistics are available for how common polyamory is. Proponents of polyamory believe that humans experience varying degrees of loving others. They see the barrier between friends and lovers as permeable. Polyamory follows rules of poly-fidelity, or fidelity within a closed system. In polyamory, the primary relationship takes on the characteristics of a spousal relationship with a high degree of commitment; all other relationships are subordinate. Secondary relationships involve both emotional and sexual intimacy and are enduring, but the secondary relationship does not carry the power or authority of the primary relationship.

One man spoke of his twenty-five-year relationship with his partner, who became impotent after surgery for cancer of the prostate. Although he continues to love his partner, he also loves another man with whom he engages in a daily, long-term Internet relationship that includes webcam sex, as sexually intimate as it can be in two dimensions.

Variations are seemingly endless. Many find it difficult to comprehend that a man can love a woman while preferring to have sex with another man. Many of these men claim to have a good sex life with women, all the while knowing that for them sex with a man is more satisfying. I know of several pairs of heterosexually married couples in which the two men have developed ongoing, long-term sexual relationships with each other. They sought these relationships as a way of dealing with their same-sex attractions. The families are friends, travel together, and seem content. Others I know have been open with their wives about their male sexual partners; their wives have agreed to share their spouse with a man rather than accept a divorce. Even in those situations where they do divorce, these men may never define themselves as gay.

The most common problems in these relationships are predictable. When someone new is brought into the system, there is an intense sexual focus on the newest member, and triangulation of relationships results in possessiveness and jealousy. Frequency of sexual intimacy between the primary spousal partners may diminish. Existing schedules and an overriding commitment to children complicate these relationships. To be successful, all relationships within the system must be respected. They must be based on honesty and authenticity rather than sex alone. Members must also be assertive to get their own needs met, while boundaries and limits must be respected.

Sexually Transmitted Diseases

When I moved to Des Moines in 1986, Jim was one of my first patients, and the first person I had treated with HIV/AIDS. He had never come out to his family but now knew he had been outed by a virus. He wanted me to help him negotiate the process of telling his family not only that he was gay but also that he would likely die from his illness. Jim was a cautious man, and he never did anything impulsively or carelessly. Except once. He knew exactly when he had been infected and by whom. For one brief moment, his judgment had failed him, and he had unprotected anal sex with a man who had a busy and indiscriminate sex life. It was at the beginning of the AIDS epidemic. No one knew much about the spread of HIV other than that it was spreading throughout the gay community. As he left my office, I remember feeling afraid to shake his hand, although I did. I knew what he really needed was a hug.

Statistics can be hypnotic, but please, stick with me here. HIV/AIDS has impacted all communities, all races and ethnicities, and all levels of society. Men who have sex with men, sometimes just called MSM, include all men who have sex with other men regardless of how they identify themselves (gay, bisexual, heterosexual, or other). According to the Centers for Disease Control, in 2010, MSM make up over half (53 percent) of all people living with HIV/AIDS, even though the CDC estimates that MSM comprise only an estimated 4 percent of the entire adult population. The rate of newly diagnosed infections in MSM is forty-four times the rate of the general population. The CDC estimates that more than one million people are living with HIV in the United States, and more than 576,000 people with AIDS have died since I first met Jim in 1981 at the beginning of the epidemic. Had I come out before I did, I likely would have been one of them.

The previously mentioned study by Francis and Mialon of Emory University found that as acceptance for homosexuality increases in the United States, the incidence of HIV decreases. The incidence of HIV decreased considerably during the 1990s as attitudes toward gays liberalized, but the incidence of new cases has been increasing again. The highest number of new infections is in the age group of thirty to thirty-nine, with forty to forty-nine the next highest. Sexual risks account for most HIV infections in MSM, particularly having anal sex with someone other than a primary HIV-negative partner. The highest risks appear to fall on those casual sexual partners who have sex without a condom ("bare backing"). Older men with a large number of sexual partners, young men who use "circuit party" drugs, and older men who use "poppers" or nitrate inhalants carry a high risk of exposure to the virus. Older men continue to be a very significant source of HIV transmission to young gay men.

One in five people living with HIV is unaware of his or her infection. Young African American MSM in the study were especially likely to be unaware of their HIV infection. A lack of knowledge is tragic because many MSM reduce their risky behaviors after they test positive for HIV. Knowing they are positive could help protect their sex and drug-using partners from HIV infection. And those who are unaware of their HIV infection cannot take advantage of medicine that could help them live longer.

Many MSM continue their false belief that they are at low risk of becoming infected or infecting their partner. Treatment successes have hidden many of the negative aspects of HIV, leading to false assurances about the risks of death or, for that matter, how difficult living with HIV can be. Young gay and bisexual men, unlike older gay and bisexual men, have not witnessed the ravages of the HIV/AIDS epidemic.

In meeting with the local HIV education group, I learned that some young men seek out a positive HIV status as punishment for guilt about their homosexuality, and some just want "to get it over with." Some HIV positive men engage in "serosorting," which means only having sex with a partner whom they believe is also HIV positive. Serosorting prevents transmission of HIV to others, but it does not reduce the risks from the introduction of a new and different strain of the virus.

Hepatitis B (HBV) is a sexually transmitted liver disease spread like HIV. HBV is found in highest concentrations in blood and in lower concentrations in other body fluids (e.g., semen, vaginal secretions, and saliva). HBV can cause severe liver disease, including cirrhosis (liver failure) and liver cancer. HBV can be prevented by HBV vaccines and safer sex practices. In the United States, chronic HBV infection results in two thousand to four thousand estimated deaths per year.

Syphilis and gonorrhea increase the risk of HIV infection and they indicate participation in high-risk sexual behavior that can facilitate the transmission of HIV infection. Use of alcohol and illegal drugs is prevalent among some MSM and is linked to risk of HIV and other STDs because alcohol and drugs also increase the likelihood of risky sexual behavior. Sexual decision making is complex; it requires an optimally functioning brain.

Where acceptance of homosexuality is low, underground cruising areas, such as public parks, beaches, restrooms, and other public areas, become the predominant venue for MSM activity. Rates of high-risk sexual behavior are higher in those venues. It is only safe to have sex— oral, anal, or vaginal—with someone whose HIV and HBV status is known to be negative. Easy to say, but all of us run the risk, like Jim, where sexual drive overpowers rational thought.

A rapid test is a screening test that produces results in approximately twenty minutes. Rapid tests use blood from a vein or from a finger stick, or oral fluid, to look for the presence of antibodies to HIV. Positive results from a rapid HIV test must be confirmed with a follow-up test before a final diagnosis of infection can be made.

Several companies market HIV tests, but as this book is being written, only the Home Access HIV-1 Test System is approved by the Food and Drug Administration. Keep in mind that HIV is not necessarily transmitted every time you have sex. Many places provide testing for HIV infection, including local health departments, HIV clinics, LGBT resource centers, offices of private doctors, hospitals, and other sites set up specifically to provide HIV testing. Your HIV test result reveals only your HIV status. Your negative test result does not reveal whether or not your partner has HIV.

If you answer yes to any of the following, you should be tested for HIV at least once a year (those who engage in high-risk behaviors, such as unprotected anal sex with casual partners, should be tested more frequently).

- Have you injected drugs or steroids or shared equipment (such as needles, syringes, works) with others?
- Have you exchanged sex for drugs or money?
- Have you ever been diagnosed with or treated for hepatitis, tuberculosis (TB), or a sexually transmitted disease (STD), such as syphilis?
- Have you had unprotected sex with someone who could answer yes to any of the above questions?

Chapter 9
In Your Weariness: In the Morning You Start Again

Everybody wants to go to heaven,
But nobody wants to die.
—"Everybody Wants to Go to Heaven,"
Peter Tosh (attributed)

The universal description of the midlife crisis includes a time of personal turmoil, sudden changes in personal goals and lifestyle, realization of aging and physical decline, and feelings of entrapment in roles that are seen as unwelcome and too restrictive. I was well past the over-the-hill-at-thirty gay man when I came out. It used to be that forty was considered midlife, but that is a bit outdated. One man wrote, "I'm not forty yet, still getting there. People who think about life being over at thirty years old are simply silly. We are lucky to be alive whether we're twenty, thirty, fifty, or eighty, and we should do our best to enjoy it. I will not say my life was better when I was younger, but definitely totally different. In ten years it will be totally different again."

All people have a moment when mortality finally becomes personal. We realize that there is less time remaining than has already passed, and we begin to check things off our "to-do" list without ever having done them. Midlife is a time when we review our life experiences and begin to consider the need to develop a legacy, a suitable ending to our life story. It is a time of disengagement from the world of the young to pursue a greater range of social roles. It is also a time of higher cognitive complexity, when values and institutions are seen with more ambivalence and uncertainty. As we mature we become more critical of groups and institutions that once had a great influence in our lives.

The exact ages for midlife seem to be quite elastic, with some even extending it from the thirties through the sixties. According to the U.S. National Center for Health Statistics, life expectancy for all races of men is 75.4 years. I prefer to think of midlife as the middle of *adult* life, which would put it in our fourth decade. Whatever age range one chooses, it seems that all people reach a point where they begin to have some awareness that they are aging, that time is passing by and that they are "halfway home."

Midlife can be a tumultuous time where every aspect of a person's life comes into question. Much of what is revealed is horrifying, including the destructiveness in others and the recognition that we have been responsible for some of the pain experienced by those we care about. What we aspired to be versus our current achievements may be significantly different. We are stretched between a strong investment in maintaining the status quo and the urgency of modifying our life, to test out, to explore.

The period of midlife transition is characterized by disillusionment as we recognize that long-held assumptions and beliefs about the self and the world are not true. This can be experienced both as a loss and as liberation. Without something to replace our former self-image, it is daunting to deconstruct the straight and narrow, nice-kid-next-door pose that was often assumed for decades before coming out in midlife. In maturity, a person begins to act in ways that are more in concert with his reconstructed internal values rather than reverting to the old patterns of pleasing others. Priorities have changed, and the external world is no longer the reference point for what is correct.

One man described his late coming out this way: as mature people, we have highly personal value systems constructed from the best parts of different systems to which we have been exposed. Prior to maturity, we simply adopt the value system of our parents and peers, or we reactively reject those values completely and develop values that are directly in opposition to them. In either case, our values are still dominated by the values of our parents. Midlife allows us to integrate those values with our own later experiences.

As men undergo the psychological changes of midlife, they begin to reconsider the qualities of life that make it worthwhile. Men often become more sensitive to the misfortunes of others. They no longer fear intimacy, and they begin to question the validity of doing, making, having, and never admitting weakness. Even more important, such ideas are no longer considered to be expressions of being "queer."

In midlife we are able to recognize that what we learned about being a man and what is expected of us may not be a definition we have to cling to. It may not be who we really are. Paul, a man I interviewed, is an

172

excellent example. Paul is an identical twin and was a Lutheran minister until he was outed in 1991. At the age of forty-six at a church leadership retreat he disclosed that he experienced sexual attraction to other men.

From the age of thirteen Paul had felt called to the ministry, and the increasing struggle he felt about his sexuality led him to believe that if he were exposed, he would lose everything important to him. For Paul, coming out put all of his family, social networks, and vocational relationships

> **In midlife, men recognize that what they once learned about being a man no longer defines who they are.**

at risk. During the years before he came out, he dealt with suicidal feelings and the fear of being exposed.

Although the group at the retreat had taken an oath of confidentiality, two people went to his bishop. The bishop demanded Paul's resignation. Losing his job meant coming out to his teenage children, an experience he anticipated would be devastating. Instead, it turned out to be "a wonderful experience because each of my three children said that they still loved me." Paul began to accept that he was gay and believed that God accepted and affirmed him as a gay man.

Prior to coming out, Paul had only experienced limited, casual sexual encounters with other men. Paul and his twin brother had explored their sexuality with each other from the onset of puberty through high school. His first date with a woman was for the homecoming dance his senior year in high school. He dated a woman in college, but when she wanted to have sex, he refused, rationalizing that it was because his moral standards were higher than hers. He had never had sex with a woman before his marriage. He felt his wife was a good choice for him, but even as he was getting married, he began to feel he was making a terrible mistake.

Paul describes his late-arriving homosexual "adolescence" in this way: "In 1984, after finally coming to terms with being gay and accepting my sexuality as a positive thing, I think, as is common for gay men who are accepting their sexuality, I acted like a teenager. For me that mainly manifested itself as looking for a lot of sexual encounters and also shocking people by inappropriate revelations of my sexual adventures." Paul discovered in his coming out that his identical twin, who also had been married, was also gay and had a very parallel sexual development.

173

Paul is now legally married to the man he has been with for nearly twenty years.

Eight of the men in my study came out in their eighties, four of them having been outed like Paul. Like Paul and me, they always felt very sexual, but acting on those feelings with women evoked considerable anxiety. We avoided heterosexual dating as much as possible, using justifications like "morality," "need to work," or "Southern gentility" to explain our restraint. What other young men were learning by trial and error with women, we never learned. Our deficiencies, however, were remedied when we began dating men. Each of us sought to tame the wild horse of Plato's allegory.

"My Dad's a Faggot"

On our first vacation together as a couple, Doug accompanied me and my children to the Cayman Islands. My children hardly knew him at the time. A few days into the vacation, one of my daughters had a disagreement with Doug. Caught squarely between them, I attempted to mediate. My daughter's response was, "It's just like having a stepmother!" Unfortunately, I failed to recognize her genuine distress. I thought her comment was precious, so I shared it with Doug. "Precious" was not the word Doug used to describe how he felt about being compared to an evil stepmother.

> Dating an older man with children is complicated because the children will always come first.

Some men find fathers attractive partners. They consider them less self-oriented and better at compromise, but bringing kids into the mix adds a layer of complexity to a relationship. People underestimate the central role of children in the lives of gay men. For gay men, just like heterosexual men, the children always come first. The birth of Alfredo's son permanently bumped me into a subordinate place in his affection.

In 1997, Gilbert Herdt, Jeff Beeler, and Todd W. Rawls studied a group of previously married gay men and women in Chicago. They found that people who have been married tend to self-identify as gay an average of ten years later than those who never married. Marriage also delays the age of coming out to both parents, although mothers were generally told earlier than fathers. The difficulty in coming out to my mother far surpassed the difficulty in telling her I wanted to be a psychiatrist.

174

One man I interviewed was retired from the military. He had married and divorced twice even though he knew he was gay much earlier in his life. He said that his deployments for military combat enabled him to remove himself from the conflict that he experienced about his sexual orientation while at home. He was the custodial father of his two daughters. Not yet out to his daughters, he was struggling to find a new life as a gay father.

Gay fathers have some unique problems. The image of the affluent gay man who hedonistically indulges himself doesn't fit most newly divorced gay men. Many go through several years of legal and financial problems often compounded by a wife who feels deceived and cheated. Because of child support and alimony, they may have very little discretionary income. Kids make significant demands on the time of gay fathers. This can be a big source of conflict with a partner who has never had children of his own.

Marital history and the timing of important life events significantly impact the coming-out trajectory. According to Herdt and colleagues, gay men who have been in heterosexual marriages have much more in common with each other than they do with gay men who came out early in their lives. The development of gay men who have children is shaped in a much different way than those who do not because children are central in their lives.

When I joined the gay fathers' support group, I felt an immediate sense of brotherhood with the other men in the group. Gay fathers have clusters of common experiences that make it easy to relate to each other, but those experiences may complicate relating to men who have always known they were gay and thus never married.

Gay men who come out in later life, whether previously married or not, are rookies in a game they've never played before. Their lives are turned upside down. Some trade a comfortably familiar, heterosexual life in the suburbs for a new life in a gay urban environment. Their previous straight social network has been sidelined. They are out of sync with developmental tasks appropriate to their age. With little or no previous experience in the gay community, they battle with tasks that are typically associated with late adolescence and young adulthood rather than middle age. They lack certainty about their new world. Without a clear sense of their new identity, they compete in the game, but there is no rule book. Many are not prepared to begin life anew as a single man.

Coming Out to the Kids

For many gay fathers, the biggest barrier to coming out is telling their children. Gay fathers know that they are different; they also know that their being different will define their kids as different. Fathers worry about how their homosexuality will impact their children's relationships with other kids. All parents want to buffer their kids against the pain inflicted by teasing, accusations, and rejection. Guilt stabs gay fathers when their kids hear slurs like, "Your dad's a faggot." I worried that my daughters' boyfriends would be scared off when they said to them, "There's something important I need to tell you about my dad."

For most gay fathers, telling their children is by far the biggest barrier to coming out.

Gay fathers worry about whether or not to tell their children's teachers and their coaches. They wonder, "Will I embarrass them if I bring the man I'm dating to watch their softball games? Will parents of my kids' friends allow them to come for sleepovers to the home I share with my partner? Will other kids think they can get AIDS because I'm gay?" I accepted the prospect that I might be shunned for being gay, but I dreaded the thought that I might be responsible for my daughters being rejected.

I don't have a distinguished record for coming out. One of the few times I faced that responsibility head-on was when I came out to my daughters. I agonized about how to approach it for quite some time. I decided that I would take them out for a picnic on my sailboat one Wednesday afternoon when the lake would be deserted. I sailed the boat to the farthest corner of the nearly abandoned lake, out of earshot of everything except the wildlife. Anxiously, I lowered the anchor, opened the picnic basket, and said, "I have something serious to tell you. I'm gay."

"Oh, Dad, we've known that for a long time," my daughters responded. "Can we eat now?" Many years later, I learned that they had discovered books and papers in my library about homosexuality. They had figured it out and were waiting for me to say something to them. Their generation's acceptance of homosexuality is considerably different from my generation's attitude about it.

Although coming out to their children occasionally sparks a wildfire, many gay fathers have had experiences of coming out to their children similar to mine. One who has three adult sons said his children responded, "Pop, why didn't you tell us this ages ago?" They told him they loved and respected him even more because he demonstrated to them qualities he had been unable to see in himself. He regretted that he'd been too afraid to tell them when he first became confident that he was gay. Losses loom so much larger than gains.

Amity Pierce Buxton, who wrote *The Other Side of the Closet: The Coming-Out Crisis for Straight Spouses and Families*, offers advice to fathers considering coming out to their children. Most kids believe that the sooner a gay parent comes out to them the better it is. After the spouse has been told, children will already be aware of the tension in the household. Buxton suggests that children not be told at the time their parents separate; coming out should wait until both parents are somewhat comfortable with the revelation. Then both parents are in a better position to be supportive of the children when they are told. Depending upon their age, they may have already observed telltale signs of their parent's sexual orientation.

> Every important venture in life starts without feeling adequately prepared.

Children should be told at a time when they can react, reflect, and ask questions. The goal is to lovingly help them understand. Many older children will have some idea of what it means to be gay. The divorce may be a more difficult issue to accept than sexual orientation. But as my daughter said, "Children who have a gay parent must come out to our friends, too. Telling friends about a divorce is a one-shot thing, but coming out to our friends never ends." In some cases, estrangement may occur. It takes time, consistency, and work to reestablish damaged relationships.

I have never started an important venture feeling adequately prepared. It isn't necessary to do everything perfectly. Sometimes just doing an acceptable job may be adequate, and just because something is painful doesn't mean it is dysfunctional. It may help to know that you're not in this alone, but it may not help much. Sometimes things are as bad as they seem, but often they are not. In dealing with any conflict, only three options are available: change it, put up with it, or get out. Since changing sexual orientation is not possible, putting up with it or getting out are the only two remaining choices.

Hating Adonis

As we age, both men and women experience a gradual decrease in the attributes that are considered attractive. But from my research, women and gay men experience it more dramatically and earlier than heterosexual men do. For a while past the age of fifty, men get a free ride. Age may even enhance some aspects of men's attractiveness and work to their advantage in some relationships. That said, the psychological impact of physical changes can be significant.

Central to the fear of middle age are attitudes about changes in the body. Those who are most deeply invested in their physical appearance encounter the greatest difficulty, fearing the loss of their external, youthful sexual attractiveness. As Rebecca Mead wrote in *The New Yorker*, "The new idea offered by the contemporary culture of cosmetic surgery is that it is the vessel itself that we must value, rather than the soul or spirit that it contains." This physically attractive body is the person we present ourselves to be, and some have lived behind the façade with little concern about learning how to relate to others in ways beyond the physical. Middle age, and the loss of that youthful body, can be shocking, and some gay men feel they've lost their former social self.

Stereotypes describe gay men as either limp-wristed and effeminate or obsessed with attaining the beautiful masculine body. Julie Jones and Steve Pugh, in the article "Aging Gay Men: Lessons from the Sociology of Embodiment," describe the relationship gay men have with their body image. While the extremes are captured by the exaggerated femininity in the form of drag and the exaggerated masculinity in the musculature of the gym rat, between these extremes there are an infinite variety of aesthetic preferences, but the unifying factor is the presentation of an attractive, attention-grabbing body. Some gay men consider their bodies their most significant asset, and they seek affirmation through admiration and envy from others. Rarely alone, but sometimes lonely, they believe their bodies are their ticket to power and success, and the goal is perfection.

Showering in a gym is surely as oppressing for a stocky, skinny, or aging gay man as it is for a woman trying on a new swimsuit. Joan Collins once famously said, "After a certain age, you get the face you deserve." Chiseled good looks are achieved by very few and remain only a dream for the majority. Not being able to achieve those good looks is sometimes perceived as a lack of

> **The body is approached as a project that must constantly be improved lest it revert to its natural homeliness.**

commitment to body maintenance or a lack of self-control. The body becomes a project, perpetually in need of development to prevent it from reverting to its natural homely state. Continual fixation on body image sometimes means attempting to radically alter the way we look by "having a little work done," including the use of pectoral implants, steroids, and penile enlargers.

Our body image is the result of the difference between the perfect body and the way we see our body. To be satisfied with our body image, we must first have a realistic expectation about what our body can be. Then we must see it as it actually is rather than focusing exclusively on our "deficiencies." The saddest and angriest gay men are those who have failed to come to terms with their bodies; they feel as intimidated by beautiful gay men as they do by straight men. The enemy for these men isn't their body—it is their unrealistic expectations of what their body can be, or must be.

Gay men's connection to physical attractiveness or preoccupation with fashion can be perceived as superficial or even threatening to heterosexual men. The American masculine ideal dictates that real men must not be concerned about matters of style and taste, but all the while they are being blasted by images of men reshaped by computers and wearing Calvin Klein briefs. The word "metrosexual" was coined to describe a man who blends an interest in style, fashion, and culture, while not letting go of ball scratching and beer guzzling. These men have always been a part of wealthier crowds, but now frosted hair and manicures have become accessible to the average man. In Europe, these men don't need a special category to justify their emphasis on physical grooming, but this crossover is something we're not yet comfortable with in the United States; it is just too queer.

Because of the importance of physical attractiveness in the gay community, middle age comes sooner to gay men than it does to heterosexual men. The midlife gay male must work daily to maintain the appearance of youth, but the labor must also be hidden so no one knows how difficult it is to keep up. Harold Kooden wrote in *Golden Men: The Power of Gay Midlife* that the concept of a linear aging process is misleading. He suggests that gay men have four ages: chronological (clock age), biological (body age), experiential (heart age), and sexual (gay age). He proposed that we age in each of these four areas at different rates and times; chronological age represents only one portion of our authentic age.

Another age might be added to Kooden's list: geographical age. Age functions quite differently in urban and rural communities. Because men who have sex with men may undergo conflict about their sexuality, their sexual age may lag behind their clock age, body age, and heart age. Geographical age may add another incongruity—men who grew up in the city may arrive at a homosexual identity at a younger age.

Crisis Competence

Some have suggested that coming out serves as a training ground for successful future crisis management, a phenomenon referred to as "crisis competence" by D. C. Kimmel. The idea suggests that working through the conflicts of coming out creates a buffer against later traumas and the capacity to deal with the stresses of midlife with a higher degree of skill: "If I survived that, I can survive anything." Crisis competence consists of our innate ability to recover from adversities and learned coping mechanisms from earlier life experience. Crisis competence can mitigate feelings of loss, help us develop some immunity to traumatic events, and hasten our recovery. Kimmel suggests that gay people may age in a more positive way because living through the crisis of coming out facilitates their resolving future crises.

I don't buy it. It doesn't seem applicable to my life. First of all, the concept of crisis competence is based on a linear description of aging, and the coming-out process is seen as if it were a training ground for crisis management. Individuals vary considerably in their psychological strengths, whether or not they have come out. A man with low self-esteem, who feels that he has little control over his world to begin with, may have difficulty making a decision and taking action. And significantly, a man may have dealt competently with many crises earlier in his life and for a variety of legitimate reasons has not addressed his conflicts about sexual orientation.

More than that, should a man who waits until midlife to come out be labeled "crisis incompetent" and judged less capable of adapting to the changes that come with old age? It's far more likely that innate personality characteristics determine coping talents—some people have greater resiliency than others, and individuals vary widely in their susceptibility to stress, and consequently to anti-gay attitudes.

The Spirit Is Willing

The usual belief about a midlife crisis is that it involves a dislocation or change in one's basic personality. Men are expected to go through this crisis as they begin to experience physical and psychological changes as they age. One of the things I examined in my research was the presence of stressful events in the lives of mature men who have sex with men. The greatest stresses of midlife often are attributed to the loss of physical vitality, but emotional stresses are far greater: illness or death of parents, siblings, or contemporaries; marital discord, separation, or divorce; extramarital affairs; children leaving home; disappointment in children's achievements; or feeling caught between the demands of aging parents and children. However, my research and the findings of other researchers dispel the idea that midlife is a universally stressful time. Traditional beliefs about aging, and in particular gay aging, overestimate the frequency of a midlife crisis, and serious emotional disturbances are the exception rather than the rule.

The medical literature is not much help when seeking to understand the midlife transition for gay men. Researchers ignore older people and are ignorant of the fact that they might still be having sex. Gay boomers are difficult to research because having been raised in an era when homosexuality was criminalized and pathologized, many gay men and lesbians have never let go of their fear of exposure. Consequently, they reject the labels that might sideline them from the general population. Having lived in a world of severe sanctions against their sexual orientation, many have lived a hetero-normative life, concealing their sexual orientation either by choosing to live a celibate life or by feigning disinterest in sex.

However, midlife can be liberation. It is a time to stop pretending a commitment to inherited values and instead integrate only that which is valuable from your roots and later life experiences. It means shifting away from using the external world as the main reference point and focusing on what is correct for you and your developing image of the future. Midlife has allowed me to realize that attractiveness is not measured by only one standard or from only one perspective; it includes a personal value system, a *mature* adult physical attractiveness, and a richness of personal history.

The Birth of Mortality

When I turned forty, a sense of urgency to deal with the parts of myself that I earlier had neglected, ignored, or put on hold swept over me. One of those was my sexual orientation. I had been committed to meeting obligations I had to my family and career. Worrying about how I looked, when I was going to have sex and whether I'd be dancing the night away were the least of my concerns. But then I began to ask myself, "Am I too old to start over as a gay man?" I

> **I asked myself, "At what point do you become too old to start over as a gay man?"**

shuddered at the alternative to coming out that seemed to predict a series of meaningless and clandestine sexual encounters with faceless men, the risk of disease, and eventual public humiliation.

The common misunderstanding of the midlife crisis is that it focuses on physical changes, but psychological aspects induce the greatest stress. What I faced were losses. I was divorced and the noncustodial parent, a role as difficult as the name is ugly. Many people I loved were dying, including my mother, my brother, my stepfather, and friends the same age as me. Professionally, I had reached the apex of my career; younger physicians, filled with the energy and passion I once had, pushed me aside. For the first time in my life, I had medical concerns. Erik Erikson wrote that "despair expresses the feeling that the time is short, too short for the attempt to start another life and to try out alternate roads to integrity." Was it possible for me to find integrity rather than despair in a new life as a gay man?

Coming out in midlife is characterized by deconstructing inherited values and reconstructing your own. Having a mentor, someone who is further along in that process, is invaluable. Many mature men who have sex with men have lived for years in a heterosexual world where they have passed as straight. Sometimes they have had only a partial or conditional acceptance of their homosexuality and their commitment to their sexual orientation was surpassed by their commitment to values of a heterosexist society. Because they have lived in a straight world and concealed their sexual orientation for so long, they risk losing their straight friends by coming out while they still only have underdeveloped relationships with gay people. Because their self-esteem is so damaged, people who do not undergo an internal transformation of their homo-negativism may isolate themselves to a greater and greater degree.

One man, a married father and Muslim from Egypt, said he cries himself to sleep each night, wishing some kind of treatment could make him stop wanting to have sex with a man so that he could go on with loving his wife and two children without those intrusive thoughts. He has no support in his community, explaining, "I am afraid I will be killed if my attraction is exposed." He hungers for a connection with like-minded men and his only link is via the Internet, but those relationships are often with other emotionally starved men. Frequently these connections focus on sex to the exclusion of the emotional intimacy he craves. He is adamant that he doesn't need more sex. What he needs is an emotional hug from men in a compassionate and understanding community. His is a familiar story.

Regrets

The most common regrets people face in midlife are related to education, career, romance, family, and negative attitudes and behaviors. We are forced to make all of life's most important decisions without enough information—information that we receive only as our lives unfold. We should not regret a decision that we made in good faith, with the best information available at the time, even when information later received proves the decision wrong. The decision about coming out can be just like that. Although few regret it, there is no way to know whether the people we love will accept us. But not making a decision is a decision that bears its own unpredictable consequences.

Recently, while I was waiting for a flight in the tiny airport in Flagstaff, Arizona, a young soldier in desert fatigues got off a plane and was greeted by his family and his infant daughter, who he was seeing for the first time. It took me back to when the Navy moved my wife and me to Maine shortly after my wife became pregnant. I was soon to be deployed to Italy, and Lynn would experience her first pregnancy alone. I would miss grabbing the suitcase and rushing to the hospital to await the arrival of our first child, Whitney. Lynn returned to Nebraska to be with her family, and they were the first to hear Whitney's cries. I was present for the birth of my second daughter, Krista. I spent a few moments alone with her in the hospital room. Knowing what it was like to be without a father, I promised her that nothing would ever separate me from her. I broke that promise. She forgave me long before I forgave myself.

My decision to separate from my family when my daughters were in high school was a painful one for all of us. Living thirty miles away, I had difficulty coordinating my schedule with theirs. One agonizing evening I went to see a high school play Whitney was in. Throughout the performance I sat among many former friends who would have nothing to do with me. At the end of the performance I went backstage to congratulate her, only to find that she'd already left with friends. I called her mother, sobbing, grief piling in on me, not just from that evening but for broken promises and every wonder of their lives I had missed and would continue to miss.

Whitney's graduation party was held at her mother's home. Her mother's boyfriend appropriated my role as a cohost and greeted me at the door as if I were just another guest. He invited me into a room filled with former in-laws whom I had not seen since the divorce. I could not identify a single ally in the room. I headed directly for the bar, gulped down three glasses of wine, and was heading back for more when my ex-wife's sister, also divorced, invited me to go outside with her. She helped me realize that I was not an intruder, that I really belonged at Whitney's open house. My ex-wife was truly sorry about what had happened, and when Krista graduated, we agreed to hold the party on neutral ground where I could have my legitimate role as cohost.

Some things we sacrifice with regret, some with relief. I do not regret my leaving; I believed then—as I do now—that the consequences would have been worse for everyone if I had stayed.

Loren A. Olson, M.D.

Midlife: A Time to Grow

The rapprochement with my former wife gained momentum with my daughters' weddings. Our relationship first began to improve when Krista got married. We agreed that whatever differences remained were too insignificant to turn her dream into a nightmare. At the rehearsal, I finally understood that whatever else had happened, Krista had only one dad, and I was the only one who legitimately could walk her down the aisle. I would always be the father of the bride for my daughters. No other man could replace me. By the time Whitney was married, her mother and I could once again appreciate the things about each other that had drawn us together in the first place.

As we mature, we can begin to perceive that with loss comes an opportunity for personal growth, and failure to adapt to loss may lead to bigger losses. Our losses can strengthen us, and those experienced by people we love strengthen our capacity for compassion for others. We learn to accept that love and risk are inseparable. We finally realize that it is safe to openly express our pain and sorrow. We seek to age well, to be vibrant, well adjusted, and involved in sexually intimate relationships.

In midlife, issues that divided families can diminish in importance and be reconciled. Families of choice may even be expanded to include some members of the family of origin. It is even possible to reconcile with deceased members of the family with whom relationships may have been strained; we can learn to forgive the mistakes they made. As we mature in midlife, the issues that our parents faced in their midlives are seen from a fresh vantage point.

Each of us must direct our own development through midlife. The first step in helping a mature man in the coming-out process is to help him understand his history in a new way, to help him understand decisions and choices he's made in the past. The process of development for gay men does not end with coming out, and as we age we must incorporate positive attitudes about aging. For a man to deal well with midlife, it is important for him to have good relationships with others. He needs peers with whom he feels equal but from whom he also feels separate. He needs friends who accept and respect his individuality and are not just connected based on common activities or similarities. Maturity is a process of individuation where a person changes in relationship to himself and to the world.

185

The formula for self-esteem is having confidence in what you think and feel and responding to your own perceptions in a positive way. You can move out from behind the mask of concealment you've worn for so long, and speak with your own voice. You can learn to have confidence that your opinions are worthwhile, and trust that what you think and feel is valid. You can stop living according to the expectations of others and not wear neckties or go to parties you don't like. It is all about observing and trusting your own perceptions and developing your own vision for whatever future remains.

Chapter 10
Accidental Sex: Never Pass Up a Hard-on

God gave men both a penis and a brain, but unfortunately not enough blood supply to run both at the same time.
—Robin Williams

I blew out my knee having sex. I wish this story became more exciting at this point, but it doesn't. It was routine sex, the kind couples have after they have been together for a long time. When I injured my knee, Doug and I had been together about twenty years. Sex had grown predictable. I don't mean to sound like I'm complaining. It was good sex, just not unusual or extraordinary. Let's face it: if I hadn't injured my knee, I wouldn't be writing about it at all.

I went to an orthopedist, who confirmed that I had torn a meniscus in my right knee and would need surgery to relieve the pain. In order for my insurance to authorize payment, they demanded additional information. Their inquiry opened with, "Was this problem the result of an accident?" The sex wasn't accidental, but then I hadn't planned to tear up my knee either, so I answered, "Yes." Since I had responded affirmatively, the insurance company responded, "In order to determine if your injury is covered under the terms of your policy, we will need more information. Please explain in some detail how this accident occurred." I responded, "Having sex." I left the rest of the questions blank, signed the form, and sent it in. I received an approval for the procedure with no further questions.

Embracing Maturity

Shrinking time forces men who have passed the middle of their lives to take inventory. It seems there isn't much time remaining to catch up with where they might have expected to be. Social views, personal values, and ambitions evolve, and the focus changes from concern for self to concern for others. Men can no longer hide from the fact that they've made some bad choices and likely will do so again. Making dramatic changes causes others to accuse them of acting childishly and not dealing with reality, abandoning all moral values, and the most devastating of all, selfishly hurting their families just when they need them the most. Some even shame them for leaving the ones they love exposed and vulnerable. Helplessness, hopelessness, and a feeling of loss of control may lead to depression.

Victor Hugo said, "Forty is the old age of youth; fifty is the youth of old age." Is sixty, then, the midlife of old age? Developing pain in my arthritic right shoulder produced more of a crisis for me than coming out. I was hit with the emotional tsunami of being an old man. It began to dominate my thinking and I generalized it to everything I did. It resurrected my anxieties that had been dormant for many years about being fifteen years older than Doug. I tried Viagra for erectile difficulty, but it only made me feel as if my penis belonged to someone else; I had no pleasurable sexual sensation while using it. It helped me sustain an erection, but what's the point of an anesthetized erection?

Nothing I had done so far, including coming out at forty, had prepared me for my sixtieth birthday, the worst birthday of my life. As my sixtieth birthday approached, all I could think were negative thoughts, like "impotence," "senility," and "death." My only wish was to survive to see it. I could think of nothing to celebrate as I started sliding down the back side of my life, so I told Doug and my daughters that the only gift I wanted was for them to ignore it. I had no idea they actually would.

When the day arrived, I realized I had made a terrible mistake, but I was quite certain that Doug, the rest of my family, and friends would have ignored my plea. All day long I peered around corners for some evidence that they had remembered. Nothing. I then thought, "Since no one has said anything at all, not even happy birthday, it must mean they are planning a surprise party." I spent the rest of the day wondering just how they were going to pull it off and when people would jump out from behind the drapes and sofas and shout, "Surprise!" Nothing. Doug called me late in the afternoon and said that two of our best friends had called him and invited us to dinner. He wondered—"under the circumstances"—if I wanted to go. I strained to contain my excitement, and thought, "I knew they wouldn't let this one go by." A sense of calm settled over me because I had friends who recognized what a transitional moment this was in my life. Acting reserved and uncertain while smiling inside, I said, "Oh . . . okay."

I was so excited that I left work early and then realized that I was going to arrive at the restaurant early. Nothing spoils a surprise party more than having the guest of honor arrive before everything is in place, so to kill time, I stopped at McDonald's for a cup of coffee. I laid two one-dollar bills on the counter to pay for it, and the fourteen-year-old, pimple-faced server pushed one of them back at me, saying, "It's only thirty-nine cents—for *seniors.*" If I hadn't been so excited about the surprise party, I probably would have questioned how she'd been raised and insisted on paying full price.

I slowly drank the coffee, delaying an extra fifteen minutes, and then left to go to the restaurant. Sitting at a table for six were Doug, the other couple, and their two preteen sons, who never looked up from their video games. No tables were pushed together for a bigger group. No streamers, no confetti or party hats. No one mentioned my birthday. I still held out hope that the servers would put some crazy hat on my head, surround the table, and sing "Happy Birthday" as they brought a cake with lighted candles. I finished my meal in silence. No singing waiters, no cake. All around me I could hear doors of lost opportunities slamming shut, and I wasn't even sure that I wanted to open any of the few doors that were in front of me.

Fortunately, my sixtieth birthday lasted only a day and I was able to once again put it all in perspective. I had to count my blessings: I had Doug, a family and friends who had done exactly as I'd asked them to do, however ill advised they were by me. Sixty years plus one day old allowed me to have a whole new attitude.

But the Flesh Is Weak

Lest I appear that I don't give a damn about my physical appearance, I must admit that after receiving a small windfall of money, I began to seriously consider seeing a plastic surgeon to correct the problem of "man boobs" that had plagued me ever since early adolescence. Nurses always know who the best doctors are, so I asked a nurse, "I have a friend who is considering plastic surgery. Who would you recommend?"

Seeing right through me, she said, "Oh, are you going to do something about the hooding over your eyes? With that much baggy tissue over your eyes, it is probably obstructing your vision, and you can get Medicare to pay for it." I was doubly insulted. "Hooding? Medicare?" I was still several years away from Medicare, and I didn't even know that I had hooding! I went home and looked in the mirror, and there it was. My upper eyelids were drooping down below the eyelashes. I became obsessed with the hooding that until then I hadn't even seen. I immediately consulted the surgeon she had recommended. He told me that he could fix the hooding and the gynecomastia all in one procedure, so I scheduled the surgery. One of my friends who later had his eyes done referred to it as having his eyes circumcised.

Wrinkling and graying serve as constant reminders that my body wasn't what it once was. The mature man begins to realize that he has fallen below earlier physical peaks of performance as his bodily powers decline. Aches and pains plague him and death asserts itself. Although fortunately I have never felt as old as my birth date tells me I am, situations remind me with increasing frequency that I am growing older. Once Doug and I were buying tickets for a movie, and the attendant diplomatically asked, "Will *either* of you require the senior discount?" For a long time, I resisted accepting those discounts.

Several months ago I was using the monorail system to change planes at the Dallas–Fort Worth airport. As I pushed my way into the crowded monorail car, I saw one seat remaining. Two of us remained standing. Pain burned in the right knee that I needed replaced, and I looked at the seat. Then I looked at the other person standing, a very obese African American woman, who I can only imagine was diabetic and hypertensive. Her luggage and her shopping bags loaded her down. I looked at her and she looked at me. At the same moment we eyed the empty seat. I nodded my head for her to take it. She acknowledged my courtesy but silently motioned for me to take it. I pondered two unappealing explanations: either this is some flashback to the Jim Crow era of Southern deference of blacks to whites, or I just look very old. Unwilling to accept that my age might give me a priority for the seat, I once again insisted she take it, but she refused. Our martyrdom repaid us with pride as we both stood up for the entire trip.

A few months later while sitting at the dining room table and sifting through an enormous stack of Christmas catalogs, I burst out laughing. "Hey, Doug! Look at this." I couldn't contain myself as I looked

190

at an ad in the Vermont Country Store catalog. I had come across a tool they called the Easy Wipe Extender, a long handle with a grip on one end and a pincher mechanism on the other. I pictured some huge person overflowing a toilet seat, needing that extender to take care of one of his most intimate matters of personal cleanliness. I was still laughing as I read the description, "You fasten a piece of toilet paper to the end of it, to extend your reach so you can clean yourself properly, reaching where you can't, ensuring good personal hygiene." By then I could hardly breathe enough to ask, "Who would ever . . . ?" Remembering the lost range of motion in my right shoulder, I stopped and blurted out, "Oh, my God! *I need that now!*"

Although I had pictured someone much larger than me whose arms couldn't reach far enough around to deal with his personal hygiene, it suddenly struck me that there were other reasons why someone might have that difficulty. The tool was designed to assist older folks with a limited range of motion. I was hit with another emotional wildfire: I have become one of those people!

I injured my right shoulder when I was in my thirties, married and with two small children. It was the 1970s and we were living in Maine. All of our friends were expats of consumerism. We had gardens, heated our homes with wood, and kept small farm livestock. One of the problems with small-scale livestock farming is that you tend to fall in love with your animals and forget that the reason you raised them was to fill the freezer. One of my friends, also a psychiatrist, said he preferred to freeze other people's pets.

We had purchased two six-week-old piglets and named them Sweet and Sour. Sour had already met her predetermined fate, but I decided that Sweet should at least have an opportunity to have a litter of pigs in order to leave some legacy of her time on earth. We found a man who agreed to bring his Duroc boar over to get Sweet bred, and after a few short weeks, she had six of the cutest little pigs.

Following the instructions in *Small-Scale Pig Raising*, I knew that I needed to cut off the early teeth in the piglets' mouths when they were about two weeks old. Sweet was a dear animal who had grown to about six hundred pounds. She insisted on having her ears scratched by everyone, including a photographer who had come to take the family's Christmas photo in our pasture. Sick of Sweet's interference in the photo taking, the photographer threatened to have her made into a new camera bag. Sweet's name perfectly suited her nature because she was so docile we even allowed our daughters, aged two and five, to ride on her back.

After the piglets were a few weeks old, I climbed into the pen with Sweet and her precious piglets. I carried with me side-cutting pliers, ready to perform the minor dental procedure. As I picked up one of the little pigs, he squealed as if I were going to put an apple in his mouth and roast him right then. The power of maternal instincts exploded before me when with every ounce of strength in her body Sweet came at me like an out-of-control locomotive, demonstrating a side of her personality I'd never seen before. If anyone was going to be served on a platter, it was me.

I dropped the piglet and went flying for the nearest fence, cartwheeling over it. Excruciating pain in my right shoulder immediately announced that I had dislocated it. I began to bang my arm against the fence in an attempt to put my shoulder joint back in its socket, and I experienced relief almost instantly as I felt it slip back into place. It is interesting how midlife punishes us for those indiscretions of our youth. In my sixties the pain and restricted range of motion of my right shoulder proved to be another legacy of Sweet's brief time on earth.

> **Midlife punishes us for youthful indiscretions, and the punishment just keeps coming.**

Shortly after Sweet raised her little pigs, she was sent to slaughter. Although she had been gentle as could be, we were unwilling to have her around our little girls after that instinctual maternal attack. We brought her home from the locker in several large boxes; a six-hundred-pound pig produces a lot of meat. As Lynn fixed a meal of plate-size pork chops, the smell of the fresh pork made us both feel uneasy; freezing meat buffers the reality that the meat was once a part of a beloved pig. The children sensed our discomfort because as we sat down to eat, Whitney, our five-year-old daughter, looked at us and asked, "Is this our pig?"

Lynn and I looked at each other anxiously, turned to Whitney, and said, "Yes, this is Sweet."

Whitney took a bite, thought for a moment, and then asked, "Does she hurt when I chew her?" The remainder of Sweet stayed in the freezer for a very long time.

As one ages, each physical problem cascades into a series of physical deteriorations. As my shoulder grew more and more arthritic, I began to have more and more pain and an increasing loss of range of motion in my dominant right arm. Doug has to assist me to get my belt through the back loops of my trousers, and I have difficulty with those most intimate elements of personal hygiene. I compensated for these problems, but one problem seemed to have no redress: during sexual activity, I have pain.

Attention to my minor medical problems precipitated an absorption in other realities related to late life: fears of institutional living, financial insecurity, loss of family of origin and family of choice, lack of independence and mobility, and the possibility of discrimination in accessing social services and entitlements like Medicare. I have observed bizarre dynamics develop in families during times of grief, especially when families of origin and families of choice fight over end-of-life issues and inheritances. Although Doug and my family have always gotten along extremely well, I began to wonder how their grief following my death would alter their relationships. I wondered whether my family and our gay friends would be there to support him when I die.

As I pondered these things, I learned that the younger partner in a mixed generational gay couple in our social group was dying. Until I learned about their situation, I had never considered that I might be the one forced into the caregiving role. I could be the one left alone. Could I find the will and compassion to assume the role of Doug's care provider? Was my love strong enough? Would I begin to resent him if the demands were very high?

Erik Erikson writes that aging is just another step in personal development and cannot be understood in isolation from the rest of our lives because each stage builds on the developmental changes of previous stages. In this context each family member and each generation of the family must be understood in relation to developmental changes within the others. We expect parents to structure the development of their children, but we fail to realize that children also mold the development of their parents.

Erikson's perception of aging reassured me; this wasn't the decline of my life—it was another part of my development. For my sense of well-being, aging demands a robust and active lifestyle. I was determined that I was not going to become a depressed, lonely old queen who aged prematurely and was oversexed but incapable of having a sexual partner. I was not going to waste whatever time remained. I stopped wearing neckties. I decided I would never go to a cocktail party where I was sure there would be no one there that I really liked. I decided I would never finish a book I didn't like, nor would I ever sit through a bad lecture or a boring movie. I warned my minister that his sermons had better be good. This was the beginning of a new sense of freedom. I intended to trust my own judgment; I would take charge of my own thoughts. I began to search for ways to approach this time in my life as the beginning of the next part of my life rather than the beginning of the end of it.

The Hard Facts

Men who are seeking long-term relationships occasionally question how soon to introduce sex into a relationship. There is no universally correct answer. Many gay relationships, both romantic and platonic, have been established following a casual sexual encounter. Doug and I spent the first night we met together, and we have devoted almost every night in the twenty-four years since we met to each other. Doug said, tongue in cheek, that gay couples should mark their anniversary as the second night they sleep together; the first night is a hook-up, but the second is the beginning of a new relationship.

After several years of being together, sexual excitement ebbs in all relationships. I don't mean to imply that sex is reduced to monotony, but as couples become more and more familiar with each other, sex doesn't hold many surprises. The dopamine rushes don't match those when the relationship was young. Sexual frequency declines as the length of the relationship extends. Whether gay or straight, the more time partners share a sexual relationship, the more perfunctory it can become.

Dan Ariely, who wrote *The Upside of Irrationality: The Unexpected Benefits of Defying Logic at Work and at Home*, addresses the issue of "hedonic adaptation" or "emotional leveling." He describes how pleasure can deviate in either a positive or a negative direction from the baseline, but over time always returns to the baseline. About three months after I'd purchased my most recent new car, I began throwing empty Diet Coke cans in the backseat, just like I did with the old car. Neither the excitement of new romance nor the painful consequences of a broken

194

relationship endure forever. The inability to accept the hedonic adaptation in relationships condemns a person to always chasing the high that comes with the next new man, only to be disappointed when the high once again doesn't last.

Like a stone thrown into a pond, the effects of my knee injury rippled far beyond the point where it broke the surface: my body was aging. I thought about sex less frequently, and sometimes when I thought about sex, I tried to dismiss it. When there was a choice between sleep and sex, I opted for sleep. I had more difficulty achieving and maintaining an erection, and when I lost an erection during sex, I felt defeated, and I beat up on myself pretty severely. I became dissatisfied not only with my sex life but also with my life in general. According to a 2008 study by Carmita Abdo published in the *Journal of Sexual Medicine*, erectile dysfunction and reduced sexual satisfaction are linked to lower life satisfaction and a compromised quality of life. Sexual dysfunction lowers self-esteem and can lead to depression, anxiety, anger, and shame. It also results in obsessive concerns about performance.

Scientists neglect the study of human sexuality. Funding isn't available and subjects who will speak openly about their sexuality are difficult to find. We know very little about some of the fundamental questions related to sexual desire and arousal and how desire affects judgment. The origins of sexual identity are heatedly debated, and studies of homosexual arousal, desire, and sexual activity make people green about the gills. In particular, we know almost nothing about why people who understand sexual risks choose to act in

Sexuality exceeds the boundaries of a universal biological drive.

ways that are potentially destructive. Freud and Kinsey both hypothesized that sex is a universal drive, and now neuro-imaging has substantiated an anatomical location for it. But can science really answer the questions "Who am I?" and "Why do I do the things I do?"

Sexuality exceeds the limits of just being a universal biological drive. Cultural forces shape it, socialization modifies it, and environmental influences impact it. Ariely wrote, "In the same way that the chemical composition of broccoli or pecan pie is not going to help us better understand what the real thing tastes like, breaking people up into their individual attributes is not very helpful in figuring out what it might be like to spend time or live with them."

Late-Blooming Gay Baby Boomers

Back in the days before reliable birth control existed, abstinence was promoted for all adolescents, as well as for adults, as a means to limit family size. We were admonished to build a strong family: "Don't go getting some girl pregnant you would never want to be the mother of your children. Your life will be miserable." While I was in medical school, the contraceptive pill was introduced, and women were finally released to have sex for pleasure, too. Now I had no reason to hold back, but in reality, I lost one more excuse for avoiding sex with women.

I tried to fall in love with Kathy, a nurse, when we were both twenty-three. Her doctor did not buy into the "sex for pleasure" revolution for single women. He refused to put her on the Pill. Even though her doctor didn't sanction it, everything pointed in the direction that we would have sex anyway. I went into the neighborhood drugstore to purchase some condoms. It was a different era. No one said the word "pregnancy." Instead it was either "in a family way" or just simply "PG." Kotex boxes were wrapped in plain paper, and condoms were hidden behind the pharmacy counter.

I nervously approached the counter of the pharmacy and said to the pharmacist, "I need some condoms."

The pharmacist, who was a much older man, asked, "What size do you want?"

Not knowing how to answer, I thought of locker room comparisons, and I said, "Average." I wanted to add, "at least."

"Lubricated?"

Again, not knowing the answer, I responded, "Yes."

"Reservoir tip?"

"Yes." If his goal was to make me uncomfortable, he succeeded.

Kathy lived with another nurse in a one-bedroom apartment. That night with her roommate asleep in their bedroom, Kathy and I began to get intimate on the couch. She lay across my right arm, immobilizing it. I'd never put on a condom before, so with my left hand I searched to retrieve the foil package from my pocket. I could not tear the package with one hand, so I resorted to using my teeth. My clumsiness embarrassed me as I struggled to roll the condom onto my erect penis with one hand. It kept popping off before I could get it unrolled, and I was pretty sure that if I tried much longer, I would cum before I got the damn thing on.

I began to wish that I had bought extra condoms to practice this exercise a little earlier. Now was not the time for a condom dress rehearsal; it was the main event. Did all of this come easily to other men? Men fix machines; they should know how to condomize a penis. I wondered if I could have numbed my excitement if I had masturbated before the date.

For the first time, at age twenty-three, I was having sex with a woman. As I began to move my hips in the much-anticipated way, her roommate walked out of the bedroom through the tiny living room where we were and into the open kitchen. She opened a Coke, lit a cigarette, and then walked back into the bedroom without saying a word. The following morning I stared at myself in the mirror and examined my chest hairs to see if they had grown. I wore a smile fit to accompany a swagger. I had finally crossed to the other side, but inside my head I could hear the haunting voice of Peggy Lee singing, "Is that all there is? Is that all there is, my friend?" I broke off the relationship with Kathy shortly thereafter, but my loneliness led me back to her. Was Kathy my hedonic baseline, the baseline to which I would keep returning? After a few weeks I called her once again. She hesitated, and then made me promise that if she started seeing me again I would not end it as I had before. Desperate to have someone in my life, I agreed but immediately realized that I had made a very bad decision. I ended it once again.

While I was dating Kathy, her roommate got pregnant. Back then, single women who were pregnant took up residence in homes for unwed mothers. Omaha had three such homes (they all went out of business shortly after introduction of the Pill). Medical students delivered most of the babies born to the expectant young mothers. I discovered there was a possibility that I might deliver Kathy's roommate's baby. Her pregnancy provided a lingering reminder of my mother's admonishments about premarital sex. Her roommate relinquished custody of her infant, as most of the young mothers did at the time, whether they wished to or not.

I often wondered about whether those adopted children would search for their birth parents, and I felt a great deal of empathy toward them, because I had had my own "search" to know my father, after he died. As fate would have it, I would indeed cross paths with just such an adopted child.

Twenty years later, and a few months after Doug and I had been living together, I received several phone messages at home from a woman whose name I didn't recognize. She persisted in her attempts to reach me. One evening she called while I was home.

The young woman asked, "Are you Dr. Olson?"

"I am."

"Did you graduate from the University of Nebraska Medical School?"

"Yes."

"In 1968?"

"Yes."

"Did you know a woman named Barbara?"

"Yes."

"I think you're my father."

Stunned, for a moment I could say nothing. Then I stuttered, "I don't think that's possible." The shock of what had just happened made me sound much more tentative than I actually felt. The list of women with whom I could have fathered a child before I was married was very short: Kathy. Even though I knew I couldn't possibly be her father, I empathized with her need to know who he was. As we talked, and I tried to assure her that I wasn't her father, her disappointment grew increasingly evident. I knew she thought I was lying. For a moment I thought, "Perhaps I should tell her I am her father because I know what it's like not to have one." Her disappointment evolved into anger, and she hung up. I never heard from her again.

As I was writing this chapter on sexuality, in the back of my mind was an accusation made by a young gay man. He had been quite harsh in his criticism, saying that it wasn't possible that I had no idea I was gay until I was forty. He went on to say that my marriage was a sham and that I had just been a hypocrite using my wife and kids to protect my secret. I began to wonder if he might have been right. I decided I needed to know from my wife how she had experienced our sex life; basically, I wanted to know whether she felt I was totally present in our sexual relationship. After some difficult years immediately following the divorce, our relationship has become one where we both can accept some responsibility for the failure of the marriage and no longer blame the other. I decided to ask her how she felt about my sexual performance while we were married.

She readily agreed to talk with me about it. I asked her if my lack of confidence about being a man was apparent to her during the years of our marriage. She responded, "When we were first married, we were both sexually inexperienced. I believed that what we had was as good as it could get. You were always as sensitive to my needs as you were to your own. Now that we're older and more experienced, I *know* you were an excellent lover." She had no reason not to be honest with me. I came away from that conversation knowing that my anxieties about whether I had been a good lover, whether I had been man enough sexually in our relationship, were unwarranted. My shoulders felt broader and the swagger returned to my gait. I was reassured that indeed we had loved each other—and in many ways we still do. She did not feel that I had used her to shield myself against the assaults from my own doubts. As my anxieties lifted, I could return to my writing.

As the Twig Is Bent

Men typically believe they know far more about their sexual functioning than they actually do. They also fail to admit that they don't know much, even when they don't. Drive, vigor, and performance form the core of men's sexuality. Society dictates that a man must always be ready, always be successful, and never leave a job half finished. A man fails with anything less. Although men learn the basics of sex experientially, they often do not understand some of the common explanations for failure and how their sexuality changes as they age. In order to understand sexual dysfunction, one must first grasp the fundamentals of normal sexual function. Four major "domains" constitute male sexual response: sex drive, erectile functioning, ejaculatory functioning, and general sexual satisfaction. Below are the concerns older men have about each domain.

Areas of concern for mature men regarding their sexual functioning:

1. Sex drive—frequency and intensity of sexual interest
2. Erectile function—the most common area of concern

3. Ejaculatory functioning—usually of little concern
4. General satisfaction with sexual activity—although sex drive, erectile intensity, and ejaculatory function decline with age, those changes do not significantly impact mature men's general satisfaction with their sex lives

The Massachusetts Male Aging Study (MMAS), a rare random sampling of ordinary men who lived in the community, studied a complex set of sexual variables, both physical (erections, masturbation) and emotional/cognitive (desires, fantasies, satisfaction). The study, conducted from 1987 to 2004, found that older men reported lower erectile function, including less frequent erections, fewer morning erections, and trouble achieving and maintaining erections. Prevalence of erectile dysfunction (ED) increases with age, but it is not an inevitable consequence of aging.

Most of the age-related effects on drive, erections, and ejaculation begin past the age of fifty and increase over time. Although sexual function declines with age, sexual satisfaction often does not. Men do not seem to worry much about ejaculation, even though in older men ejaculation diminishes and sometimes may not even occur at all during sexual activity. In the MMAS, men in their sixties reported levels of satisfaction with their sex life and partners at about the same level as men in their forties.

> **Men in their sixties have levels of sexual satisfaction at about the same level as men in their forties.**

Aging brings on changes, but not all of the changes are bad. Body changes, hormonal changes, medication, disability or illness, change of sex partner, and changes in life responsibilities may all interfere with sexual function, but they do not eliminate sexual pleasure. In reporting on their work in *Sexuality across the Life Course*, McKinlay and Feldman cautioned that older men should not be held to a level of interest and performance more appropriate to younger men. Health care providers and therapists must be taught that older men are not only interested in sex but also capable of having good sex. That said, goals must be realistically set.

Plenty of studies have shown that many men in their late seventies and eighties are sexually active. As we age, lifestyles and relationships begin to change, but some things actually get better. For older men, frequency of sex diminishes, but when men learn that sensuality, touch, and emotional intimacy are all forms of sexual expression, they discover that sex can be satisfying and can be even better than it was when they were younger and equated good sex only with a powerful orgasm. The younger men I interviewed generally believed that older men emphasize emotional intimacy more than genital sex. They begin to cherish their relationships and put more time into them than younger men do. Although penetrating sex and ejaculation may become less frequent, kissing, caressing, and more prolonged sexual intimacy may contribute to greater sexual satisfaction and quality of life in old age. It may take a little longer to stoke the fire, but the flames may go higher.

For all men, sexual performance consists of a complex interaction of mood, health, thought, and physiological mechanisms. Sexual response occurs in five steps: excitement, plateau, climax, resolution, and refractory period. Sex drive is an innate force that motivates and impels a person toward sex partners and relationships. Often nudity, erotica, or the prospect of a willing partner inaugurate the period of sexual excitement and provoke the thought, "I need to have sex."

Sexual excitement taps into the memory banks of the amygdala and the hippocampus of the brain, producing arousal. If sex were purely a rational act, we would foresee all of the potential alternatives, analyze and calculate their value, and choose to respond in a way that maximizes our immediate and long-term interests. Instead, when these areas engage the prefrontal cortex to plan the appropriate response, our hormones often show an appalling lack of respect for the logic and reasoning of the prefrontal cortex.

During the excitement phase, a man experiences the sensation that his penis is beginning to swell. Physical touch to an erogenous area enhances arousal. Dopamine, the "pleasure molecule," floods into the brain. As excitement intensifies and as prospects of success increase, the penis grows in size and firmness according to the degree of stimulation. Increased blood flow to the penis engorges the spongy tissue on the underside of the penis that contains the urethra, which leads from the bladder to the opening in the head of the penis. In response to touch and sometimes to arousal alone, the scrotum pulls the enlarging testicles toward the body. The tension of the muscles in the body increases, heart rate accelerates, and blood pressure rises.

Stages of male sexual response:
1. Excitement—As blood accumulates in the penis, the penis becomes larger and more erect and the testicles may be pulled toward the body.
2. Plateau—The time between the full engorgement of the penis until climax when pre-ejaculate (pre-cum) is released from the opening of the urethra in the head of the penis.
3. Climax—A feeling of "ejaculatory inevitability" is followed by orgasm, which may or may not include ejaculation of semen from the penis.
4. Resolution—A return to the unexcited state.
5. Refractory—A period of time during which restimulation cannot occur.

During the plateau phase, the head of the penis continues to enlarge and the testicles are drawn even closer to the body. A clear lubricating seminal fluid called pre-ejaculate or "pre-cum" begins to flow at varying rates from the head of the penis. A big price is paid for mechanical and indifferent sex. Men who learn to prolong the plateau phase with extended periods of cuddling and body contact greatly increase their pleasure. At first, sexual pleasure does not insist on pushing one toward climax or orgasm, but similar to a tightening spring, the strength of the urge intensifies. Then, like a set mousetrap, the spring seeks to uncoil. This need to release the tension interferes with rational thought and has ensnared countless numbers of men.

As the plateau stage progresses, a man experiences a feeling deep within the pelvis that orgasm is on its way. It is followed by a sense of ejaculatory inevitability, a feeling often celebrated with a verbal announcement. Almost immediately the genital muscles begin to contract, expelling semen with varying degrees of force through the urethra. During the resolution phase, blood leaves the penis in a process called detumescence. The penis shrinks to about half its erect size. Sexual activity concludes with a refractory period during which no amount of stimulation can produce an erection.

Maturity modifies these stages. In adolescence, young men are in a perpetual state of excitement with an almost petrified erection. A young man might walk around most of the day with an erection, even when it is quite embarrassing. As men mature, the excitement phase is longer and less intense; it generally requires richer fantasies and a higher degree of direct stimulation to the genital area. Unfortunately, it is also more easily interrupted.

An older man, if distracted during the excitement phase, may lose some or all of his erection several times, only to regain it again once he experiences a renewed sense of sexual excitement. Often, however, loss of an erection replaces excitement with despair. For an older man, orgasms shorten and they lack youthful insistence. Expulsive force and volume of seminal fluid decrease with age, and detumescence occurs more quickly. The refractory period, during which no erection can occur, lasts longer. One comedian joked that his wife wanted to have sex every day for thirty days to try to get pregnant. He responded, "I'm thirty-nine years old. The only way I could have sex thirty times in thirty days would be with thirty different women."

Fatigue, work, depression, finances, and illness also undermine excitement. Although at first I didn't recognize it, pain from my torn meniscus should have been only a temporary distraction. Instead, fears about failure displaced all sense of pleasure. My focus shifted from pleasure to ruminating about my performance failure.

The Blue Magic Bullet

Erectile difficulty happens occasionally to every man. Impotence is the persistent inability to get and hold an erection of adequate firmness to permit satisfactory sexual performance in the absence of any significant psychological problems. Although the term "impotence" remains in use outside of the United States, in America in the 1990s it was deemed pejorative. It connoted weakness rather than just erectile dysfunction. Men began to dread this indictment because it hints at a permanent loss of all masculine capabilities. After former senator Bob Dole became the pitchman for the blue, diamond-shaped Viagra pill, erectile dysfunction—now just ED—generally replaced the term impotence. ED implies reversibility, and the term has attenuated the emotional significance of erectile difficulties.

Fifty million American men bear the diagnosis of ED. While a man who fails to have an erection more than 50 percent of the time carries a clinical diagnosis of ED, a man who fails to have an erection less than 20 percent of the time does not. ED occurs when something interferes with the reflex activation of the system that enhances blood flow to the penis. These are often due to physical changes in the body, such as vascular insufficiency, neurological problems, diabetes, high blood pressure, lack of exercise, medications, hormonal changes, alcohol and drugs, and cigarette smoking. Psychological problems rather than physical ones account for about two-thirds of sexual dysfunction. The negative impact of ED on quality of life is independent of its explanation.

Some reports suggest that ED occurs in as high as 90 percent of depressed people, most commonly expressed as a lack of interest in sexual activity. Unfortunately, many of the medications used to treat depression also reduce libido. Other psychological factors that impact libido include a lack of good sexual information, negative attitudes toward sexual expression, low levels of general happiness, and low self-esteem.

The length and the quality of a relationship are also important psychological factors. Unresolved anger, especially if directed at the partner, can lead to significant problems with ED. People who are passive also suffer more problems. Some struggle with ED because of the lack of an available partner.

Performance anxiety significantly complicates sexual functioning. Men who are preoccupied with performance to the exclusion of emotional intimacy may be devastated by the loss of an erection during sex. Social messages browbeat men into believing that real men don't fail at sex. When performance is the primary criterion for judging success of male sexual functioning, erectile failure generates considerable anxiety. Anxiety, acting like an anti-aphrodisiac, further blocks the spontaneous flow of sexual thoughts and feelings.

It is not surprising that men sometimes refer to their penises as "tools," because in male sexuality the emphasis is on instrumentality. Functional measures and frequency count more than intimacy, and the bonds of sexual connectedness dominate social ideals of masculinity. Memories of earlier failures replace excitement with anxiety, causing men to avoid sex and another possible failure. After having erectile failure, men frequently begin to perform sexual autopsies on their performance, and pleasurable sexual interaction becomes virtually impossible. Have you ever been afraid you were about to run out of gas, so you drove faster and faster to get to your destination? It is a counterproductive strategy. Sexual performance anxiety is like putting the pedal to the metal. Many men, after they have that fleeting fear of losing their erection, force sex faster and faster, further compounding the problem. Unless this emotional ambush is resisted, it can lead to loss of self-esteem, relationship discord, and greater sexual dysfunction.

After I tore up my knee having sex, a complex set of factors blunted my sexual functioning. A lack of confidence in being a man formed the bedrock of my difficulties. I experienced both the physical changes of aging along with a preoccupation about the meaning of those changes. My worries expanded beyond the boundaries of reality. Instead of recognizing that my erections could be restored, fear of failure immediately set in. I obsessively analyzed my failures. I focused solely on the difficulty with my physical performance to the exclusion of the joy of emotional intimacy. Everything I did accelerated me toward failure.

Preoccupation with erectile functioning has not gone unnoticed by the health products industry. One young man, writing on a health blog about the blue Viagra pill, praised it as a "wonder drug." He said that it has brought about a change in sexual morality and sexual behavior throughout the world. "This isn't just another drug; it's the magic bullet we've been waiting for." Drug representatives detailing Viagra have even been robbed of their samples. Following its introduction, the brand name, Viagra, immediately became a part of our sexual lexicon.

Viagra was a drug marketer's dream. With its promise to allow men to have sex anywhere, anytime, and with anyone, Viagra use exploded. With the iconic image of the Marlboro man fixed in our brains, men began to use the blue magic bullet not only for ED but also to guarantee a world-class erection every time. The promotion of sexual enhancement products burgeoned as the industry preyed upon our fears. Pharmaceutical companies added Cialis and Levitra to the formularies. The Federal Drug Administration mandated that product information contain a precaution about priapism (a continuous and painful erection). Clever marketing converted what is seen as one of the risks of these products into an apparent strength. Men began to hope they might be the one to have an erection that lasted three hours and fifty-nine minutes.

According to Dr. Abraham Morgentaler, a urologist, the frequency of priapism "is vanishingly low." As use of Viagra expanded beyond ED to include sexual enhancement, some men have conditioned themselves to believe they cannot have an acceptable erection without it.

The Renaissance Man

All that gay men think and talk about is sex, or so some believe. Although we struggle to shed that stereotype, in some ways sex does define us. We're each vastly unique but do have one thing in common: we want to have sex with someone of our own gender. Older men who are just beginning to explore their homosexuality may experience sexual excitement to a much greater degree than they did in their familiar heterosexual relationships. After I accepted my homosexuality, I experienced sexuality in a new and exciting way. I thought of sex constantly, and I began to feel as sexual as I did when I was a teenager. I was eager to make up for lost time. For men of all ages who come out, sexuality overshadows everything as they experience what has been referred to as a "coming-out crash." The penis is turned on autopilot as hormones erase all rational thought. In his role as Edward Cole in *The Bucket List*, Jack Nicholson advised older men of three things: Never pass up a bathroom. Never pass up a hard-on. Never trust a fart. The older man who is just coming out knows precisely what he means.

> **Mature men who are just exploring their homosexuality experience sex as new and exciting, much as they did when they were adolescents.**

When I met Alfredo, I had been married for sixteen years. Although I had a good sexual relationship with my wife, by then it had become somewhat routine and predictable. My relationship with Alfredo was an entirely new sexual experience, with passion and intensity. Once while driving down the road in Des Moines with Alfredo next to me, I reached over and began to touch him. As he responded to my touch, he began to touch me as well. As we continued to drive down the street, we opened each other's flies and our arousal quickly intensified. Finally, the spring on my sexual mousetrap was so tight that I knew there was only one way to release the tension. I pulled the car off the road, drove into a wooded park, and we ran to a patch of weeds while holding up our still-open trousers.

When I arrived home, I realized that I had lost my wallet while my pants were around my ankles. Having no excuse to leave my home that night and drive thirty miles back to Des Moines, I waited nervously until the next day. The next morning, I found my wallet still in the weeds, with only a few bits of evidence of our lovemaking. Our relationship had passion, although it lacked trust and the ability to resolve conflict, which are the characteristics of more mature relationships.

The late English novelist Aldous Huxley is quoted as saying, "Habit converts luxurious enjoyments into dull and daily necessities." Through the process of hedonic adaptation, the excitement of any new relationship returns to baseline. But after my relationship with Alfredo I established an entirely new baseline.

The Anti-Aging Tonic

Popular culture equates testosterone with virility and a macho male physique. A doctor speaking at a medical conference I attended hyped testosterone replacement therapy (TRT) as "the amazing, medically proven" way to reverse aging. He promised that it would revitalize sexuality, strength, and stamina. He assured us, "You'll lose weight and gain muscle. Your memory and mental focus will improve." Apparently, TRT guarantees us that we will all bathe in the fountain of youth in the twenty-first century. But growth in its reputation and its increased use has outstripped scientific evidence of its potential benefits and risks.

Testosterone, sometimes referred to as androgen, is a hormone produced in large amounts in the testicles (testes), with smaller amounts produced in the distant adrenal glands. As anyone who has been an adolescent boy knows, production peaks in the teens and early twenties. In high school, I would sit in the doctor's waiting room before my football physicals, begging God to take away my erection before seeing the doctor. Men don't run out of testosterone, but it does decline with age. Levels of testosterone continue to remain high between ages twenty and thirty, but somewhere about thirty-five levels begin to decline and continue to slide as we age. Diseases like diabetes and liver disease, chronic alcohol use, and some cancer treatments also reduce testosterone levels. Symptoms attributed to testosterone deficiency include decreased sexual function, lower vitality, loss of muscle mass and strength, increased fat, depression, anemia, and cardiovascular disease. These symptoms, however, can occur with normal levels of testosterone, and in some cases the symptoms may not occur even when testosterone levels are low.

Dr. Abraham Morgentaler, in his book *Testosterone for Life: Recharge Your Vitality, Sex Drive, Muscle Mass, and Overall Health*, writes, "Testosterone is critical, not only for how the brain responds to sexual thoughts and stimulation, but also for the proper function of the penis, by affecting its ability to get hard, to release the necessary chemical signals, and to maintain the proper types of cells that are essential for good erectile function." The possibility that TRT might be an anti-aging tonic appeals particularly to older men, whose sexual functioning sags along with their muscles and energy.

Symptoms of testosterone deficiency:
- Decreased sexual function
- Lower vitality
- Loss of muscle mass and strength
- Increased fat mass
- Mood changes and depression

Doctors debate the topic of male menopause. I don't like the term because the physiological changes that occur for men are distinctly different than they are for women. In women, menopause occurs when hormone production stops completely, ending their period of fertility. For men, hormone production falls, but it does not stop. Testosterone helps maintain sex drive and sperm production well into late life, and most men are capable of impregnating well into late life.

When we think about the characteristics of testosterone, we usually think about its sexual power rather than its potential impact on mental processes. But all of our body's attributes change with age, and unfortunately mental functions are no exception. We can learn new truths; it just takes a little longer. New information is processed less carefully and details often slip away. Memory is the most fragile of mental functioning, and testosterone and memory begin their decline at about the same time.

In my sixth decade, I was hit by an emotional tsunami. The decline in my sexual performance resurrected my earlier fears about unfinished masculinity. Men fix machines and they don't fail at sex. Worries about failing at sex just about guaranteed that I would fail. I had never experienced a significant loss of sexual interest or satisfaction. Then I remembered the presentation on testosterone and began to consider that lowered testosterone levels might account for some of the problems I was having.

My doctor determined that my testosterone levels were borderline (I had gone in for a routine physical and asked my doctor to help me determine if testosterone replacement might help with some of the sexual, mental, and physical dullness I had been feeling). "I think it would be worth a trial of replacement therapy," my doctor told me. I readily agreed.

Laboratory studies often ordered prior to initiating testosterone replacement therapy:
- Testosterone level
- Thyroid function
- Luteinizing hormone (a pituitary hormone that tells the testes to produce more testosterone)
- Prostate-specific antigen (PSA)

In many cases TRT helps relieve the symptoms of testosterone decline, whether it comes from aging or other causes, but it remains unclear whether or not restoring testosterone to youthful levels is of benefit. In addition, my doctor informed me, therapy may restore testosterone levels without improving the symptoms attributed to testosterone decline. Only a few small short-term studies have examined whether therapy might improve mental function in healthy older men, but studies have found some connection between higher testosterone levels and better performance on cognitive tests. The primary impact of TRT on sexual function is related to increased sexual drive. Having more interest in sex has an added benefit of making us feel more sexual, and helps restore some loss of confidence in our sexuality. Larger randomized clinical trials in older men will need to be completed before we can determine with confidence the benefits and safety of TRT. As with all medications, the balance of risks and benefits, personal preference, side effects, and costs must be considered.

There are several treatment options for testosterone replacement therapy (TRT): injections, patches, or a gel that is spread on the skin. One of the most effective and convenient forms of treatment is injection of long-acting testosterone pellets under the skin of the buttocks. TRT by injection is given about once every two weeks, and treatment produces good levels of testosterone for three to five months. However, injections are inconvenient and therapeutic levels and symptom relief may fluctuate between the injections.

Patches are applied nightly. The gel is rubbed onto the skin of the abdomen, chest, arms, and shoulders. The gel is less irritating than the patches, but it is possible to transfer the TRT agent to a sexual partner, or even a pet, through skin-to-skin contact. The buccal treatment is a pill that is applied to the upper gums.

I opted for the TRT gel. Almost immediately, I began to feel some improvement. How much of my response was placebo and how much was an effect of the TRT is hard to say. I knew that something convincing was happening. I thought more about sex, I was more successful at it, and the success restored my confidence. Even my aches and pains became more of a nuisance than a barrier to sex. I began to believe I could ride out the tsunami.

Potential Risks and Benefits of Testosterone Replacement Therapy

Potential Benefits	Potential Risks
Improved muscle mass and strength	Possibility of stimulation of prostate cancer
Thickened body hair and increased oiliness of skin	Noncancerous enlargement of the prostate and difficulty with urination
Reduced depression and irritability	Testicular shrinkage and reduced sperm production
Improved sexual drive	Breast enlargement
Increased bone density	Stimulation of breast cancer if present
Increased energy	Aggravation of sleep apnea
	Potential heart problems
	Acne

A physician must carefully monitor progress on TRT, especially for those who are taking insulin, steroids, or medications that cause blood clotting. Other health care providers should be informed that TRT is being given. Just as Viagra is not a magic bullet, TRT is not gunpowder for the problems of aging. Lifestyle changes that focus on diet and exercise must accompany TRT. When sexual dysfunction is primarily related to psychological factors, counseling may be required and in some cases antidepressants may be indicated.

An entire industry has developed around TRT, but it will never return you to your sexual prime. TRT may cost several hundred dollars a month, and it may not be covered by all insurance plans. Claims for feeling sexier, stronger, and healthier are exaggerated, but claims about reversing low energy and improving muscle strength and libido have been proven. Improvement in sexual performance creates improved mood and a sense of well-being. An improved attitude in itself contributes to better sexual performance. TRT didn't fix my aging body, but awakening with morning wood brings a smile to my face.

Thin Slicing

Writing in the *New York Times* in 2004, Benedict Carey said, "Sexual taste is a wild card, in short, and one that many people would prefer be kept face down." Research on the subject of why people are attracted to a particular type of individual has reached a consensus about a few things:

1. Physical attractiveness is viewed as important for friendship, marriage, and financial success.
2. When a person is physically attractive, his or her attractiveness is usually apparent at a very young age.
3. Younger people are considered more attractive than older people.
4. Age has a greater impact in women than it does in men; it also has a greater impact in gay men than straight men.

Even as we discover more about the biology of the brain, the concept of the unconscious is experiencing a renaissance. As Malcolm Gladwell suggests in *Blink: The Power of Thinking Without Thinking*, we always believe more data will lead to better decisions, but excessive analysis paralyzes us. We undervalue decisions based on feelings. Gladwell states that the unconscious finds patterns in situations and behaviors based on little information, something he calls "thin slicing." The unconscious leaps to conclusions much like a computer that quickly processes a great deal of data. Gladwell believes decisions made very quickly can be every bit as good as decisions made cautiously and deliberately.

Most animals choose their mates in a nonrandom fashion through assortative mating. Some animals favor mates with certain characteristics, e.g. traits that they themselves possess, or alternatively, traits they feel they lack. In this process, they reduce their field of selection of potential mates. Similarly, whether in a gay bar or an Internet chat room, a gay man will scan his environment. Within a few seconds, he will unconsciously "thin slice" all available men, narrowing his choices into his short list of prospects—without ever realizing he has been engaged in a selection process.

To impress a potential mate, male animals spread their feathers or puff up their chests to appear to be the strongest, most masculine, and most attractive they can be. In their mating rituals, men also exaggerate their virtues and minimize their weaknesses and vulnerabilities. They deceive others about things they feel make them unattractive. For gay men, cruising for casual sex frequently focuses on something sexually explicit—not unlike heterosexual casual sex. When the pursued man responds in a sexual way, sexual arousal is heightened. The interaction progressively focuses more and more on sex, dislocating any rational thought. Any exchange of information about who the two are as individuals is ended. Those who are searching for a relationship that is more than just sex may be left feeling a little empty.

On a business trip to Washington, D.C., I left an O Street male strip club late at night to return to my hotel. A younger man who had left a little before me walked in the opposite direction. He looked over his shoulder at me, sensing that I was looking back at him. He walked a few more paces, stopped, and looked back at me again. I was still watching him. He then leaned against a car, lit a cigarette, and continued to look in my direction. In this brief nonverbal mating dance, we had communicated just enough.

Men with Rounded Corners

One tall and handsome lean young man told me about his sexual attractions. He said he is only attracted to heavier men with big bellies and hairy chests. Unconscious forces operating in his brain "thin slice" his sexual attractions only to older men with mature bodies; younger men hold no appeal. What both may fail to recognize is that their own physical appearance may be exactly what will show up in the other's thin slices.

Fifteen years separate the ages of my husband, Doug, and me, but we rarely talk about it. When we first started seeing each other more than twenty years ago, I was quite certain that he would sooner or later dump me for a younger man. One day I mentioned my concerns to him, and he replied, "I've always been attracted to older men. As a kid, I wasn't attracted to my friends; I was attracted to their fathers." At first I had trouble believing that, but I rarely thought about it again, at least until recently as I approached retirement.

Getting older magnified the age difference. Dormant and patched-over fears of abandonment crept back into my mind. Would Doug jump ship for a younger man? If I became physically unable to be his lover, would he find what gentle folks call a "friend with benefits," but what gay men often call a "fuck-buddy"? Would his loyalty shift to this new playmate? If I need care that I could not reciprocate at some point, would he begin to resent me? How would we deal with the financial problems if I were to retire sooner than he did? Could he find a job in his mid-fifties? Would he be able to manage both a job and any care I might need? What if he died first? In Tim Turner's play *Out Late*, Charles says to the much younger Evan, "I sure wish I'd met you thirty years ago," to which Evan responds, "Thirty years ago, you would have been too young for me, and I wouldn't have been born." Intergenerational relationships (IGRs) are relationships between two men whose ages are separated by a difference of at least fifteen to twenty years, and the younger man is at least the age of consent. There are really no meaningful statistics about how often IGRs occur between men. Most in the straight world don't know that intergenerational gay relationships exist, and many in the gay community don't understand them.

Almost daily, younger men question me, "Why do I find myself only attracted to men who are older than me?" Young men who prefer older men are often backed into a corner to defend their choice, but they don't understand their attraction either. Frequently they have looked for an answer in their relationship with their father or their grandfather, just as I had done for an explanation of my attraction to men. Sometimes they say, "My relationship with my father (or grandfather) was so wonderful; I just want to try to recreate that with a man." At other times, they say, "I had no relationship with a father figure, and I think my attraction to older men is to fill that void." When there are two contradictory hypotheses for the same phenomenon, looking for the explanation in their relationship with their father is too simplistic.

Family and friends confront them with their belief that the relationship cannot be based on love but must be based on other ulterior motives. Often fully capable of taking care of themselves, these men are hurt by accusations that they are looking for a "sugar daddy." As I talked with young men, I repeatedly heard things like, "I don't need stuff! I want more than an orgasm. I want a relationship with someone who is sensitive, caring, and romantic, self-assured and satisfied with his life." All stereotypes have validity for some, but not all. While there certainly are young men seeking a sugar daddy and older men seeking an Adonis-like, aggressive sex partner, people mistakenly assume that all IGRs are based on exploitation. Younger men are accused of exploiting the financial security of the older man, and the older man is accused of wanting a trophy.

One young gay man has never been attracted to men of his own age. He explained, "All those guys who are under sixty years old might as well have vaginas because I have no interest in them." One of my gay friends is in a relationship with a man who is forty years older than he is, and he's tired of defending his relationship. Although his family has come to accept their relationship, his gay friends are the most critical. One of his friends asked him, "What does a young, good-looking guy like you see in an old man who is well past his expiration date?"

I must confess I have been guilty of asking young men about their interest in older men, too. Even though I am now married to a man fifteen years younger than me, I still had difficulty understanding IGRs. Why would a young man who works hard to achieve that hard-bodied, gay ideal find himself physically attracted to someone who looks like Dick Cheney, politics aside? We demand an explanation from these younger men, but why does it matter? A young man I spoke to said, "I am going through a kind of second coming out and have started psychoanalysis in order to understand my patterns of relationships and my choice of partners, who are always much older than me." It is unlikely he'll find the answer. Older men are rarely asked to defend their choice of a younger man. The older man has chosen up; the younger man chose down. The fact is that research hasn't determined why we are drawn to the people we're attracted to, and most likely, the explanations are very complex.

When I asked one young man about his attraction to older men he replied, "I like older men because they have all of their corners rounded off." It brought to mind a class I'd taken on antiques. The instructor suggested that buying old furniture is better than buying new. "You hate to get a new piece scratched, but a mark on an old piece of furniture just adds character."

David Sedaris, writing in *Me Talk Pretty One Day*, states, "When asked what we wanted to be when we grew up, we hid the truth and listed who we wanted to sleep with when we grew up. A policeman or a fireman or one of those guys who works with high-tension wires." The young men I interviewed who are attracted to older men say they have been aware of their attraction from the very first time they recognized sexual attraction of any kind. They say that the attraction persists, even as they become older. One man said, "It sucks because I have buried three of my lovers." Another older man joked, "I could do all my cruising in a nursing home."

> **"I like older men because they have all of their corners rounded off."**

Older men who are attracted to younger men can't explain their choice either, although they often say that temperamentally they feel much younger than their chronological age. If an older man is attracted to a masculine man with ripped muscles, it's reasonable that he would find it difficult to believe that the muscular young man could find his too fat, too short, too wrinkled body attractive. Some older men resist the idea that younger men will find them attractive even to the point of being suspicious of the younger man's motives. One commented, "I do not need to raise another son. I don't need a helpless kid to protect." Other older men express fears of abandonment because they may be unable to satisfy the younger man's greater sexual appetites. Younger men frequently respond that they find the other essential characteristics of the relationship of more importance than the sexual compatibility.

We project our own attractions and expectations onto a prospective mate, expecting that the things they love and cherish are exactly the same as our own. If an aging man hates the changes in his body, he expects that any potential partner would abhor them just as much. If his sexual drive and potency have diminished, he may not trust that the younger man will find his interest in slow and sensual lovemaking desirable. Why would anyone want a fat, indolent, and decrepit man?

In *The Upside of Irrationality: The Unexpected Benefits of Defying Logic at Work and at Home*, Dan Ariely writes, "To a large degree, beautiful people date other beautiful people, and 'aesthetically challenged' individuals date others like them." He goes on: "In terms of what they were looking for in a romantic partner, those who were more attractive cared more about attractiveness, while the less attractive people cared more about other characteristics (intelligence, sense of humor, and kindness). . . . The aesthetically challenged people were much more interested in going on another date with those they thought had a sense of humor or some other nonphysical characteristic, while the attractive people were much more likely to want to go on a date with someone they evaluated as good-looking."

This may not be too reassuring to those who feel "aesthetically challenged," although Ariely did admit there are significant exceptions as well as a disclaimer: "We are also a scent, a sparkle of the eye, a sweep of the hand, the sound of a laugh, and the knit of a brow—ineffable qualities that can't easily be captured in a database."

In 2005, GrayGay.com conducted an online "mini-poll" called "What Attracts You to Older Men?" Although the survey is not a scientific sampling, the results are interesting and informative.

Looks, demeanor, physique	32%
Sexuality, role-play, dominance	19%
Wisdom, knowledge, experience	14%
Softness, spirituality, calmness	12%
Father figure, father substitute	10%
Money, power, sugar daddy	7%
Stability, assets, comfort	5%

Therapists engaged in efforts to "recover" men from homosexuality exploit the idea that the younger man searches for a father figure, but only 10 percent of the respondents addressed the issue of the father figure. Younger men do analyze their relationships with their fathers to find an explanation for their attraction, but their accounts are contradictory. Common responses are, "My father was a wonderful man, my best friend. I want a man just like he was." It is also common, however, to hear, "I didn't have a good father. I want someone to give me what I didn't have," or "My father left at a very young age. I never witnessed much of father/son activities. I missed out on so much during childhood."

The GrayGay.com survey suggests that over 50 percent of younger men are attracted to older men because of their looks—the rounded corners of both their physique and their temperament. Words used to describe them were "lovely, gorgeous, raw beauty, manhood," or more simply, "They just make me horny." The older men are sometimes described as "daddies," a word that connotes the qualities of maturity, stability, and emotional safety rather than some deeply Freudian maladjustment. "Daddies" are seen as nonthreatening, while the sharp edges of their contemporaries are more menacing. Young men perceive older men to be more sensitive, caring, romantic, self-assured, and satisfied with their lives. They want relationships based on emotions rather than stuff.

Humans have a powerful need to attach to a spouse, family, friends, pets, and even objects. Physiological and environmental cues drive us to interact socially. Paul J. Zak, in an article called "The Neurobiology of Trust," reported that the hormone oxytocin enhances an individual's propensity to trust a stranger when that person exhibits nonthreatening signals. Oxytocin has been dubbed the "cuddle hormone." It promotes social interaction, bonding, and romantic love in addition to its key procreative functions, including uterine contractions and lactation. As oxytocin rises, anxiety over interacting with strangers is reduced. A safe, nurturing environment may stimulate the release of more oxytocin. Research by Sarina Rodrigues and Laura Saslow has suggested that oxytocin's effects on empathy and countering stress may be the result of a single gene. Could it be that a single gene impacting the effects of oxytocin accounts for a younger man's attraction to older men?

Relationships between older and younger men are but one variation in attraction between men. "Chubbies" and "chubby chasers," "bears" and "cubs," and "dominants" and "submissives" are others. We excessively analyze the reasons for these choices, imposing an undue emphasis on categorization, rather than accepting the great diversity of homosexual attractions. Explanations for our attractions may be simple but more likely are complex and perhaps unknowable. All research runs the risk of reductionism. It can focus attention on genital sexual activity alone, to the exclusion of considerations of affection and affiliation. Alfred Kinsey, in *Sexual Behavior in the Human Male*, wrote:

> Males do not represent two discrete populations, heterosexual and homosexual. The world is not to be divided into sheep and goats. Not all things are black nor all things white. It is a fundamental of taxonomy that nature rarely deals with discrete categories. Only the human mind invents categories and tries to force facts into separated pigeon-holes. The living world is a continuum in each and every one of its aspects. The sooner we learn this concerning human sexual behavior, the sooner we shall reach a sound understanding of the realities of sex.

Emotions always accompany behavior. Concentrating exclusively on genital sex causes us to miss the real significance in relationships. Sex is a nice, momentary boost, but having someone who cares about you and is there to support you, even as a close friend, is much more valuable in any long-term view. One younger man seems to have gotten it right when he said, "Don't question the whys. They will be answered in the growth of the relationship. Decisions will be made as we grow together or apart. He likes you, you like him, and you're both legal. Go for it. Life experience is the issue, not age."

Chapter 11
Outed at Eighty: The Infancy of Old Age

Try to keep your soul young and quivering right up to old age, and to imagine right up to the brink of death that life is only beginning.
—George Sand

It was a perfect day to die, if ever there is such a thing. Spring of 1999 had delivered a dazzlingly beautiful morning for my mother's last day. The sun that burst through the window spotlighted the three dozen multicolored tulips on her bedside table. Doug, who loved my mother almost as much as I did, had sent the tulips with me as I made the seemingly endless trip from Des Moines to my hometown in Nebraska. A few days before, my mother had suffered a debilitating stroke that left her speechless, unable to swallow, and paralyzed on one side, but until near the very end, her mind remained clear.

My family gathered around my mother as she lay comatose in her bed in the small Catholic hospital in rural Nebraska. Sister Gertrude, the grief counselor for the hospital, was a whisper of a woman whose vitality filled a room and belied the fact that she was much older than my mother. She had come in that morning to tell us what we already knew, that my mother's death was very near. When the doctor visited, he suggested that we call her pastor for the Lutheran equivalent of the last rites. After the pastor arrived, he read the 23rd Psalm and offered a prayer to our tearful but resolute family. As he began to close his meditation with the Lord's Prayer, my mother opened her eyes, looked at us, and smiled as if to say, "Not yet." It was the same smile she had when she'd drop the Queen of Spades while playing hearts after a holiday meal.

The stroke had not come as a surprise, because it was the last of several. Her first stroke occurred during a University of Nebraska football game. When my mother and stepfather arrived at the hospital by ambulance, he apologized to the doctor. "I held her up during the National Anthem. Maybe I should have called the paramedics right away."

The doctor replied with a smile, "With Nebraska football, most Cornhusker fans would have waited until the end of the game."

After one of her earlier strokes, she could not speak. She had been a church organist and choir director for years and discovered that although she couldn't speak she could still sing. When the doctor visited on morning rounds, she sang her progress to him to the tune of "Twinkle, Twinkle, Little Star."

I had resisted her aging. A few years before she died, I walked into her kitchen one day and for the first time in my life saw her as a frail and vulnerable old woman. I had always tried to prove to my mother that I was as good a man as she believed my father had been. She never demanded it of me, but I always knew what she expected. I had delegated to her enormous power over me as a consequence of my need to please her. The first time I really challenged her expectations of me was when I told her I wanted to be a psychiatrist. My decision to be a psychiatrist disheartened her because she knew that I wouldn't return to my hometown to be its only doctor. Perhaps it also triggered memories of my grandfather's suicide.

As a physician, I assumed the role of the family's spokesperson with the doctor. When I first consulted him after her stroke, the doctor told me that my mother would not recover from this stroke as she had from her earlier ones. He asked, "Do you want a feeding tube?"

"No," I responded immediately. She had been a strong and vibrant woman, fully engaged in her life, and she had a strong belief in an afterlife. I was confident I spoke for her and my siblings: "No feeding tube."

"Intubation and resuscitation?" I assured the doctor she would not have wanted either.

"How about antibiotics?"

Again I said no.

"Then what about IVs?" I hesitated. The questions had gotten progressively more difficult. I was torn between knowing what could be done medically and what should not be done ethically. Convinced the end was inevitably near, I said no. My siblings and I agreed that we knew how our mother would want to spend the last days of her life. She would not have wanted to spend them in some depository for the dying. All she would have wanted was the loving touch of the family she adored.

Her death was certain, but the timing of it was not. Even without those lifesaving interventions, she died more slowly than any of us had hoped. I could tell from the dark, amber color of the urine in her catheter bag that she was getting very dehydrated. Several times a day we would wipe her mouth with large cotton swabs. She would suck on the first of the swabs to extract every drop of the lemon-flavored liquid. Then she would accept another to relieve her parched mouth, but she always refused the third. She could neither speak nor sing her progress, but I believed she communicated her wishes to us.

After I returned to Des Moines following my mother's funeral, I saw one of my patients who had AIDS. End-of-life decisions preoccupied my thoughts, so I asked him if he and his partner had discussed terminal life care in the event that either of them had to make some tough decisions. He said, "I don't want *anything* done to me . . ." and after thinking for a moment, he added, "except a feeding tube. I don't want to starve to death." For me, the feeding tube had been the easiest intervention to refuse, but his response made me wonder, "Did I just starve my mother to death?"

Early one morning a few weeks after my mother's death, the ringing of the phone startled me from a sound sleep. It was my sister-in-law. My brother, aged sixty-two, had died in his sleep. He was a quadriplegic, and for many years before he married, my mother had cared for him. Even after he married, he spoke with my mother daily. He died of pneumonia, his immune system depleted by my mother's death.

The grass on my brother's grave had scarcely sprouted before I received another call announcing that my ninety-year-old stepfather had died. He had lived alone in the home he shared with my mother after she died, but he didn't know how to live alone. Following her death, he had lost his will to live. After his burial, my capacity to grieve was exhausted. I could not have squeezed one more tear out of my eyes.

For older men and women, losing emotionally important family and friends harbors life's most difficult challenges, but midlife frees us to express our pain and sorrow more openly. We gain strength through our own losses, and we grow in compassion for others through their losses. By facing the reality of death, we learn to accept that love and loss are inseparably joined.

During the late summer of 2009, Congress debated the Affordable Health Care Act. Sarah Palin, who had been the Republican vice-presidential nominee, popularized false but intractable rumors that the bill contained provisions for "death panels." In a town hall meeting in Iowa,

Iowa's veteran Republican senator Charles Grassley spoke of "pulling the plug on Grandma." In an attempt to derail the real issues of the debate, social conservatives had twisted the bill's proposed optional consultations for end-of-life care to suggest that committees would decide who was worthy of living and who would die. Tragically, Medicare payment for the optional end-of-life counseling was stripped from the legislation as a compromise to move it forward. Doctors were to be paid for keeping people alive, not for helping them die with dignity.

I was incensed with what I considered to be immoral propaganda. I had personally experienced the importance of discussions about end-of-life care. Families wrestle painfully with decisions about when to stop care. Sister Gertrude's counseling had been a gift to us as my mother lay dying. End-of-life counseling can give serenity to patients, families, and physicians knowing that the wishes of the dying are being respected. I pulled the plug on my mother, but only to allow my mother to die as she had wished.

I've Fallen and I Can't Get Up

A groundbreaking report called "Improving the Lives of LGBT Older Adults" was released at the Aging in America Conference in Chicago in March 2010. It was prepared by Services and Advocacy for Gay, Lesbian, Bisexual & Transgender Elders (SAGE) and the Movement Advancement Project (MAP). The report examined three particularly difficult areas for LGBT elders:

1. LGBT elders are poorer and less financially secure than are American elders as a whole.
2. LGBT elders find it more difficult to achieve good health and health care than do American elders as a whole.
3. LGBT elders' health disparities are overlooked.
   a. There is limited government support for the families and partners of LGBT elders.
   b. Health care environments are often inhospitable to LGBT elders.
   c. Nursing homes often fail to protect LGBT elders.

I am still troubled by a report I received of a preoperative male-to-female transgender person in her seventies who had Alzheimer's disease. Her social worker was unable to find placement for her within one hundred miles of her hometown in Nebraska. Transgender people often face the question, "Which bathroom will she use?" In late life they must also confront the question, "Who would want to be her roommate?"

In 2006, MetLife published "Out and Aging: The MetLife Study of Lesbian and Gay Baby Boomers." According to the study, LGBT seniors face inequitable laws and social programs that fail to address barriers to social acceptance, financial security, and better health and well-being. The MetLife study found that less than half of their respondents had confidence in being treated with dignity and respect by health care providers. Slightly more than half of the respondents had not completed wills or living wills, even though those documents are particularly important for gay men and women because their relationships often have no legal recognition. The case of the preoperative transgender person exemplified the realities of the MetLife study—nursing homes and assisted living facilities frequently do not know how to address the special needs of LGBT elderly.

Although there are a wide variety of social programs and services to support the elderly, none of these programs recognizes or supports LGBT seniors. According to the MetLife study, only about 20 percent of LGBT seniors are as likely as their heterosexual peers to access such needed services as senior centers, housing assistance, meal programs, food stamps, and other entitlements. Social service

> **LGBT seniors are less likely than their heterosexual peers to access needed services, and may feel forced to re-closet themselves.**

agencies almost always operate with a presumption of heterosexuality. Caregivers often do not understand the nature of the informal support groups that many gay people have. In order to access the services of social agencies, many elderly gay men and lesbians feel forced to re-closet themselves. Retreating back into the closet reinforces isolation.

Older LGBT people must begin to face the death of their partners, but they also fear their spousal relationships won't be recognized. Families of choice are often not afforded legal protections. Most institutions that care for the elderly expect children and extended families to provide for the needs of the elderly. The traditional heterosexual hierarchy called upon for assistance is spouse and children, parents and siblings, in-laws and spouse's family. In a traditional family structure, friends are usually the last to be called upon, but LBGT people rely far more heavily on these nontraditional but often legally and socially unrecognized caregivers. Until April 2010, when President Obama asked the Department of Health and Human Services to establish a rule that would prevent it, hospitals could deny visitation privileges to gay and lesbian partners. Still, same-sex partners may be denied participation in decisions about end-of-life care and cannot share a room in most care facilities.

After a death has occurred, LGBT partners cannot receive Social Security survivor benefits. Medicaid regulations protect the assets and homes of heterosexual spouses when one partner enters a nursing home, while assets of gay couples are not protected. While married people can inherit unlimited assets without triggering federal estate taxes, tax laws discriminate against gay seniors.

Two or Three Times Hidden

Gay elderly have been the most invisible demographic. Most gay men generally are indistinguishable from their heterosexual contemporaries except for those who represent the extremes of the LGBT community: drag queens, leather men, and activists. In most contemporary images of gay men, those who are identifiable are also young. The rest of us fade into the background. Mature gay men and women have been called "twice hidden" because of both their age and their sexual orientation. Those men who have chosen not to reveal their same-sex attractions or prefer not to be labeled gay are buried even deeper.

Little thought has been given to the special needs of LGBT elderly. Researchers have failed to include questions about sexual orientation in their studies. In the research that has been done, affluent, white gay men from urban areas have been overrepresented. Women, people of color, and those with low incomes have virtually been ignored. No one seems to even know about the existence of non-gay-identified men who have sex with men. Herdt and colleagues suggested gay elderly are a much more diverse group than was once thought; they are diverse in culture, ethnicity, physical ability, income, education, marital and child-rearing histories, place of residence, and the importance of an LGBT identity.

Several studies suggest that between 3 percent and 8 percent of the population is gay. A growing tidal wave of aging LGBT people is ready to inundate the United States as baby boomers, born between 1946 and 1964, reach retirement age. About 40 percent have previously been married in heterosexual marriages, something that is much more common in the senior cohort group than in younger ones. This group is also the first post-Stonewall group to have experienced a high LGBT visibility.

Gay men who come out in midlife or later not only lose the favored status of the heterosexual life they've been living, but they also must face compounded ageism from the youth culture of our society. Youth bias in the broader culture and among LGBT people in particular is reflected in our standards of beauty. This emphasis on youth accelerates the effects of aging for gay men.

Older men who wish to come out face other complex issues. The 2010 report "Improving the Lives of LGBT Older Adults" estimated that 11 percent of the LGBT population lives below the poverty line. They are two to three times more likely to have fair to poor health. The gay community is just now beginning to realize its impact, but policymakers have had a hands-off approach. With aging comes a need to access social services. Aging service providers are not ready to face this flood of gay baby boomers. Although there are a wide variety of social programs and services to support the elderly, none of these programs recognizes or supports the families of LGBT seniors.

Gay elders are often segregated from the LGBT community. Until recently, gay seniors have frequently been excluded from community discussions, and senior issues have been absent from the LGBT political agenda. There has been a lack of outreach to gay seniors. Older gay men and women do not advocate for their own interests very well. Some who grew up prior to Stonewall simply have never learned to be comfortable expressing their sexual orientation publicly. Older people in general have less fire in their bellies; they have fought the good fights and now have political fatigue.

Although gay men are said to experience themselves as older than their chronologic age—and to be seen as older by the larger LGBT community—perhaps this is changing. During a visit to Las Vegas, I rode in a beautiful vintage Cadillac with a group of men from the Las Vegas Prime Timers. As the car edged its way through the crowd, the streets were lined with young gay men and women and LGBT supporters who shouted their support to us and gave us the thumbs-up. This sense of separation between the older and younger members of the LGBT community wasn't apparent at that Pride event.

"Doctor, Meet My Friend"

I once cared for an aging lesbian who began to have memory problems. She went to a neurologist who said bluntly, "Get your affairs in order. You have Alzheimer's disease." My patient was confused, devastated, and depressed. She asked a companion to accompany her on her return visit. This time the neurologist said, even more bluntly, "I never told you that you have Alzheimer's disease!" Enraged, her companion suggested that she get a second opinion. The second neurologist compassionately confirmed the diagnosis of Alzheimer's disease.

Most Americans, especially those over sixty, worry about the quality, access, and affordability of health care. In general, the sicker you are, the less satisfied you are with the care you receive. Writing in the *Archives of Internal Medicine* in 2008, Jennifer Wolff and Debra Roter suggested that having a companion accompany you to your doctor visits allows even the frailest and most vulnerable to have more confidence in their doctor's skills, to feel better about the information they receive, and to have a better relationship with their doctor. According to the findings, companions facilitated communication, recorded physicians' instructions, provided medical history, asked questions, and explained instructions to patients. In addition, they offered moral support, provided transportation, and handled details like appointments and paperwork. The more functions the companion performed, the higher the patient's satisfaction for the services received.

> Taking a companion to visits with a physician will improve both quality and satisfaction with the medical care received.

It is difficult to age well without a social support system, and families often act as a protective buffer. For many LGBT seniors, prejudice disrupted their lives and their connections with their families of origin. When LGBT individuals become estranged from their families, that buffer is removed. They are also less likely to have children of their own. The MetLife study found that more than three-quarters of gay men and women rely on the emotional and social support of their "families of choice" rather than their families of origin.

Both the "Improving the Lives of LGBT Older Adults" report and the MetLife study suggest that those who are partnered have a greater sense of well-being. They tend to have fewer sexual problems, lower levels of regret about their sexual orientation, and less depression. Because gay relationships are misunderstood, when caregiving decisions are made, the roles of the family of origin trump those of the family of choice. Kristijan, whom I wrote about earlier, told me that as his lover lay dying, his lover's sister pushed Kristijan aside during the final days. She had been estranged from her brother since learning several years before that he was gay, but during his final days she rushed back into his life. The gay community consists of a wide variety of family structures. There are marriages, civil unions, partners with and without children, single parent families, and reconstituted families that were once estranged. It is tragic that Kristijan's lover's family of origin, like so many other families, doesn't accept this.

My friend Bernie described his experience with caregiving in this way:

> I did not divorce until after Mom died. My good former wife, Wilma, often said—once she "caught on" [that I was gay]—that if Mom were alive I would have remained married. Talk about my avoidance of who I was then! Later she "came around" and really liked a couple of my partners, especially Carl.
>
> My wife died six years ago of a nonmalignant brain tumor—a slow death over seven years. When she needed constant care and was wheelchair-bound, I took care of her on some weekends to give our oldest daughter some respite. Wilma gracefully lived with Carl and me. She adored Carl, and she often asked him to sing for her. Once I had to go out of state for a speaking engagement and I asked Wilma if she would mind my leaving her in Carl's care. Without a moment's hesitation, she chimed, "Go ahead; Carl and I can get along better than you and I used

to deal with each other." Happily, their friendship deepened.

So here is the dilemma for gay people: medical care improves when you have a companion, but more than half of gay men between sixty and seventy-nine years of age live alone. Aging gay seniors also must become assertive about developing a good support system and a family of choice when there is no family of origin available. But the LGBT community must also begin to recognize the needs of gay people who are isolated, alone, and unable to advocate for themselves. This is an increasingly serious challenge for our LGBT community.

Given an Inch

I once heard a Libertarian say on National Public Radio, "I believe in personal responsibility; each person must take responsibility for themselves. I know that sounds harsh toward poor people, but that's what I believe. Given an inch, they'll take a mile." Has he never been exposed to anyone who was incapable of taking care of himself? Or does he have no capacity for empathy? Are we so self-absorbed that we cannot recognize and respond to the pain in other peoples' lives? How will the Libertarian respond if his mother has a debilitating stroke?

The MetLife study reported that one out of every four LGBT adults has provided care for an adult friend or family member, a rate that is higher than for the population as a whole. LGBT adults cared for parents (33 percent), partners (18 percent), and friends and nonrelatives (26 percent). The percentage of gay men who were caregivers was much higher than in the general male population. Some gay men become caregivers for parents because they are single and assumed to be the logical sibling to do so. Even though at least 75 percent of the respondents to the survey expected to become caregivers for someone, nearly one in five was unsure who would take care of them when the need arises.

All caregiving produces stress. As we leave midlife and move into our senior years, we progress closer either to requiring care or to being a caregiver for someone else. One of the great challenges for a caregiver is to find ways to replenish emotional reserves consumed by the caregiving role. During caregiving, emotional energy flows only in one direction, away from the caregiver. When caregiving depletes emotional reserves, care and compassion can be transformed into anger and resentment.

Come Out, Come Out

To many older gay men, coming out seems almost routine for young people today. The life of pre-Stonewall men and women is nearly unimaginable to the young. Those who grew up in the pre-Stonewall era were accustomed to being considered sick, sinful, perverse, or arrested in their development. They lied to their parents, teachers, coworkers, and the military. They often denounced other gay men and women. They risked loss of stature, employment, social and economic standing, housing, friends, and family. Religion condemned them. Law enforcement brutalized them. Society stripped them of their dignity. Their social lives were disguised and addressed only in secret code. They found safety in marriages and in the priesthood while secretly having sex with men outside those relationships. They hid their identity, their relationships, and the depth of their sexually intimacy with their same-sex partners.

> The hidden lives of pre-Stonewall gay men and women is unimaginable to younger LGBT people.

In a classic 1991 article about aging gay men and women, R. A. Friend described three adaptational styles by which older gay people cope with their gay identities:

1. Stereotypical—Those that conform to the negative stereotypes of isolation, loneliness, self-hatred, depression, and low levels of sexual intimacy
2. Passing—Those who largely pass as heterosexuals, have a marginal acceptance of homosexuality, and have a conditional self-acceptance. They become depressed and negative, not aging well and not involved in the LGBT community.
3. Affirmative—Those who are socially active with a positive gay identity, a vibrant and well-adjusted social life, and a sexually vigorous adjustment to aging.

In general, the older one is, the more reticent one is to reveal sexual orientation. Greater awareness of LGBT culture and increasing civil rights protection along with fewer repressive social constraints have all created new opportunities for older men to come out in the latter half of life. As men age, they have greater financial independence, are further along in their education and career, and have greater access to social options. Older gay men may have lacked access to positive gay role models. They have been actively blocked in the process of identity development by societal messages about the validity of their same-sex attachments. Mature gay men have had less capacity to resist the internalized negative societal messages about their sexual identity. Men who come out in midlife or later often were well adjusted and lived lives more consistent with heterosexual development sequences. Their social associations have been heterosexual, and their lives have been concealed. Remaining closeted later in life (or being forced back into the closet because of homophobic social services) leads to lower self-esteem and greater feelings of isolation.

It Ain't All Bad News

Not all elderly people, gay or straight, are depressed and lonely. We live our older years in much the same way we lived our younger years, and later life reflects all the stages that came before it. Prior life experiences such as education, occupation, and social class influence how people experience their declining years. A piece by Kirk Johnson in the *New York Times* in 2010 described how some older people engage old age as a never-ending adventure. Some senior adrenaline junkies hike in South Africa, travel to Antarctica, walk on the wings of planes, skydive, and tour New England on bicycles. For them, getting old is just the next stage of exploration of their lives. Catering to these elderly people, entrepreneurs are developing businesses based on education, adventure, and culture.

Many of the men who responded to my survey are quite healthy and active. Many have been married and have children; others who are estranged from their families have friends who have become their "family of choice." But a significant number are in poor health, live alone, and have no one to drive the car to the hospital or doctor's office. Here are some findings from my survey of men over the age of sixty with same-sex attraction:

- Many are quite healthy and active.
- The percentage of men having fair to poor health increased with age from 11 percent between sixty to sixty-nine years of age to 38 percent for those over eighty years of age; however, half of the men over sixty reported their health as very good to excellent.
- Those perceiving their health to be a major life stress increased from 28 percent in the sixth decade to 50 percent into their eighth decade.
- Fifty to 60 percent of gay men between sixty and seventy-nine years of age live alone, although unexpectedly this percentage decreased with increasing age.
- The number of men who live alone but have a partner is surprisingly high: 58 percent. This dropped to 38 percent for those seventy to seventy-nine years old, and even lower for those over eighty.
- More than half of the respondents are or were married, and between half to two-thirds of those who had been married had children.

It's a Wrap

"Why would a forty-year-old man come out, anyhow? He's too old to have sex." I was speaking to someone at the Services and Advocacy for LGBT Elders (SAGE) office in New York City where I had gone to discuss my book. She said that one of their young male staffers had asked that question during a discussion of older LGBT who are just coming out. The young staffer was unaware of three things:

1. Forty is the infancy of old age.
2. Men and women have sex well into late life.
3. Being gay is about far more than just having sex.

Over and over through the years, I have said to my patients, "All of life's most important decisions are made without enough information." As I have reflected on the two questions I'm often asked—"How could you not know you were gay?" and "Wasn't your marriage just a sham to protect yourself?"—I can say confidently that my marriage was not a sham. I did not use my wife and children as a shield from the possible consequences of my being gay. I loved her as much as I was capable—just not enough for either of us. I simply didn't have all the information I needed to make a different decision. I do not regret my marriage or my children; my only regret is the pain my being gay has caused them. I do not wish I had done it all differently, nor could I have done it differently. Many aspects of the heterosexual life I left behind brought me great joy.

Those of us who enter midlife before coming out have only begun to confront the cognitive complexities of paradox, ambiguity, and uncertainty in our lives. We discover the world is no longer black and white as we once believed. Mortality becomes personal as we experience the liver spots and erectile

> **Loving someone and bereavement are two sides of the same coin.**

changes. By midlife we have discovered that loving someone and bereavement are two sides of the same coin. Social status and religious support may be threatened while we seek the emotional freedom and release of coming out. The depths of sexual intimacy may appear elusive. A man who comes out in midlife or beyond must tack his ship in heavy winds and high seas, sailing from port to port as he off-loads the heavy baggage of the straight world he lived in.

Justin Spring, in his book about the life of Samuel Steward, wrote:

Each generation of writers reinvents its perception of sexuality through novels, poetry, and autobiographical writing, and in the process rebels against the perceptions and experiences of the generation before. For male homosexuals in the twentieth-century United States, these shifts in perception have up to now been largely described merely as "pre-Stonewall" and "post-Stonewall." But clearly there have been other equally significant generational breaks between pre–World War II and post–World War II; pre-Kinsey and post-Kinsey; pre-McCarthy and post-McCarthy; pre-AIDS and post-AIDS; and, most recently, pre-Internet and post-Internet.

At sixty-seven years of age I have lived through all of that and more. I would add to Spring's list pre-DNA and post-DNA and pre-brain-imagining and post-brain-imaging. We now know that DNA and the human genome function as a GPS that guides development in universal ways from the point of conception until our return to dust. On a global level, our brains are all alike, and yet the intricate networks that develop in our brains make us all unique. Little by little scientists uncover secrets about our brains, and more will be revealed as the study of the brain dominates science in the twenty-first century. But will they answer the question, "Why do some stars shine brighter when I see an attractive man and not as brightly when I see an equally attractive woman?" Life cannot be defined by genetic codes, neurotransmitter substances, or hormones. We do not connect with the entirety of humanity on a purely biological level.

Pre-Freud and post-Freud might also be added to Spring's list. Sigmund Freud was an extremely good biologist, but the embryonic nature of biology constrained his exploration of the mind. Perhaps the unconscious isn't the mystical id, ego, and super-ego, but simply all of the truths about the brain that are not yet known. Fear of disapproval from family and society and observance of the canons of religious establishments help explain why some gay people "live straight," even though compliance to the dictates of family and religion make them feel guilty and worthless. Studying Freud, much like studying the Lutheran catechism, served me well. But it served me better when I became mature enough to understand that I could challenge the dogma and unlearn some of what I had been taught. Not all truths have been revealed.

I have grieved my father's death and I have sought out male mentors to figure out how to be a man. But I now understand that it wasn't my father's death that made me gay. Of course, his death was a tremendous loss for all of my family and impacted each of us in various ways, but I no longer feel I need to try to be a better man than he was just to feel as if I am his equal. I can also understand that my mother held me close after he died because she needed someone to touch and hold on to, especially after my grandfather took his own life. And it took me a while, but I finally learned that I would never lose her love simply by making choices for my life that were different than the ones she would have made for me.

The question, "How could you not know you were gay until you were forty?" is much easier to answer now. I was a child in an era when the Nazis were performing experiments on homosexuals in Germany. I was an adolescent when our own government associated homosexuality with Communism and believed that gay men and women needed to be exposed and eliminated. I had a therapist who suggested that my homosexuality might lead to jumping off a bridge, as it did so tragically for Tyler Clementi, a young Rutgers student. I have experienced the AIDS epidemic and hearing people say that my friends deserved to die because God was punishing them for their abominations. I have had a friend murdered by someone who felt that killing a gay person might bring power to his powerless existence. Living in a world so hostile to homosexuality inhibits development and creates contradictions and dissonance that demand repression. In fact, it seems almost surprising—even heroic—that anyone comes out at all.

Mature men who have sex with men but who have not yet come out have asked me, "Is it too late for me?" Author Carlos Castaneda wrote, "We either make ourselves miserable or we make ourselves strong, the amount of work is the same." In my lifetime, older gay men were once thought to be poor, to live in the Bowery, to seek oblivion in cheap alcohol, and to regress to a point where they preyed on small children. But a new image of mature gay men is emerging. Having confidence in what we think and feel, and responding to our own perceptions in a positive way, allows us to move out from behind the mask of concealment and live life authentically.

Some older men resent the push by gay activists for them to openly and fully acknowledge their sexual orientation. Degrees of outness are not predictors of happiness in old age. As men become older they often distance themselves from an all-encompassing gay identity. Sex diminishes as the central organizing force of one's life, and these men may choose to come out only to the point of self-acceptance.

The essential coming-out tasks for mature men who have sex with men are:

- Finding a stable acceptance of yourself
- Constructing a new reality
- Assertively meeting your needs

- Seeking a satisfactory sexual and social life
- Publicly acknowledging your same-sex attractions *except* where it might interfere with access to resources

Several months after Doug and I got married, I spoke with my favorite uncle, the one man I believe is most like my dad would have been. Speaking about our marriage he said, "What you did almost broke my heart." For a while I felt sad for having caused him pain, but it did not undermine my confidence that what I had done was right. I am confident that my opinions are valid and worthwhile, and I know that he will continue to love me even though he may never approve of my marriage. Poet Hugo von Hofmannsthal said, "To grow mature is to separate more distinctly, to connect more closely."

> **For years I thought that I was not a man because I was gay; now I know that I am a man because I accept the validity of being gay.**

For years I thought that I was not a man because I was gay. Now I know that being a man means accepting that I am gay and knowing that I am the person I want to be.

Dr. Mihaly Csikszentmihalyi, a psychology professor at the University of Chicago, wrote, "Happiness is not something that happens. It is not the result of good fortune or random chance. . . . Happiness, in fact, is a condition that must be prepared for, cultivated, and defended privately by each person." Your future can be different from your past, but you have a role in making that happen. What is stopping you from moving ahead? What do you want that future to be? What have you tried? What worked? What didn't work? What are you willing to sacrifice for it? We pay a price for taking action, but there is a significant price paid for not taking action.

At sixty-seven, I haven't started feeling old, but I now can see old age lying ahead of me. Aging has compelled me to ponder the question, "What do I value most?" But it also allows me the freedom to discard what I least value. The transition from living straight to becoming gay began with unlearning things that I once thought were true. Then I discovered an entirely new reality. I don't expect to ever confront having to start another lawnmower. I can choose to practice only those parts of psychiatry that I continue to love. I can save my energy to work on my new marriage and the relationships with family and friends whom I love. I've written my first book.

"Would you tell me, please, which way I ought to go from here?"

"That depends a good deal on where you want to get to," said the Cat.

"I don't much care where—" said Alice.

"Then it doesn't matter which way you go," said the Cat.

"—so long as I get somewhere," Alice added as an explanation.

"Oh, you're sure to do that," said the Cat, "if you only walk long enough."

—Alice's Adventures in Wonderland,
Lewis Carroll

References

Introduction

Dececco, J., *Gay and Gray: The Older Homosexual Man* (Haworth Gay & Lesbian Studies) (2 Sub ed.). New York: Routledge, 1995.

Drescher, J., *Psychoanalytic Therapy and the Gay Man*. Hillsdale, NJ: The Analytic Press, 2001.

Groseclose, S. L., DVM, Ed., "First Report of AIDS." *Morbidity and Mortality Weekly Report*, 50:21 (2001): 1.

Gross, J., "Aging and Gay, and Facing Prejudice in Twilight." *New York Times*, October 9, 2007, www.nytimes.com/2007/10/09/us/09aged.html?scp=1&sq=Aging,%20gay,%20and%20facing%20prejudice&st=cse.

Lehrer, J., *How We Decide*. New York: Mariner Books, 2010.

O'Leary, M. P., et al, "A Brief Male Sexual Function Inventory for Urology." *Urology*, 46:5 (1995): 697–706.

Paris, J., *Prescriptions for the Mind: A Critical View of Contemporary Psychiatry*. New York: Oxford University Press, 2008.

Chapter 1: I Am Not Gay, but I Might Be a Little Bit Queer

American Psychiatric Association, "Therapies Focused on Attempts to Change Sexual Orientation," May 2000, www.psych.org/Departments/EDU/Library/APAOfficialDocumentsandRelated/PositionStatements/200001.aspx.

Carey, B., "Long After Kinsey, Only the Brave Study Sex." *Science Forum—Scientific Discussion and Debate*, November 9, 2004, www.thescienceforum.com/viewtopic.php?p=242344.

Centers for Disease Control, "HIV and AIDS among Gay and Bisexual Men." *CDC Fact Sheet*, September 2010.

Chauncey, G., *Gay New York: Gender, Urban Culture, and the Making of the Gay Male World 1890–1940*. New York: Basic Books, 1994.

Hawks, H. (director), *Bringing Up Baby* (motion picture), 1938.

Howard, J., *Men Like That: A Southern Queer History*. Chicago: University of Chicago Press, 2001.

Kinsey, A. *Sexual Behavior in the Human Male*. Philadelphia: W.B. Saunders Co., 1948.

Pathela, P., et al, "Discordance between sexual behavior and self-reported sexual identity: a population-based survey of New York City men." *Annals of Internal Medicine*, 145 (2006): 416–25.

Satinover, J., "Is Homosexuality Genetic?" MissionNOW.com, retrieved August 3, 2010, from www.mission.org/jesuspeople/thegaygene.htm.

Spring, J., *Secret Historian: The Life and Times of Samuel Steward, Professor, Tattoo Artist, and Sexual Renegade*. New York: Farrar, Straus and Giroux, 2010.

Chapter 2: It's Just Common Sense
Bailey, J. M., and R. C. Pillard, "A genetic study of male sexual orientation." *Archives of General Psychiatry*, 48 (1991): 1089–96.
Buddha (trans. Taitetsu Unno), *Dhammapada*. Shin Dharma Net, retrieved October 10, 2010, from www.shindharmanet.com/worship/dhammapada.htm.
Darwin, C., *The Works of Charles Darwin, Volume 21: The Descent of Man, and Selection in Relation to Sex* (Part 1). New York: New York University Press, 2010.
Drury, A., *Advise and Consent*. New York: Doubleday, 1959.
Haidt, J., S. H. Koller, and M. G. Dias, "Affect, culture, and morality, or is it wrong to eat your dog?" *Journal of Personality and Social Psychology*, 4 (October 1993): 613–28.
Hu, S., et al, "Linkage between sexual orientation and chromosome Xq28 in males but not in females." *Nature Genetics*, 11 (1995): 248–60.
Plato, *Phaedrus* (Oxford World's Classics). New York: Oxford University Press, 2009.
Schindler, P., "Pope's views against gays are long and detailed." *Downtown Express*, Volume 17, Number 49 (April 29–May 5, 2005), www.downtownexpress.com/de_103/talkingpoints.html.
Spring, J., *Secret Historian: The Life and Times of Samuel Steward, Professor, Tattoo Artist, and Sexual Renegade*. New York: Farrar, Straus and Giroux, 2010.
Warneken, F., and M. Tomasello, "Altruistic Helping in Human Infants and Young Chimpanzees." *Science*, 311:5765 (2006): 1301–303.

Chapter 3: God Hates Fags: In Bondage to Dogma
Aslan, R., *No god but God: The Origins, Evolution, and Future of Islam.* London: William Heinemann, 2005.
Borg, M. J., *Meeting Jesus Again for the First Time*. New York: HarperCollins, 1998.
Chellew-Hodge, C., *Bulletproof Faith: A Spiritual Survival Guide for Gay and Lesbian Christians*. San Francisco: Jossey-Bass, 2008.
Haldeman, D. C., "Gay rights, patient rights: the implications of sexual conversion therapy." *Professional Psychology: Research and Practice*, 33:3 (2002): 260–64.

Martino, S. C., et al, "Virginity Pledges Among the Willing: Delays in First Intercourse and Consistency of Condom Use." *Journal of Adolescent Health*, 43:4 (2008): 341–48.

Pelosi, A. (director), *The Trials of Ted Haggard* (documentary), 2009.

Saad, L., "Americans' Acceptance of Gay Relations Crosses 50% Threshold." Gallup, May 25, 2010, www.gallup.com/poll/135764/americans-acceptance-gay-relations-crosses-threshold.aspx.

Chapter 4: Out from the Shadows: You're Not the Man You Thought You Were

Cass, V., "Homosexual identity formation: a theoretical model." *Journal of Homosexuality*, 4 (1979): 219–35.

Fowler, J., and N. Christakis, "Dynamic spread of happiness in a large social network: longitudinal analysis over 20 years in the Framingham Heart Study." *BMJ*, 337 (2008): a2338.

Friedan, B., *The Feminine Mystique*. New York: W. W. Norton & Company, 1963.

Grossman, A. H., A. R. D'Augelli, and S. L. Hershberger, "Social support networks of lesbian, gay and bisexual adults 60 years of age or older." *Journal of Gerontology Psychological Sciences*, 55B (2000): 171–79.

Kooden, H., *Golden Men: The Power of Gay Midlife*. New York: Avon Books, 2000.

Lynch, F., "Non-Ghetto Gays: A Sociological Study of Suburban Homosexuals." *Journal of Homosexuality*, 13:4 (1987): 13–42.

Russo, R., *Bridge of Sighs*. New York: Random House, 2007.

Satyal, R., *Blue Boy*. New York: Kensington, 2009.

Schindhelm, R. K., and H. J. Hospers, "Sex with men before coming-out: relation to sexual activity and sexual risk-taking behavior." *Archives of Sexual Behavior*, 33:6 (2004): 585–591(7).

Chapter 5: Are You Shooting at the Wrong Target? Detox and Rehab for Addiction to Approval

Allport, G. W., *The Nature of Prejudice: 25th Anniversary*. New York: Perseus Books Group, 1954.

Bettelheim, B., *Good Enough Parent: A Book on Child Rearing*. New York: Vintage, 1988.

Brewer, M., "The psychology of prejudice: Ingroup love or outgroup hate?" *Journal of Social Issues*, 55:3 (1999): 429–44.

Centers for Disease Control and Prevention, "HIV and AIDS among Gay and Bisexual Men." *CDC Fact Sheet*, retrieved August 2, 2010, from www.cdc.gov/nchhstp/newsroom/docs/FastFacts-MSM-FINAL508COMP.pdf.

Coffin, W. S., *Credo*. Louisville: Westminster John Knox Press, 2005.

DeParle, J., "Rude, Rash, Effective, Act-Up Shifts AIDS Policy." *New York Times*, January 3, 1990, www.nytimes.com/1990/01/03/nyregion/rude-rash-effective-act-up-shifts-aids-policy.html?scp=1&sq=ACT+UP+%2B+rude+%2B+rash&st=nyt.

Dick, K. (director), *Outrage* (documentary), 2009.

Gottman, J., *The Seven Principles for Making Marriage Work: A Practical Guide from the Country's Foremost Relationship Expert*. New York: Crown, 1999.

Hiller, A. (director), *Making Love* (movie), 1982.

James, S., "Many Successful Gay Marriages Share an Open Secret." *New York Times*, January 28, 2010, www.nytimes.com/2010/01/29/us/29sfmetro.html?_r=1.

Kahneman, D., and A. Tversky, "Prospect Theory: An Analysis of Decision Under Risk." *Econometrica*, 47:2 (1979): 263–92.

Lehrer, J., *How We Decide*. New York: Mariner Books, 2010.

Levit, A., "Out of the Office Closet." *Wall Street Journal*, July 19, 2009, http://online.wsj.com/article/SB124796073372262319.html.

Spring, J., *Secret Historian: The Life and Times of Samuel Steward, Professor, Tattoo Artist, and Sexual Renegade*. New York: Farrar, Straus and Giroux, 2010.

Tobias, A., *The Best Little Boy in the World*. New York: G. P. Putnam's Sons, 1973.

Chapter 6: Ain't Nobody's Business: Tricks of the Trade

Boswell, J., "The Church and the Homosexual: An Historical Perspective, 1979." Fordham.edu., www.fordham.edu/halsall/pwh/1979boswell.html.

"CBS Reports 1967: The Homosexuals." *Music Videos, Politics, and Funny Videos at Vodpod*, http://vodpod.com/watch/3028357-cbs-reports-1967-the-homosexuals.

Dougary, G., "Lord Browne: 'I'm much happier now than I've ever been.'" *Sunday Times*, February 6, 2010, http://business.timesonline.co.uk/tol/business/movers_and_shakers/article7014787.ece.

Engel, G. L., "The need for a new medical model: a challenge for biomedicine." *Science* 196:4286 (1977): 129–36.

Faderman, L., *Odd Girls and Twilight Lovers: A History of Lesbian Life in Twentieth-Century America*. New York: Penguin, 1992.

Fitzgerald, J., "Interview with David Kuria." *The Equal Rights Review*, 5 (2010): 86–90.

Gerassi, J. G., *The Boys of Boise: Furor, Vice & Folly in an American City*. Seattle: University of Washington Press, 2010.

GLBTQ: An Encyclopedia of Gay, Lesbian, Bisexual, Transgender, and Queer Culture, "McCarthyism," www.glbtq.com/social-sciences/mccarthyism.html.

Hiller, A. (director), *Making Love* (movie), 1982.

London, R. J., GayUganda. Retrieved October 10, 2010, from http://gayuganda.blogspot.com.

Myers, S. L., "Irving Bieber, 80, a Psychoanalyst Who Studied Homosexuality, Dies." *New York Times*, August 28, 1991, www.nytimes.com/1991/08/28/nyregion/irving-bieber-80-a-psychoanalyst-who-studied-homosexuality-dies.html.

Oliver-Miller, S., "CCIES at the Kinsey Institute: Papua New Guinea." *International Encyclopedia of Sexuality*, www.iub.edu/~kinsey/ccies/pg.php#homoerot.

Russo, V., *The Celluloid Closet: Homosexuality in the Movies*. New York: Harper & Row, 1981.

UC Atlas of Global Inequality, "Uganda and HIV," http://ucatlas.ucsc.edu/health/aids/uganda_hiv.php.

Williams, W. L., *Spirit and the Flesh: Sexual Diversity in American Indian Culture*. Boston: Beacon Press, 1986.

Chapter 7: How to Have Sex in a Tree

AARP, "Sex, Romance, and Relationships: AARP Survey of Midlife and Older Adults," May 2010, http://assets.aarp.org/rgcenter/general/srr_09.pdf.

American Psychiatric Association, *Diagnostic and Statistical Manual of Mental Disorders DSM-IV-TR Fourth Edition (Text Revision)*. Arlington, VA: American Psychiatric Publishing, 2000.

BBC News, "Vatican 'clarifies' cardinal's homosexuality abuse link," April 14, 2010, http://news.bbc.co.uk/2/hi/europe/8620135.stm.

Mosher, W. D., A. Chandra, and J. Jones, "Sexual behavior and selected health measures: men and women 15–44 years of age, United States, 2002." *Advance Data*, 362 (2005): 1–55.

Munzenrieder, K., "Rent Boy Customer Dr. George Rekers' Damage Control: Jesus Hung Out with Prostitutes Too." *Miami New Times* blogs, May 2010, http://blogs.miaminewtimes.com/riptide/2010/05/rentboy_customer_dr_george_rek.php.

Paris, J., *Prescriptions for the Mind: A Critical View of Contemporary Psychiatry*. New York: Oxford University Press, 2008.

Satyal, R., *Blue Boy*. New York: Kensington, 2009.

Schachter, S., and J. E. Singer, "Cognitive, social and physiological determinants of emotional states." *Psychological Review*, 69 (1962): 379–99.

Timmons, S., *The Trouble with Harry Hay: Founder of the Modern Gay Movement*. Los Angeles: Alyson Publications, 1990.

Whiteman, H., "Gay outrage over cardinal's child abuse comment." CNN World, www.cnn.com/2010/WORLD/europe/04/14/vatican.homosexuality.pedophilia/index.html.

Chapter 8: Hook-ups and Not-Quite-Sex

AARP, "Sex, Romance, and Relationships: AARP Survey of Midlife and Older Adults," May 2010, http://assets.aarp.org/rgcenter/general/srr_09.pdf.

Atwood, J. D., and L. Schwartz, "Cybersex—The new affair treatment considerations." *Journal of Couple & Relationship Therapy,* 3 (2002): 37–56.

Badgett, M. V., *When Gay People Get Married*. New York: New York University Press, 2010.

Bernard, T. S., and R. Lieber, "The High Price of Being a Gay Couple." *New York Times*, October 3, 2009, p. A1.

Boykin, K., *Beyond the Down Low: Sex, Lies, and Denial in Black America*. New York and Cambridge, MA: Da Capo Press, 2006.

Centers for Disease Control and Prevention, "HIV in the United States," July 2010, www.cdc.gov/hiv/resources/factsheets/us.htm.

Coffin, W. S., *Credo*. Louisville: Westminster John Knox Press, 2005.

Dee, T. S., "Forsaking all others? The effects of same-sex partnership laws on risky sex." *Economic Journal*, 118 (July 2008): 1055–78.

Druckerman, P., *Lust in Translation: Infidelity from Tokyo to Tennessee*. New York: Penguin Press, 2008.

Elford, J., G. Bolding, and L. Sherr, "Seeking sex on the Internet and sexual risk behaviour among gay men using London gyms." *AIDS,* 15:11 (2001): 1409–15.

Harasim, P., "Some question sexual addictions." *Las Vegas Review Journal*, April 18, 2010, www.lvrj.com/news/some-question-sexual-addictions-91350124.html.

Hart, T. A., et al, "Sexual behavior among HIV-positive men who have sex with men: what's in a label? *Journal of Sex Research*, 40:2 (2003): 179–88.

Justice, E., "Study Links Gay Marriage Bans to Rise in HIV Rate," Emory University News Release, June 4, 2009, http://shared.web.emory.edu/emory/news/releases/2009/06/study-links-gay-marriage-bans-to-rise-in-hiv-rate.html.

King, J. L., and K. Hunter, *On the Down Low: A Journey into the Lives of "Straight" Black Men Who Sleep with Men*. New York: Broadway Books, 2004.

Neresian, E., "Can a Tiger Rehab His Stripes?" *Women's Health Magazine*, retrieved August 19, 2010, from www.womenshealthmag.com/life/tiger-woods-and-adultery.

Rieger, G., M. L. Chivers, and J. M. Bailey, "Sexual arousal patterns of bisexual men." *Psychological Science*, 16:8 (2005): 579–84.

Spring, J., *Secret Historian: The Life and Times of Samuel Steward, Professor, Tattoo Artist, and Sexual Renegade*. New York: Farrar, Straus and Giroux, 2010.

Turner, T., *Out Late* (unpublished play), 2007.

Chapter 9: In Your Weariness: In the Morning You Start Again

Ariely, D., *The Upside of Irrationality: The Unexpected Benefits of Defying Logic at Work and at Home*. New York: Harper Collins, 2010.

Buxton, A. P., *The Other Side of the Closet: The Coming-Out Crisis for Straight Spouses and Families, Revised and Expanded Edition*. New York: Wiley, 1994.

Centers for Disease Control and Prevention, "Life Expectancy." Retrieved August 6, 2010, from www.cdc.gov/nchs/fastats/lifexpec.htm.

Erikson, E. H., *Identity and the Life Cycle* (Reissue ed.). New York: W. W. Norton & Company, 1994.

Herdt, G., J. Beeler, and T. W. Rawls, "Life Course Diversity Among Older Lesbians and Gay Men: A Study in Chicago." *Journal of Gay, Lesbian, and Bisexual Identity*, 2 (1997): 231–46.

Jones, J., and S. Pugh, "Ageing Gay Men: Lessons from the Sociology of Embodiment." *Men and Masculinities*, 7:3 (2005): 248–60.

Kimmel, D. C., "Adult Development and Ageing: A Gay Perspective." *Journal of Social Issues*, 34:3 (1978): 113–130.

Kooden, H., *Golden Men: The Power of Gay Midlife*. New York:

HarperCollins, 2000.

Mead, R., "Proud Flesh: The Cult of Cosmetic Surgery." *New Yorker*, November 13, 2006, www.newyorker.com/archive/2006/11/13/061113crbo_books?current Page=1.

Chapter 10: Accidental Sex: Never Pass Up a Hard-on

Abdo, C. H., et al, "Sexual satisfaction among patients with erectile dysfunction treated with counseling, sildenafil, or both." *Journal of Sexual Medicine*, 5:7 (2008): 1720–26.

Ariely, D., *The Upside of Irrationality: The Unexpected Benefits of Defying Logic at Work and at Home*. New York: Harper Collins, 2010.

Carey, B., "Long after Kinsey, only the brave study sex." *Science Forum*, November 9, 2004, www.thescienceforum.com/viewtopic.php?p=242344.

Erikson, E. H., *Identity and the Life Cycle* (Reissue ed.). New York: W. W. Norton & Company, 1980.

Gladwell, M., *Blink: The Power of Thinking Without Thinking*. New York: Back Bay Books, 2007.

Kinsey, A., *Sexual Behavior in the Human Male*. Philadelphia: W.B. Saunders Co., 1948.

Morgentaler, A., *Testosterone for Life: Recharge Your Vitality, Sex Drive, Muscle Mass, and Overall Health*. New York: McGraw-Hill, 2008.

Mykletun, A., et al, "Assessment of male sexual function by the Brief Sexual Function Inventory." *BJU International*, 97 (2005): 316–23.

O'Leary, M. P., et al, "Distribution of the Brief Male Sexual Inventory in community men." *International Journal of Impotence Research*, 15 (2003): 185–91.

Reiner, R. (director), *The Bucket List* (movie), 2007.

Rodrigues, S. M., and L. R. Saslow, "An oxytocin receptor genetic variation relates to empathy and stress reactivity in humans." *Proceedings of the National Academy of Sciences*, 106 (2009): 21437–441.

Rossi, A. S. (editor), *Sexuality across the Life Course*. Chicago: University of Chicago Press, 1999.

Sedaris, D., *Me Talk Pretty One Day*. New York: Little Brown & Co., 2000.

Turner, T., *Out Late* (unpublished play), 2007.

Zak, P., "The Neurobiology of Trust." *Annals of the New York Academy of Science*, 1032 (2004): 224–27.

Chapter 11: Outed at Eighty: The Infancy of Old Age

Csikszentmihalyi, M., *Flow: The Psychology of Optimal Experience*. New York: HarperCollins, 2007.

Friend, R. A., "Older Lesbian and Gay People: A Theory of Successful Aging." *Journal of Homosexuality*, 20:3/4 (1991): 99–118.

GrayGay.com, "What Attracts You to Older Men?" July 2005, www.graygay.com.

Johnson, K., "Seeing Old Age as a Never-Ending Adventure." *New York Times*, January 8, 2010, p. A1.

MetLife, "Out and Aging: The MetLife Study of Lesbian and Gay Baby Boomers," November 2006, www.metlife.com/assets/cao/mmi/publications/studies/mmi-out-aging-lesbian-gay-retirment.pdf.

National Gay and Lesbian Task Force Policy Institute, "Outing Age 2010: Public Policy Issues Affecting Lesbian, Gay, Bisexual and Transgender Elders." November 2009, www.thetaskforce.org/downloads/reports/reports/outingage_final.pdf.

SAGE, "Improving the Lives of LGBT Older Adults." SAGE Resources, http://sageusa.org/resources/resource_view.cfm?resource=183.

Spring, J., *Secret Historian: The Life and Times of Samuel Steward, Professor, Tattoo Artist, and Sexual Renegade*. New York: Farrar, Straus and Giroux, 2010.

Wolff, J., and D. Roter, "Hidden in Plain Sight: Medical Visit Companions as a Resource for Vulnerable Older Adults." *Archives of Internal Medicine*, 168 (July 2008): 1409–15.